Religion

and the

Human Sciences

Daniel A. Helminiak

Religion
and the
Human Sciences

An Approach via Spirituality

STATE UNIVERSITY OF NEW YORK PRESS

Some of the material in Chapter 4 is from *Eye to Eye: The Quest for the New Paradigm* by Ken Wilber, © 1983, 1990, 1996. Reprinted by arrangement with Shambhala Publications, Inc., 300 Massachusetts Avenue, Boston, MA 02115.

Production by Ruth Fisher
Marketing by Nancy Farrell

Published by
State University of New York Press, Albany

Library of Congress Cataloging-in-Publication Data

Helminiak, Daniel A., 1942–
    Religion and the human sciences : an approach via spirituality /
Daniel A. Helminiak.
        p.   cm.
    Companion volume to The human core of spirituality.
    Includes bibliographical references and index.
    ISBN 0-7914-3805-8 (hardcover : alk. paper). — ISBN 0-7914-3806-6
(pbk. : alk. paper)
    1. Spiritual life—Study and teaching. 2. Religion and the social
sciences. 3. Religion—Study and teaching. 4. Psychology.
5. Interdisciplinary method. 6. Philosophy of Science. I. Title.
BL624.H386   1998
291.4—dc21   97-36986
                                                                            CIP

10 9 8 7 6 5 4 3 2 1

For Celia and Allan
much loved and loving
sister and brother

CONTENTS

LIST OF FIGURES

PREFACE

This book is a companion volume to *The Human Core of Spirituality: Mind as Psyche and Spirit* (Helminiak, 1996a). Together these books propose an elaborate theory of spirituality as an academic discipline and, indeed, as a science—specifically, a specialization, not in theology, but in psychology. These two books originally constituted one massive manuscript. I completed that original draft in late 1991.

I had begun developing the theory in 1978 when I taught an introductory course in spirituality at Weston School of Theology, and I continued to elaborate and nuance the theory as I taught systematic theology and spirituality at Oblate School of Theology in the early 1980s. This theory lay behind my essay *Spiritual Development: An Interdisciplinary Study*, which was an application to a specific topic in spirituality. Once I completed the comprehensive manuscript, I used my dissertation requirement at The University of Texas at Austin to test the theory in a standard empirical research project on adult development. The result was *Men and Women in Midlife Transition and the Crisis of Meaning and Purpose in Life, a Matter of Spirituality* (Helminiak, 1994a). This project provided supporting evidence for major suppositions of the theory.

In the meantime I looked for a publisher for my manuscript. Reactions were consistent: the work was too big. Reflecting the intellectual mood of our times and the economic realities of contemporary publishing, other comments were more revealing and more disconcerting: Publishers would have gobbled up a manuscript like this twenty-five years ago, but the market for serious scholarship in spirituality is virtually nonexistent today. And: The fact that a comprehensive study of this kind has never been produced perhaps suggests that it ought not to be tried.

Facing reality—one hallmark of authentic spirituality, as I understand it—I decided to split the comprehensive manuscript in two. I reworked the central chapters into *The Human Core of Spirituality*, a study of the substantive issues. And I reworked the introductory and concluding chapters into the present volume, a treatment of the methodological issues. I had originally argued— and I still believe—that when spirituality is the subject, the methodological and the substantive issues cannot stand independently. In fact, to allow these two books to stand as monographs, the introductory chapter of each of them briefly summarizes the argument of the other.

In essence, the study of spirituality is about the human spirit, but it is this same human spiritual capacity that effects the studying. So one's understanding of the human spirit will both depend upon and constrain one's understanding of how one studies and knows the human spirit—or vice versa. Said otherwise, spirituality deals with the human capacity for self-transcendence, but in part this capacity is identical with the capacity for understanding and knowing, so to speak substantively of spirituality or to speak methodologically about doing spirituality is to some extent to speak of one and the same matter, human spirit. To be sure, the same consideration applies to every scientific study: what we understand about a thing will determine how we study it, and how we study it will determine what we understand about it. But this consideration is absolutely pivotal in the study of spirituality, for here (as in the human sciences) the knower and the known coincide: spirituality is about us, ourselves. The task of spirituality is to say what we, who perform this task, are ultimately capable of and how we can approach that ultimate. In this unique case, our knowing and our becoming absolutely coincide.

Nonetheless, I split the methodological considerations about spirituality apart from the substantive considerations. One result is the present volume, and despite the vicissitudes of its formation, the final product is a happy one.

Since the methodological considerations in this book are no longer explicitly one with a study in spirituality, I had to present a broader context in which to address the methodology of a scientific spirituality. Obviously, that broader context is the interrelationship of religion and the human sciences. I was well aware that this interrelationship was my topic all along, but producing an independent monograph on the topic forced me to be more deliberate and more precise about the matter. I created the first chapter and the epilogue from scratch, thoroughly edited the other chapters, and updated the chapter on Ken Wilber by adding a criticism of his latest book. Thus, the present volume became explicitly relevant to a wide range of scholars and professionals: religious leaders and thoughtful adherents (Hindu, Buddhist, Christian, Evangelical, Biblical Fundamentalist, and New Age), psychotherapists and psychologists, social scientists, pastoral counselors, spiritual directors, humanistic and transpersonal psychologists, theologians, religious scholars of all kinds, philosophers of religion, interdisciplinary methodologists, philosophers of science, and anyone concerned about the emerging postmodern culture and the global community.

Since this book was once one piece with what became *The Human Core of Spirituality*, the Preface of that first volume is also pertinent to this present one. In particular, I am repeating here the names of the many people whom I already thanked in that first volume, for their contribution to the original comprehensive manuscript also impacted this second volume.

I am grateful to J. Patrick O'Brien, S.T.D., LaRoche College, Pittsburgh, Pennsylvania, for his careful comments and repeated consultation about the present volume, and to Richard Woods, O.P., S.T.D., and the other three anonymous SUNY Press reviewers for their helpful criticism. At the State University of West Georgia: I thank Christopher Donovan, my research assistant, for his tedious work in comparing the 1996 edition of Ken Wilber's *Eye to Eye* with the 1990 edition, which I had originally analyzed, and confirming that the later edition is virtually unchanged; to Don Rice, Ph.D., Chair of the Psychology Department, for arranging my teaching schedule to allow me time to attend to this publication; to Thomas A. Beggs of Learning Resources, who prepared the camera-ready figures for this book; and to the Learning Resources Committee, which awarded me a Faculty Research Grant to cover some of the

costs of this project. I am also grateful to my dear mother and
brother for their warm welcome in our family home in Pittsburgh,
which afforded me the social support I needed while completing
final revisions on this manuscript. And I thank Lois Patton, Ph.D.,
Editor-in-Chief, and Nancy Ellegate, Nancy Farrell, Ruth Fisher,
Deborah Foreman, Judy Spevack, and the other staff at the State
University of New York Press for their part in bringing this long-
term project to completion in its former and this present volume.
At every phase of production and marketing, work with this team
has been a pleasure.

    For their substantial criticism on an early version of this work,
I again thank Homer Bain, Ph.D., Assistant Director, Ecumenical
Center for Religion and Health, San Antonio, Texas; C. Edward
Harris, Ph.D., Professor of Philosophy, Texas A & M University;
Nancy Schweers, M.T.S., former Research Consultant, Ecumenical
Center for Religion and Health, San Antonio, Texas; Carla Mae
Streeter, Ph.D., Associate Professor of Systematic Theology, Aquinas
Institute of Theology; and Frank Wicker, Ph.D., Professor of Edu-
cational Psychology, The University of Texas at Austin. And for
inviting me to teach graduate summer courses in which I devel-
oped the ideas in this book, I again thank Patrick Guidon, O.M.I.,
President (retired), and Lillian Yonker, Academic Dean (retired),
Oblate School of Theology, San Antonio, and Claudia Blanchette,
Ph.D., Emmanuel College, Boston.

    For ideas, criticisms, suggestions, leads, references, encour-
agement, information, feedback, proofreading, and other helps: I
thank Mark H. Bickhard, R. Gerald Bishop, Mary Kay Cain, Sylvia
Padilla Chavez, Charles L. Christen, John Christopher, Paul
Dauben, Frederick J. Cwiekowski, James J. Davitt, Anne DiSarcina,
Mary Donahey, Robert Doran, Thomas J. Dougherty (R.I.P.), Barnet
Feingold, Roy Eugene Graham, Kelvin Gregory, Beverly Hall,
D. Mark Hamlet, Tobin Hart, Elfie Hinterkopf, Randall Hoedeman,
Bruce Jarstfer, Toby Johnson, Beatrice Johnston, Steven Joseph,
Paul Kirkpatrick, Lacey Largent, John Macnamara, James Maney,
Rose Marden, Doris Spitznagel Marsilio, Mary and Dick Murphy,
Robert Poletto, Kaisa Puhakka, Garrett Rauwerda, Louis Roy, Eliza-
beth St. Lawrence, Michael Schatz, Randall Scott, Terry J. Tekippee,
Elisa Velasquez, Nedra Voorhies, and Gee Gee Whitehurst.

    I am filled with awe and humility as I bring this project to
completion. I have been gifted. So many people have generously

helped me. Some have been listed here, and others, unnamed, from my earliest beginnings, teachers in one form or another, offered strands of influence that interweave and lead up to my extensive graduate studies and beyond. Often I have marvelled that the ideas I finally wrote had ever occurred to me at all. How I, who sit and write now in the unfinished basement of our small mill worker's home in South Side Pittsburgh—how I could have written this book is amazing to me. All criticism of this book aside—and some negative criticism must surely be fair—this book's mere existence is testimony to the fact that I have been greatly blessed. For this I also give thanks to The One Who/That Which gives life and blesses in countless and marvelous ways.

May my eyes ever be open to such blessing. May this work be a worthy tribute to it. May all of our eyes be more attuned to what is genuinely beautiful, marvelous, and worthwhile. May this book help foster understanding about the meaning of our being together here. As we structure a global community for the third millennium, may we truly take a step forward and find a way to combine ancient marvel with modern rigor, to preserve primordial awe as we pursue critical thinking. May we succeed in uniting religion and science in a manner worthy of them both and in a manner worthy, then, of us all.

Easter and Pentecost, 1997

Chapter 1

Opening a Can of Worms

eligion used to be everything. The religions of traditional societies encompassed every facet of life—conception, birth, puberty, marriage, hunting, planting and harvesting, commerce, warfare, medicine, "science," art, music, death, burial, and the afterlife. Even surveying was originally a religious function. The markers between properties were considered sacred to the gods and, for this reason, were not to be disturbed (DeCoulanges, 1972).

The function of religion has always been to bring meaning and coherence to life—to explain what life is all about and to prescribe how life is to be lived in the face of its religious purpose. Meanings and values, beliefs and ethics, credo and commitment, vision and virtue, understandings and evaluations, are core hallmarks of religion. So religion touches every aspect of life.

Yet as history progressed, one by one, facets of life branched off and became independent. Socrates was noted—and executed—for teaching youth to question the stories about the gods. Thus, philosophy, the "love of wisdom," emerged alongside of religion. Medieval sacred music was fitted with secular lyrics and played for entertainment. Soon the troubadours were singing their own songs

1

of romance and love rather than hymns of God and the saints. Modern science once provoked heated controversy about the cosmos as understood in the Bible. Today not even the staunchest Fundamentalists insist on the biblical account, that the earth is a flat disk of land supported by pillars sunk into the deep and covered with a hammered-metal-like dome, from which hang the sun, moon, and stars. The hard sciences and religion now coexist in peace.

But the more science touches human life and its meaning, the more entangled religion remains. Biblical Fundamentalists still protest an evolutionary account of humanity, and medical advances routinely provoke ethical condemnations from religious leaders. Biology comes too close to home. Even worse are the human (or social) sciences—sociology, anthropology, political science, economics, psychology. Religion and the human sciences have been unable to draw their boundaries to anyone's satisfaction.

At the beginnings of American psychology, William James (1902/1961) allowed that religion is an important dimension of human psychology. He addressed the matter in his classic, *The Varieties of Religious Experience*. In contrast, Sigmund Freud (1927/ 1975) denounced religious beliefs as infantile wishful thinking and named his important treatment of religion *The Future of an Illusion*. For the most part, Freud's influence carried the day, and during much of its first century, modern psychology has been antagonistic to religion. A recent study shows that the majority of psychologists and psychotherapists are much less committed to religion than their clients or the population at large (Bergin & Jensen, 1990).

Nonetheless, psychology is too close to religion to be able to steal away quietly. Early on, religionists were already looking to psychology for pointers on pastoral care, and within religious circles concern about pastoral counseling and psychology of religion continued the discussion about the relationship between psychology and religion (Wulff, 1997). Most recently, even secular sources have begun to reintroduce religious—or at least, spiritual—concerns into psychology. So, for example, *American Psychologist*, the prestigious journal of the American Psychological Association, carried a series of articles arguing for the integration of some religious dimension within contemporary psychology (Jones, 1994; Kukla, 1989; O'Donahue, 1989).

It has now become respectable to attend to spiritual and/or religious concerns in psychology and especially in clinical practice and psychotherapy (Bergin, 1980, 1991; Bergin, Masters, & Richards, 1987; Canda, 1988a, 1988b; Conn, 1989; Chandler, Holden, & Kolander, 1992; Ellis, 1980; Ellison & Smith, 1991; Helminiak, 1987c, 1989a; Hiatt, 1986; Kass, Friedman, Leserman, Zutter-meister, & Benson, 1991; Manaster, 1990; McFadden, 1991; Miller, 1990; Moberg, 1978; Moberg & Brused, 1978; Paloutzian & Ellison, 1982; Schneiders, 1989; Shelly & Fish, 1988). But the "and/or" and the "especially" are significant. They point up the ambiguity surrounding the matter. While there is growing consensus that somehow psychology inevitably implicates religious or spiritual issues, there is no coherent and commonly accepted understanding of how religion and the human sciences relate. This is the problem that this book addresses.

The focus here is on psychology, though the overall topic is the human sciences. This is so not only because I am more familiar with psychology than with the other human sciences but also because religious issues come to the fore more saliently in psychology than in economics, political science, anthropology, or sociology. Of course, conflict with religion is at the roots of modern sociology. Its founders, August Comte and Claude-Henri Saint Simon, proposed that, with the full deployment of social science, the superstitions of religion would fall away and a form of positivist religion, a "new Christianity" of ethics and fraternity, would thrive in its place (Reese, 1967, pp. 99, 505–506). Moreover, sociological studies of American society, for example, have analyzed questions of meaning and value (Bellah, Madsen, Sullivan, Swindler, & Tipton, 1985), the very pair of concerns that are central to religion. And serious theoretical discussion, closely related to the religious concern for truth and goodness, surrounds the very nature of sociology as a discipline (Bernstein, 1976; Doran, 1981, 1990; Habermas, 1991/1970; Taylor, 1989; Weber, 1949; Wolfe, 1989, 1993). The question is, How is it possible for a supposedly objective and value-free science to treat of human realities? For not only are these human realities constituted by the meanings and values that people place on them. But the very scientists studying them also buy into particular world views and implicit agendas; the scientists are operating out of their own chosen sets of meaning and value. These methodological issues are the very same ones that also affect psychology (Browning,

1987; Doherty, 1995; Richardson & Guignon, 1991). Thus, while the focus here is on psychology, the methodological issues at stake are common to all the human sciences.

Three Common Approaches

In general, I discern three approaches to relating religion and psychology. By treating respectively the Evangelical integration project, Don Browning's position, and Ken Wilber's position, this book addresses these three approaches. Most globally, there is a call for dialogue. The suggestion is that both religion and psychology have something valid to offer, and conversation between the two would somehow be mutually enriching. But determining the ground rules for this dialogue is precisely the interdisciplinary challenge.

The second approach introduces more precision and specifies the domains of competence proper to science and religion. This approach accepts Dilthey's now classic distinction between the *Geisteswissenschaften* (human or social sciences) and the *Naturwissenschaften* (natural or physical sciences) (Palmer, 1969). This distinction suggests that, while the *Naturwissenschaften* provide explanation about things, the *Geisteswissenschaften* interpret the meaning of things. (Exactly what this means—and it is problematic—will be discussed in Chapter Three.) Thus, supposedly, there can be no conflict between the natural sciences and religion as long as each remains faithful to its respective role. When the question is about psychology, however, ambiguity reigns again, for both theology and psychology may fall under the *Geisteswissenschaften*. In this case, the first two approaches are combined, and psychology and religion become partners in a dialogue regarding the meaning of things (Browning, 1987). As may already be obvious, however, this combination of approaches provides no real advance, since the topic here from the beginning has been religion and the *human* sciences.

Finally, borrowed from Hinduism, Buddhism, and disparate strands of Western thought is an approach named "the perennial philosophy" (Huxley, 1945; Wilber, 1996). It suggests that the innermost nature of all things is spiritual or even divine, and thus it indicates a common link that unifies psychological and religious concerns. This approach is the theoretical core of much humanistic and transpersonal psychology, which rightly insists on broadening social science to include the transcendent dimensions of human experience. However, the coherence of this theoretical core remains a problem. As may already be obvious, this unification of disciplines is ultimately bought at the expense of all differentiation of specialized fields of study. Psychology and theology are ultimately collapsed into one.

An Alternative Approach

Detailed exposition and criticism of those approaches fill the latter half of this book. None of them appears to be adequate, but no alternative has been available.

In its first half, this book proposes an alternative; it suggests another approach. It provides a resolution to the conundrum in the relationship of psychology and religion. In its second half, this book also claims to pinpoint flaws in those other approaches and to suggest corrections for them. Accordingly, the alternative approach would appear more incisive and more comprehensive than the rest. Thus, this book is a contribution to the eventual emancipation of the last of the academic disciplines, the human sciences, from the all-embracing mother, religion. But the final result is not orphaned children, for the relationship between religion and the human sciences is also preserved.

In a volume companion to this one, *The Human Core of Spirituality: Mind as Psyche and Spirit* (Helminiak, 1996a), I have already exemplified the results of applying this other approach. As the title of that book suggests, spirituality is at the heart of the present discussion. A coherent understanding of spirituality is the key to clarifying the relationship of psychology and religion.

Spirituality is widely, almost universally, considered a religious concern, and "religious" is taken to mean "theological." This is to say, spirituality is generally thought to concern humanity's relationship with God. Pushing the matter even further—as in Wilber's (1996) perennial philosophy, for example—human spirit and divinity are thought to be one and the same thing; at its core humanity is thought really to be divine. But when human spirit and divinity are thus confounded, I submit, the interdisciplinary problematic becomes unresolvable. Surely, no one can say with certainty what God is. Then, if divinity is an essential dimension of humanity, all the human sciences face an impossible task. They can never hope to achieve a correct understanding of humankind. Their success depends on explaining what can never be understood: God. So positing spirituality as an intermediary discipline— between psychology on the human side and theology on the divine—is the key to relating the human sciences and religion.

Necessarily, that prior volume gave short shrift to issues of interdisciplinary methodology. This book attends to these issues in detail.

Outline of Chapter One

In the next section, I summarize some key concepts from that other book, for they also bear on methodology. Their mention here allows the present volume to stand as an independent monograph.

With that summary, the foundation will have been laid for a study of other attempts to integrate religion and psychology. This chapter will tentatively begin that study by unpacking the matter. This initial focus will be on two broad discussions about the relationship of psychology and religion: the so-called "integration" project of Evangelical Christianity, and the debate about the nature of religious studies in contrast to theology. These two discussions constitute the subsequent two sections of this chapter. These discussions are notorious for their failure to achieve consensus, so, unlike the positions addressed in later chapters, these two are not elaborated positions on the relationship of religion and the human sciences. Nonetheless, discussing these two will provide a useful introduction. It will exemplify the variety of approaches that have been suggested in this matter. It will raise the myriad and entangled questions at stake in this matter. And thus it will prime the reader for this book's subsequent deeper consideration of the matter.

An Overview of the Alternative Approach

A key suggestion was already made: Spirituality is the link between psychology and theology. Of course, here *spirituality* is taken to refer to an academic discipline or a field a study. It is the study of the lived experience that people call their "spirituality." Accordingly, this side-by-side listing of psychology, spirituality, and theology is already a sorting out of issues that all constitute what is globally called "religion." This sorting out is the heart of the alternative approach to relating religion and the human sciences presented in this book—an approach via spirituality—and this alternative presumes that "religion" is too diffuse a construct to be used effectively in interdisciplinary studies.

A System of Four Viewpoints

The full-blown presentation of this sorting out comprises a schema of four levels. (See Figure 1.1.) These I call "viewpoints," and they relate in an interlocking system. *Viewpoint* is a technical term and will be defined in Chapter Two. The term refers to a point of view or a horizon of concern or a stance regarding the attempt to understand something. And the something in question here is the human being and the human situation.

One stance approaches the human with concern simply to understand accurately what happens to be the case. This stance constitutes the positivist viewpoint. Another stance wonders, over and above that, whether what happens to be the case is as it ought to be. Here questions of *correct* meanings and *wholesome* values— questions of the true and the good—come into play explicitly. This stance is called the philosophic viewpoint, the stance of the "lover of wisdom." A further stance posits a fullness of truth and goodness as the terminus toward which correct human meanings and values point. This fullness is taken to be God, and this stance is called the theist viewpoint. Finally, a still further stance considers the possibility of human participation in that Fullness, which is God. The concern is to account for human union with God, and this stance is called the theotic viewpoint. *Theotic* comes from the Greek term *theosis*, which means deification or human participation in divinity. The study of deification would be called *theotics*, in contrast to *theology*, which limits its concern to God.

It is possible to study the human from within any or all of these viewpoints. Attending only to the de facto status quo of the matter, one works within the positivist viewpoint. Attending to human authenticity, one works within the philosophic viewpoint.

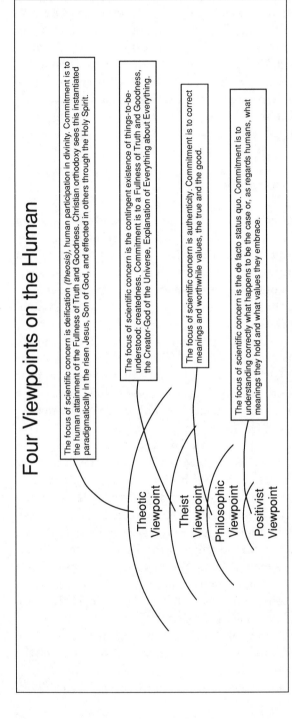

Four Viewpoints on the Human

Theotic Viewpoint
The focus of scientific concern is deification *(theosis)*, human participation in divinity. Commitment is to the human attainment of the Fullness of Truth and Goodness. Christian orthodoxy sees this instantiated paradigmatically in the risen Jesus, Son of God, and effected in others through the Holy Spirit.

Theist Viewpoint
The focus of scientific concern is the contingent existence of things-to-be-understood: createdness. Commitment is to a Fullness of Truth and Goodness, the Creator-God of the Universe, Explanation of Everything about Everything.

Philosophic Viewpoint
The focus of scientific concern is authenticity. Commitment is to correct meanings and worthwhile values, the true and the good.

Positivist Viewpoint
The focus of scientific concern is the de facto status quo. Commitment is to understanding correctly what happens to be the case or, as regards humans, what meanings they hold and what values they embrace.

Figure 1.1 This system of higher viewpoints entails a series of interlocking analytic perspectives on one and the same phenomenon. The questions inherent in each viewpoint—not a change in phenomena nor a change in the data available on one phenomenon—determine different academic disciplines or sciences. At the same time, the interrelatedness of the questions interrelates the same independent disciplines. Valid conclusions within the lower viewpoints constrain, and are retained within, the higher viewpoints. The presuppositions of the higher viewpoints confirm the validity of the presuppositions of the lower. The independent disciplines in interrelationship constitute a comprehensive human science. (Reprinted from Daniel A. Helminiak, *The Human Core of Spirituality*, © 1996, with permission of the State University of New York Press)

Attending to God and the created status of the human, one works within the theist viewpoint. And attending to human deification, one works within the theotic viewpoint.

Diverse academic disciplines are proper to each of the viewpoints. The theotic viewpoint is concerned with theotics, the treatment of human participation in divinity. Classical Christian orthodoxy (I do not mean Fundamentalism) provides a ready example of theotic concern. The three core doctrines of Christianity—the Trinity of Persons in God; the incarnation of the Only-Begotten of God as Jesus Christ and his glorification or resurrection from the dead (deification); and grace, the deifying gift of the Holy Spirit given to Jesus' human brothers and sisters—serve to account for human sharing in the divine nature of the Eternal Parent, God.

Again, the theist viewpoint is concerned with theology. Understood here in a restricted sense, theology is the study of God and God's relationship to the created universe. (*Theology* is not taken to mean any study of any issues proper to a specific religion.)

Yet again, the philosophic viewpoint is concerned with spirituality. This is the study of human beings that takes into explicit account the human need to be open, honest, and loving or, in a word, authentic. Further elaboration on this crucial matter is given below. But already it might be clear that such study of the human, differentiated from theist concerns, is a kind of social science whose vistas include the furthest possibilities of human development. So, according to the present analysis, social or human science that takes authenticity into explicit account is already spirituality.

Finally, the positivist viewpoint is concerned to explain the facts of some matter. It pertains in the natural sciences, and it also characterizes the human sciences as currently conceived.

From the positivist through the philosophic, theist, and theotic viewpoints, these four cohere as ever broader expansions of one another. To this extent they represent a coherent and comprehensive system for study of the human. They suggest where different facets of the matter fall and thus how these facets relate to the others. By the same token, the four viewpoints also determine what disciplines properly deal with these facets. The system of four viewpoints is a schema for comprehensive interdisciplinary science.

Chapter Two presents elaborate detail on this system of four viewpoints, so further explanation will not be given here. What has been said is sufficient to introduce the matter and to present the terminology.

Spirituality as an Inherently Human Phenomenon

Of course, pivotal to the matter is the understanding of spirituality. I discussed it in detail in *The Human Core of Spirituality* (Helminiak, 1996a), and here I present a brief summary.

The beginning point is to recognize the complexity of human "mind" and to differentiate within it two distinct factors: psyche and spirit. This is to say that, in contrast, the standard model of the human is bipartite. In religion the human is said to be body and soul, and in the human sciences, body and mind. (The difference between mind and soul is not significant here.) But if human mind is more than one thing, a tripartite model of the human emerges: the human is a composite of organism, psyche, and spirit. (See Figure 1.2.)

Granted that spirit is an inherent dimension of the human mind, there is already at hand a basis for treatment of spirituality apart from any implication of God. Spirituality is a fully human affair. Spirituality is built into the human experience in the very makeup of the human mind (cf. Vande Kemp, 1996). Though most people may express their inherent spiritual inclination by means of belief in God and through the practice of religion, at its core spirituality is a human, not a theological, matter; it pertains to social or human science and not to theological studies per se. Spirituality is an unavoidable consequence of being human. And all this is said without any prejudgment on questions about the existence and nature of God or about the role of belief in God in most people's lived spirituality.

The pertinent question at this point is whether this purported human "spirit" can account for all the aspects of what is called "spirituality." And the whole matter depends on the explanation of spirit.

An Account of the Human Spirit

The major inspiration of my whole approach is the thought of Bernard Lonergan (1957, 1972). The summary given here is dense, and the matter is extremely subtle. Like Lonergan's thought over-

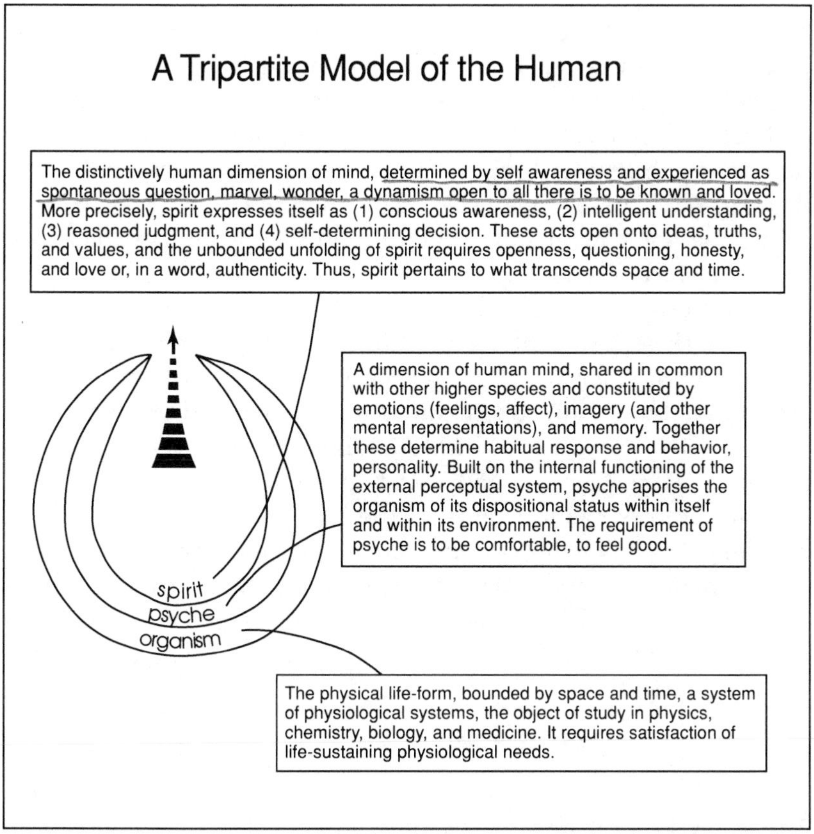

A Tripartite Model of the Human

The distinctively human dimension of mind, determined by self awareness and experienced as spontaneous question, marvel, wonder, a dynamism open to all there is to be known and loved. More precisely, spirit expresses itself as (1) conscious awareness, (2) intelligent understanding, (3) reasoned judgment, and (4) self-determining decision. These acts open onto ideas, truths, and values, and the unbounded unfolding of spirit requires openness, questioning, honesty, and love or, in a word, authenticity. Thus, spirit pertains to what transcends space and time.

A dimension of human mind, shared in common with other higher species and constituted by emotions (feelings, affect), imagery (and other mental representations), and memory. Together these determine habitual response and behavior, personality. Built on the internal functioning of the external perceptual system, psyche apprises the organism of its dispositional status within itself and within its environment. The requirement of psyche is to be comfortable, to feel good.

spirit
psyche
organism

The physical life-form, bounded by space and time, a system of physiological systems, the object of study in physics, chemistry, biology, and medicine. It requires satisfaction of life-sustaining physiological needs.

Figure 1.2 Refining the standard model, body and mind (or body and soul), the tripartite model distinguishes psyche and spirit within mind. Three factors name the necessary and sufficient to account for human reality and functioning. The factors are distinct: each entails a different intelligibility, so the one cannot be the other. Their distinction does not imply separation. Neither does their depiction here, in perceptible and imaginable representation, suggest contiguity of parts or priority of order. (Reprinted from Daniel A. Helminiak, *The Human Core of Spirituality*, © 1996, with permission of the State University of New York Press)

all, it is difficult. For this reason Lonergan is not well known, nor is his position often cited. Nonetheless, I find his thought far more incisive than any other I have studied. So I present here an instance of his possible significance, an implementation of his methodological analyses. In this and its companion volume (Helminiak,

1996a), I have tried to present as accessible a presentation as possible. Still, the reader will be challenged to think deeply and carefully. My hope is that, in the end, the reader might share my enthusiasm and believe that Lonergan's thought offers a significantly new approach to interdisciplinary questions. To test whether or not it does—to this task this book is an invitation.

Lonergan's main work was an analysis of human consciousness, the work of intentionality analysis. In places he also refers to consciousness as "spirit" (Lonergan, 1957, p. 519; 1972, pp. 13, 302), and I use these terms interchangeably. Differing from contemporary usage in psychological circles, by "consciousness" Lonergan does not refer to all the self-aware contents and processes of the human mind but restrictedly to that by which the human mind is self-aware. This particular dimension of mind is the spiritual.

Lonergan's analysis outlines the structure of consciousness or spirit: spirit is bimodal, and it operates on four levels. (See Figure 1.3.) That is, simultaneously, concomitantly, and inextricably, it is both conscious and intentional (as parallel terms I also say "nonreflecting" and "reflecting"), and in shifting emphasis its functioning is empirical, intellectual, rational, and responsible (Lonergan, 1972, p. 6–13).

The Four Levels of Consciousness

Consider first the four levels of consciousness. Note from the beginning that *levels* is a metaphor. This image does not mean that consciousness is actually built piece upon piece. If consciousness is but another name for spirit and if spirit is nonspatial and nontemporal, all talk of pieces and building and pictured levels is off base. *Levels* is but a word, and others could have been used: dimensions or aspects or facets of consciousness or factors or emphases within consciousness. The words point to distinguishable aspects of consciousness, facets that are discernibly different, though they constitute and operate within one reality, human consciousness.

Consciousness or spirit is a dynamic reality. It is driven ever forward by wonder, marvel, awe, which is inherent in humanity and constitutive of human beings. This wonder, or primordial question, expresses itself in particular formulated questions. It is at work in the child's unending curiosity and interminable queries; it

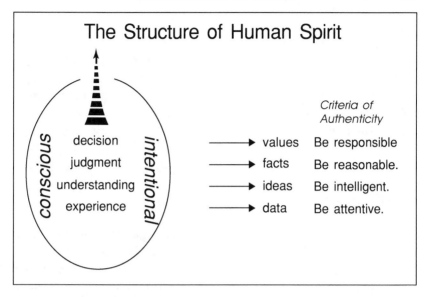

The Structure of Human Spirit

conscious
decision
judgment
understanding
experience

intentional

Criteria of Authenticity

→ values Be responsible
→ facts Be reasonable.
→ ideas Be intelligent.
→ data Be attentive.

Figure 1.3 According to Lonergan (1957, 1972), human conscious-ness or spirit is a conscious intentionality, dynamic, open-ended, and self-transcending, that operates on four interrelated levels. Acts of seeing, hearing, touching, smelling, tasting, and imagining on an empirical level constitute experience and provide data, some-thing to be understood. Acts of inquiring, understanding, conceiv-ing, and formulating on an intellectual level concern intelligibility and result in ideas, concepts, hypotheses about the data. Acts of reflecting, marshalling and weighing the evidence, and judging on a rational level concern reality, being, truth, and result in knowl-edge, facts, i.e., ideas verified in the data. Acts of deliberating, evaluting, deciding, and acting on a responsible level concern the good and express values, lived responses to experience and knowl-edge. This structure is normative, for its open-ended unfolding requires deliberate respect for its functioning on each level: atten-tion, intelligence, reasonableness, and responsibility. Together these define human authenticity and permit ongoing growth. (Reprinted from Daniel A. Helminiak, *The Human Core of Spirituality,* © 1996, with permission of the State University of New York Press)

undergirds the research scientist's attempts to understand; it emerges in the lover's profession of eternal devotion; it sustains the mystic's contemplation of the stars. The openended dynamism that makes humans human is part and parcel of every truly human experience. Humans are inherently spiritual.

On a first level, consciousness is mere awareness, and through such awareness one finds oneself confronted with data. There is something to be understood. The spontaneous dynamism of human spirit prompts the question, What is it? With this question consciousness shifts its functioning to a second level. Here, not mere awareness but understanding is at stake. After investigation and questioning, insight may occur. One has a breakthrough of understanding. Then formulation follows, and one has a hypothesis, a theory, an idea, a possible explanation.

But the presence of an idea or hypothesis spontaneously effects another shift in spiritual functioning. Wonder, marvel, and awe now express themselves in another question, Is it? or Is it so? That is to say, Is this idea correct, have I understood correctly? Or is this just another "bright" (but mistaken) idea? Consciousness is now operating on a third level. The task at hand is to check the hypothesis against the data and to determine the inherent "is" or "is not," the "Yes" or "No," regarding the correctness of the idea. This question is answered by another kind of insight, the judgment of fact that discerns whether or not there is sufficient evidence to allow the conclusion, It is so. With this conclusion, one has moved from mere experience and beyond mere idea and into reality. One has attained to fact; one has knowledge. Knowledge is correct understanding. Knowledge is understanding that is verified in the data. So human knowledge is a compound; it depends on the coalescence of data, understanding, and judgment.

The presence of knowledge in consciousness provokes yet another shift, and spirit begins functioning on the responsible or existential level, a fourth level. Here, the determining concern is expressed in the question, What am I going to do about it? Here, concern shifts from knowing to doing, from thinking to living. The same unfolding dynamic of consciousness is at work, but now it requires decision or choice and necessitates engagement with the external world. Decisions and choices result in changes in oneself and in the world, and these changes provide new data for another turn of the wheel of dynamic consciousness.

Thus, consciousness operates on four levels. Aware of data, it is empirical. Questioning to understand, it is intellectual. Marshalling and weighing evidence, it is rational. And pondering, deliberating, and acting, it is responsible.

When talking about the spiritual, I often speak simply of "meanings and values." These are the hallmarks of human spiritual functioning. Parallel and more suggestive formulations are "credo and commitment," "vision and virtue," "beliefs and ethics," "understandings and evaluations." These pairs represent a shorthand way of inferring the concerns of the four levels of consciousness. "Meanings" pertains to the first three levels, so instead of naming data, idea, and fact, I simply say "meanings." It should be noted that here *meaning* does not mean significance, as in the phrase, "the meaning of my life," for this usage already entails values and commitments. Rather, *meanings* is used in a strictly cognitive sense and suggests simply "understandings." Hence, there follow the parallels, "beliefs," "vision," "credo." In contrast, "values" relates to the fourth level of consciousness. I find these shorthand formulas useful in nontechnical presentations—as in the second paragraph of this chapter. These formulas also square well with the jargon of the social sciences and thus provide an easy entry for discussion of the spiritual in human science circles. I trust that the reader will not be confused by my shift in phrasing. A thorough grasp of any matter allows one to express it in various ways as fit the occasion.

The Correlation of Consciousness and Being

A single dynamism or intentionality is at work on all four levels of consciousness, and the ideal goal of this openended movement is to embrace the universe. We would understand everything about everything; we would love all that there is to be loved. The very nature and structure of human consciousness gear us toward all that is; they orient us toward being.

Being is taken to be all that there is to be known. Thus, human consciousness and being co-define one another. All that is can, in principle, be known, and what there is to be known is what is. What cannot be known is not, period. This is to say, "what cannot be known" is not "something" that cannot be known; rather, this supposed "something" simply does not exist; in actuality, it is nothing. If there is nothing there to be known, there is simply nothing there. And if there is something there, it can be known. The ideal reach of human spirit is coterminous with the totality of reality. Being is all that there is to be known and—granted also the fourth level of consciousness—loved.

The Inherent Normativity of Consciousness: Authenticity

Since human spirit is oriented in openended embrace toward all that there is to be known and loved, the very dynamism and structure of human spirit entail a normativity. The continued unfolding of spirit toward the universe of being imposes certain requirements. If on a first level of consciousness, people are aware, then insofar as they can determine the matter, they should be attentive. If on a second level people seek to understand, then they should be intelligent—which is simply to say, they should use whatever intelligence they have. If on a third level people seek to know, then they should be reasonable—which is to say, they should honestly make judgments on the basis of the evidence. And if on a fourth level people determine themselves and their world, then they should be responsible—which is to say, they should choose and act in accord with what they know and in a way that keeps open the openended unfolding of consciousness. The very structure of consciousness entails normative requirements. In this peculiar case, the "ought" does follow from the "is," for under consideration is the source and root meaning of "ought." Under consideration is that very reality that introduces questions of "ought" into the human situation.

The normative implications of the structured unfolding of consciousness constitute four transcendental precepts: Be attentive, Be intelligent, Be reasonable, and Be responsible. These are precepts because they impinge on us human beings and from within make demands. Violation of them entails diminishment of our own selves and inevitably, in some way or other, distortion and destruction to our world. They are transcendental because they apply across the board to whatever people do, wherever and whenever they do it.

The transcendental precepts represent a peculiar kind of requirement. Though they express absolutes, they are not absolutist.

Though they apply to every human operation, they do not prejudge or predetermine any outcome. Without ever prescribing *what* is to be affirmed or done, they require *how* every human activity should proceed: attentively, intelligently, reasonably, and responsibly. Proceeding in this way, human change moves toward unlimited fulfillment. Proceeding contrariwise, it creates its own dead end.

The transcendental precepts are absolutely openended in their purview. Indeed, in the realm of spirit they spell out the laws of nature to which Francis Bacons's famous aphorism referred: "Nature can only be commanded by being obeyed." Only obedience to the transcendental precepts assures openended human unfolding. In this, the reader should be hearing echoes of standard talk of spirituality. In contrast, only "the devil" would protest that the transcendental precepts bias human functioning.

The transcendental precepts provide the technical definition for a pivotal construct in this study of religion and the human sciences: authenticity. One is authentic to the extent that one follows the transcendental precepts. The matter is as simple and as far-reaching as that.

This understanding of *authenticity* does not completely square with the popular usage, which derives from existential philosophy. Though the word itself does suggest what is at stake in the present discussion, other connotations of the word might suggest something as banal as following one's personal whim or preference, and in some cases being authentic might simply mean being obnoxious. In contrast, Lonergan's notion of authenticity has objective validity build right into it. In Lonergan's (1972, p. 292) trenchant phrase, "Genuine objectivity is the fruit of authentic subjectivity." The presupposition is that authentic humanity is openendedly directed toward all that is, toward all that is true and all that is good. There is no possible egoism or solipsism in this understanding.

The Source of This Account

That is a popular summary of Lonergan's four-level analysis of human consciousness or spirit. I elaborated it in detail in *The Human Core of Spirituality*. The question remains, Where did Lonergan get this formulation? And there is the further question, What evidence suggests that this formulation is correct?

Historically, Lonergan arrived at his formulation through extensive study of Thomas Aquinas and the Greek philosophers, especially Aristotle, as well as study of modern philosophy and its "turn toward the subject." But the question about the evidence for his account points to another source, and in a profound sense it is the answer to both those questions.

The four-level analysis claims to formulate the structure of human consciousness. Then the only valid source for the formulation as well as the evidence to validate it must lie in consciousness itself. This analysis is correct if it accurately articulates human consciousness, and anyone should be able to test the validity of this articulation by examining his or her own consciousness. By carefully attending to inner experience, anyone should be able to detect a four-faceted functioning. Indeed, there could be no other way to test it. The only available instance of the matter in question lies within each one's own inner experience. Moreover, if the evidence does indeed lie there, this account of consciousness is empirically grounded. This account is a scientific statement. It rests on hard data—not, indeed, the data of sense, which alone narrow empiricism would credit, but real data nonetheless, the data of inner experience, the data of consciousness.

The Invulnerability of This Account

Consciousness is the ground of human subjectivity; consciousness is what make us human subjects. So another way to speak of consciousness or human spirit is to speak of human subjectivity. Now, one will never find an instance of subjectivity lying somewhere outside oneself. What is other than self or beyond self is not the subject but an object. Yet within one's own experience and only here, unless one is comatose or in dreamless sleep, one has available for examination an instance of human subjectivity. Attention to it should result in a four-factor formulation and, by the same token, result in the evidence that validates this formulation.

Are you ever aware of something to understand, so that you ask, What is it? How does it work? Why is it so? Or do you ask questions when, really, there is nothing there to be understood? And when you do ask, What is it? are you aware of trying to understand? Or have you never had the experience of insight? Have you never understood anything? And when you have an idea, do you ever wonder whether it is correct? Or does concern about correctness never occur to you? And when you determine that you are correct about something, do you begin to deliberate about the implications for your life? Do you wonder what you ought to do in this case? Or are you indifferent about the rightness or wrongness of your actions? Does it never occur to you to seek to do the right thing?

If you answered in the affirmative to the positively phrased questions, your own experience confirms the pattern of operations that Lonergan formulated in terms of four levels of consciousness. You have confirmed in your own experience the validity of this formulation. This formulation does express the very operations of your own mind. Now, you might not like the formulation. You might prefer not to speak of "levels." But regardless of how you eventually do choose to speak of the matter, it is clear that you know the reality about which Lonergan is speaking, and your formulation, despite whatever words you might use, must square significantly with his, for you speak of the same thing. In your own experience, you have evidence in support of his theory of consciousness. Moreover, the evidence in this case is telling indeed. It is the evidence of your very own experience. Fully apart from what might be the case in the experience of other people, in some way your very own self constrains you to accept Lonergan's account of consciousness. And if after consideration, other people must also admit to a similar assessment of the matter, in multiple subjects there is mounting empirical evidence in support of this account.

If, on the other hand, you answered in the negative to the negatively phrased questions, you disqualify yourself from the discussion. You unashamedly profess to be unaware, without understanding, dishonest, and irresponsible.

This is a disconcerting state of affairs. In some way it is personally offensive. It appears that this account of consciousness is telling us what we are, and we are unable to protest that we are other. In this matter we are unable to determine for ourselves what we are and what we want to be. Much to the consternation of our modern cry for autonomy and independence, we cannot but bow to this formulation of consciousness. If we refuse, we only undermine the personal dignity we wish to protect. The peculiarity of this state of affairs suggests that Lonergan is onto something. I, for one, believe that he has hit the nail on the head. His formulation of consciousness is accurate, and it cannot be subverted. Even argument to subvert it must, in the very arguing, employ the very elements that structure the account in the first place.

Thus, the evidence for Lonergan's four-level formulation of consciousness lies in the data of consciousness. The evidence lies in the very inner experience of the conscious human subject.

The Bimodal Structure of Consciousness

That fact provokes further questioning that leads more deeply into the nature of consciousness or spirit. Our daily mental functioning is filled with concern about this, that, and the other thing. We are usually quite aware of the contents of conscious experience. These contents are the things about which we think. But seldom do we attend to the process of thinking itself.

Stop for a moment and answer this question: what were you just doing?

Without much effort you will probably answer something to this effect: I was just reading the above paragraph. Or else, I had stopped reading for a moment and was thinking about what I just read. Or perhaps, my mind had drifted, and I was daydreaming about such and such. Let us assume that you answered that you were reading the above paragraph. Whatever the case, nobody could prove you wrong. You are the only person who could accurately answer that question. But the remarkable thing is that you could answer it.

Your mind was wholly taken up with what you were reading. Yet when I asked about what you were doing, you were able to answer correctly: "I was reading"—even though that is *not* what you were attending to. You could answer about the fact of your reading even though your mind was filled with whatever it was you were reading. Evidently, you were aware of two different things at one and the same time and aware of them in two different ways. You were aware of what you were reading, and you were aware of the fact of your reading. Of course, the two are inextricable, but the two contents of your awareness are different.

That is the point. Consciousness is double. By one and the same consciousness, you are aware of some object and simultaneously aware of yourself as the aware subject.

Lonergan (1972, pp. 11–13) speaks of consciousness as both intentional and conscious. It is intentional insofar as it directs us toward some object. It is conscious insofar as it makes us aware of ourselves as so directed.

In addition to using those terms, I also use parallel ones. I speak of consciousness as reflecting and non-reflecting (Helminiak, 1996a, pp. 43–59). Reflecting consciousness is intentional; through it one reflects upon, thinks about, deals with, something other than oneself, who is doing the reflecting, thinking, dealing. Non-reflecting consciousness is conscious; through it one is aware of oneself as the aware subject, who is reflecting on, thinking about, dealing with, something. Non-reflecting consciousness is not reflecting because it sets up no subject-object duality. It does not reflect on something else but is about itself.

The matter has one more complication. We can also think about ourselves. In this case we become objects to ourselves, and the object here is just as much an other as are the other things about which we could think. In every case, even while we are thinking about some object, including ourselves, there is the thinking subject simultaneously aware in another mode of its own subjectivity. I am reflectingly aware of myself when I think about myself, and simultaneously I am also non-reflectingly aware of myself as the thinking subject. Were I to raise a question about my activity, I could promote my non-reflecting awareness to reflecting awareness and begin to think about myself-thinking-about-myself. Yet even as I did this, I the thinking subject would still be non-reflectingly aware of my thinking. Reflecting and non-reflecting awareness are simultaneous, concomitant, and inextricable aspects of one and the same act of human awareness.

This discussion constantly turns back on itself, for it is nothing other than talk about human awareness or consciousness or spirit. The peculiarity of this discussion reflects the peculiarity of human spirit or consciousness. It is present to itself even as it is present to anything else. And precisely this presence to itself, concomitant to the act of being present to something else, allows for later reflection on the experience of whatever else it was present to.

Phraseology becomes difficult here. Language is made to deal with the world of objects. So talk of "presence to oneself" or "non-reflecting awareness of oneself" may be misleading. In English, prepositions take objects, so "presence to oneself" suggests that the self in question is an object. Yet the very point to be made is that this is the subject's presence "to" itself as the present subject and *not* as an object. I put quotation marks around the preposition to indicate that it is not being used in its ordinary this-against-that, subject-versus-object, sense. I use the only language available, cumbersome as it is, to speak of the presence of a subject "to" him- or herself as subject. But what cannot be expressed easily in necessarily linear language, can be grasped in understanding. At stake here is the understanding that can be grasped when one recognizes that one's consciousness is both intentional and conscious, reflecting and non-reflecting, directed toward objects and in another mode making oneself simultaneously aware "of" oneself as so directed.

It is the non-reflecting nature of human consciousness that makes us self-transcending beings. Because of our consciousness, because of our spiritual nature, we are always set already beyond ourselves. We are always more than we have articulated or can articulate, for behind every articulation is the articulating subject, whose ever-present articulating has yet to be articulated. Likewise, it is the self-transcending nature of human spirit that is expressing itself in the dynamism that results in the four levels of consciousness. The unfolding of these four levels is the filling in of the content of what has somehow already been anticipated— being, all that there is to be known and loved. And it is this same self-transcending nature that imputes normativity to this unfolding on four levels. Geared toward all that is, somehow already anticipating what is to be known and loved, already incorporating the structure of whatever will be known or loved, human consciousness urges an unfolding that will assure its own fulfillment. Of its nature, human spirit would operate in particular and required ways. For only in these ways will it attain to all being, which is its goal.

Spirituality on the Basis of the Human Spirit

That treatment of human spirit was to show that spirituality can be conceived in terms of human spirit and apart from reference to God. The discipline, spirituality, was to be distinct from theology, on the one hand, and from psychology, on the other. A test of the matter is whether or not spirituality so conceived can account for what people generally mean when they speak of spirituality. Let us engage in this test.

One hallmark of spirituality is awareness of transcendence and the experience of self-transcendence. But insofar as spirit was presented as a dynamic reality, anticipating the universe of being and directing human unfolding toward that fullness, a sense of transcendence is essential to spirit or consciousness. It is constitutive of spirit. Moreover, every movement of spirit from non-reflecting to reflecting and from one level of consciousness to the next would be an instance of self-transcendence. For every such movement would advance the human subject beyond what he or she had formerly been. This unfolding of human spirit is the key to all personal growth or development (Helminiak, 1987c). Thus, appeal to human spirit adequately accounts for the experience of transcendence and self-transcendence.

Further, spirituality is supposed to entail an openness to the infinite. But insofar as human spirit is geared to the universe of being, all that there is to be known and loved, spirit provides a basis for understanding that openness.

Again, spirituality is supposed to be characterized by the intuitive and ineffable. But insofar as spirit entails a non-reflecting dimension, it provides a basis for talk of intuition and ineffability. For what is grasped in non-reflecting awareness is, indeed, grasped; it is within awareness; but it is not objectified. To this extent, it is unspoken; it is only "intuited." Moreover, the non-reflecting dimension of spirit is by definition ineffable. Nonetheless, it is experienced, and insofar as this dimension is precisely the ever self-transcending dimension of human spirit, this ineffable dimension is an openness to the infinite. Thus, an account of human spirit provides an account of the ineffable, which characterizes spirituality.

Yet again, spirituality is supposed to deal with unusual experiences, which are called mystical. These entail some grasping, or being grasped by, that infinite and ineffable. But insofar as human spirit opens onto the infinite and provides a base for explaining the ineffable, non-reflecting experience "of" human spirit itself would be an experience of the potentially infinite and ineffable. Here, then, is an explanation of mystical experience apart from any appeal to God.

Moreover, spirituality is said to entail grace or unmerited giftedness. Of course, the term *grace* is used in a loose and popular sense. To this extent, the above account of human spirit is amenable to the vocabulary of grace. Human spirit unfolds from level to level via the experience of insight. Though one may prepare for insight by study and hard thought, insight always comes unexpectedly and as a gift. Indeed, it is the very nature of insight to transform the given such that the subsequent understanding shows the given to be other that what it was formerly taken to be. So one could speak of insight as an instance of grace. Or again, the word *grace* suggests that something has come from beyond oneself. But the very experience of non-reflecting consciousness entails an awareness of what transcends whatever is already objectified and articulated. Insofar as we tend to think of ourselves as the "me" about whom we can talk, all non-reflecting experience of ourselves, just like insight, would seem to come from beyond ourselves. Again, the notion of *grace* would be apropos.

Finally, for some traditions spirituality entails explicit emphasis on moral goodness or holiness, and to some extent or other all religious traditions include such moral validity in their understanding of exemplary spiritual achievement. But insofar as the unfolding of dynamic human spirit is a guided affair, normativity is built into it. The transcendental precepts are requisites of this very unfolding, and obedience to these precepts provides the fundamental meaning of the terms *moral, ethical, honest,* and *good.* Indeed, the philosophic viewpoint, whose disciplinary concern is spirituality, is defined by attention to these requisites. So treatment of spirituality in terms of human spirit does include explicit concern for human goodness.

Spirituality as a Psychological Specialization

Those considerations make clear that an understanding of human spirit provides a solid base for the treatment of spirituality and that such treatment can proceed apart from theology, the study of God.

Nonetheless, this treatment of spirituality does point godward. If spirituality is specified by concern for the openended unfolding of dynamic human consciousness or spirit, and if the human spirit is geared toward the universe of being, toward all that is true and good, and if God is conceived as the fullness of Truth and Goodness, then the theist believer will readily recognize that the full picture does not eschew God. There is a place for God and for the study of God, theology, but this place is not the same place as that of spirituality. Still, the theist can see that spirituality does point toward God and that spirituality and theology are related.

On the other hand, human spirit is understood to be one dimension of the human mind. To this extent, the study of spirituality can be conceived as a specialized form of psychology, which has always been defined in part as the study of the human mind. So on this understanding, far from being a theological matter, spirituality is primordially a specialization in psychology. It is that specialization that results when one studies the human being with explicit attention to the openended unfolding of the human spirit, which is specified by the inherent human requirement of authenticity.

When spirituality is delineated as a psychological specialization, it stands as a link between psychology as generally conceived, on the one side, and theology narrowly defined, on the other side. This specification of interrelated disciplines—psychology, spirituality, and theology—along with the specific concerns that define them, sorts out a number of pivotal issues that all comprise "religion" and that are generally confounded. Thus, this specification of spirituality is the central methodological maneuver for the clarification of the global notion *religion* and the resultant systematic interrelation of religion and the human sciences. Said otherwise, through the elaboration of human spirit and the specification of a psychological spirituality, the tripartite model of the human being and the system of four viewpoints intersect and lock together. Thus, they form the methodical interdisciplinary position that is the offering of this book. (See Figure 1.4.)

An Account of the Human Psyche

With the delineation of the dynamic, openended, bimodal, and four-levelled structure of human consciousness or spirit, it becomes clear that there is more to human mind than this. Psyche, the other factor in human mind, stands out in stark relief (Doran, 1977a, 1977b, 1977c, 1981).

The easiest introduction to psyche is a consideration of human dreaming. Dreams consist of images, pictures in the mind. Of

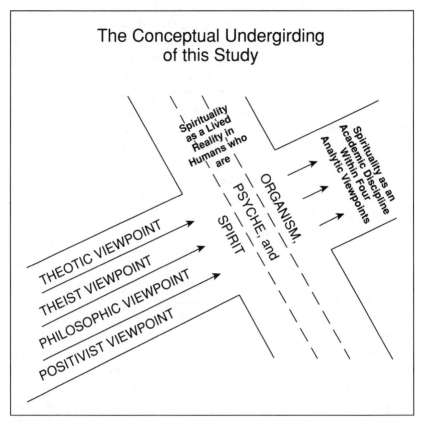

The Conceptual Undergirding
of this Study

Spirituality as a Lived Reality in Humans who are

Spirituality as an Academic Discipline Within Four Analytic Viewpoints

ORGANISM, PSYCHE, and SPIRIT

THEOTIC VIEWPOINT

THEIST VIEWPOINT

PHILOSOPHIC VIEWPOINT

POSITIVIST VIEWPOINT

Figure 1.4 Two fundamental conceptions intersect to form the undergirding of this study. First, understand human mind as double, psyche and spirit, and all human activity becomes relevant to spirituality as a lived reality. Second, distinguish higher viewpoints on the human, and academic disciplines, human sciences, are simultaneously distinguished and interrelated. Psychological study of the human within the philosophic viewpoint is already spirituality as an academic discipline.

course, the images of dreams are often more than visual. There are also auditory and tactile experiences that also qualify as "images." These appear to be internal perceptual experiences but without the external perceptual stimulation.

In addition to images, dreams also entail feelings—or emotion or affect, things like excitement, fear, anger, anxiety, gladness, expectation, and the like. Thus, in a dream one not only "sees" the imagery but also emotionally lives the dreamed experience. The feelings may be the most powerful part of the dream.

Dreams are powerful because they catch us unawares. They seem to bring up things that are a part of us but about which we are ignorant. To this extent, there is yet another aspect of psyche exemplified in dreams: memory. The record of our past emerges and mixes with images and feelings to produce the dream, a weird concoction of past, present, and future, memory and expectation.

So, as exemplified in the dream, there are three basic aspects to psyche: imagery, emotion, and memory (Lonergan, 1957). These three cohere. Their coherence is obvious in the experience of dreaming. Their coherence is also visible in what we call "personality"— our habitual patterns of response—for to a large extent emotion-laden memories and images, operating within us oftentimes unawares, determine the way we present ourselves, think, and act. (See Figure 1.5.) All these matters are the concern of psychology as generally

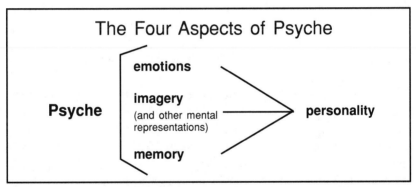

Figure 1.5 In addition to awareness, insight, judgment, and decision, all spiritual functions, human mind also entails other experiences. Emotions (feelings, affect), imagery (and other mental representations), and memory are part of an internal communication system that apprises the organism of its dispositional status within itself and within an environment. These aspects of mind relate to the inner workings of the outer-directed perceptual system. Together they constrain habitual patterns of response, personality, and constitute a mental factor distinct from spirit. (Reprinted from Daniel A. Helminiak, *The Human Core of Spirituality,* © 1996, with permission of the State University of New York Press)

understood, and contemporary psychology has a lot to say about them. Popular awareness of these things has also grown in recent years. Certainly, compared with consciousness or spirit, bimodal and unfolding on four levels, the things of psyche are the more familiar aspects of human mind.

Psyche and spirit are two factors that cohere in one human mind. But they are not parts or pieces that can be dismantled and put back together again, for they are not physical realities. In a word, they are not separable: one does not find the one without the other. Nonetheless, they are distinct: the one is not the other. One may not have an insight, a matter of the spirit, without the use of an image, a matter of the psyche. Still, simply to have the image is not the same thing as to understand. Or one may not have an insight or make a decision, matters of the spirit, without experiencing emotion, a matter of the psyche. Still, just to feel emotion is not the same thing as to understand or to decide. Psyche and spirit are really distinct. An intelligent treatment of mind requires that these two facets be distinguished. Otherwise confusion results, and there can be no coherent treatment. Human mind is double. It is psyche as well as spirit.

The Interaction of Spirit, Psyche, and Organism

Much more could be said about the psyche and its interaction with the human spirit—about the coherence of imagery, emotion, memory, and personality structures and how together they constitute but a single factor in the human being; about the core exigency of the psyche for inner comfort in contrast to the exigency of the spirit for authenticity; about the subservience of psyche to spirit when things of the psyche express meanings and values; about the friend that psyche can be when, for those who can decipher its symbolic code, it makes available new information about oneself and one's living; about the threat that psyche can also be when its spontaneous expressions unmask one's slick public self-presentation and belie one's deluded self-understandings; about the tension between spirit and psyche as the one pushes ever onward toward embrace of the universe of being and the other structures stability and comfortable present existence.

Much more could be said, and it is all actually a part of the picture when spirituality is the focus. Attention to the human spirit is only the defining feature of spirituality. Overall, spirituality entails the ongoing harmonious integration of the whole human being:

spirit, psyche, and organism in a physical and social world. The goal of spiritual concern is precisely the integration of the openended exigencies and potential of the human spirit into the permanent structures of the personality; the goal of spirituality is the integration of the human being that expresses and allows the unfolding of the dynamism of the human spirit. Thus, in a shifting compromise the exigencies of the human spirit and those of the psyche and those of the organism must somehow all be met while ever respecting the sovereign demands of the transcendental precepts. (See Figure 1.6.)

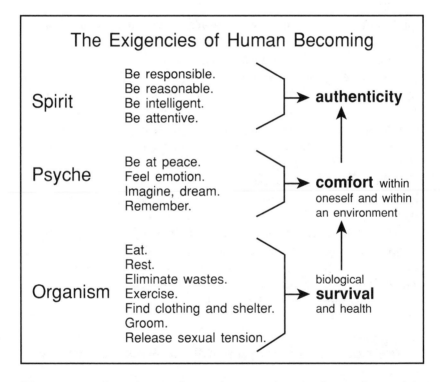

Figure 1.6 Integration demands attention, in due order and in shifting urgency, to the array of human exigencies rooted in organism, psyche, and spirit. Each person must find or create a way of being that does justice to the respective requirements for survival and comfort of his or her particular organic and psychic constitution. But the resolution of this human challenge must always respect the spiritual requirement, authenticity. (Reprinted from Daniel A. Helminiak, *The Human Core of Spirituality,* © 1996, with permission of the State University of New York Press)

But I have dealt with these matters in detail elsewhere (Helminiak, 1992, 1994a, 1995, 1996a). Besides, they are not central to the topic of this book. Although a complete treatment of spirituality cannot avoid matters of psyche and organism, differentiating spirituality from psychology and from theology turns on an elaboration of the human spirit. Thus, the present allusions to psyche and organism must suffice for the purposes of this book.

Recapitulation

Spirituality is the link between psychology and theology, and together these three enumerate diverse aspects of the global phenomenon "religion." This enumeration parallels the first three of the system of higher viewpoints: positivist, philosophic, and theist. Thus, sorting out these three is the key maneuver in the methodical interrelationship of religion and the human sciences. The overview of spirituality that has just been presented suggests what is meant by the psychological specialization, spirituality, and how it functions as the critical link between psychology and theology.

This overview has laid out the basic intellectual tools for delving into specific positions on the relationship of religion and psychology. Throughout this book these tools will be honed, and others will be brought out as they are needed. Two examples of attempts to relate psychology and religion follow in this introductory chapter. These serve to open up this interdisciplinary can of worms. The hope is that our tools will allow us to begin, at least, to untangle some of the knots.

The "Integration" Project of Evangelical Christianity

For decades a circle of Evangelical Christian scholars has been addressing the question of relating psychology and religion (Kemp, 1985). It is not easy to define the qualifier *Evangelical* with precision. Generally, it implies "acceptance of the Bible as the authoritative Word of God" (Collins, 1983, p. 4). This acceptance does not equate with the more conservative position, Fundamentalism, which usually takes the Bible literally as it reads in contemporary English. A more profoundly scholarly tradition, Evangelicalism is open to contemporary historical-critical interpretation of the scriptures. Within this circle the interdisciplinary challenge of relating psychology and Christianity is known as "integration" (Collins, 1983).

The project of integration has not been very successful, and in recent years it seems to have reached an impasse (Hill & Kauffmann, 1996; Vande Kemp, 1996). Still, this project represents a major and sustained effort to relate psychology and religion (Eck, 1996). Thus, the integration project merits serious attention. If nothing more, this attention will reveal the intricacies of the matter, raise important questions, and warn against dead ends. In a familiar and accessible form, attention to this Evangelical endeavor will introduce the matter of relating psychology and religion.

Models of Integration

Many have "written about the need for integration but [have] said little about the process and methodology of integrating Christianity and psychology" (Collins, 1983, p. 3). Some attempts merely catalogue the possible stances that one could take in making the interrelationship. For example, following H. Richard Niebuhr's (1951) classic, *Christ and Culture*, a relatively recent suggestion proposed five models of integration (Dueck, 1989). *Critique* assumes a fundamental rejection of secular wisdom; *Analogy* assumes a basic similarity between religious and secular teachings; *Translation* assumes a common vision but ponders the adequacy of the symbols with which the vision may be expressed; *Dialogue* assumes an insurmountable tension between religion and psychology but is also committed to the possibility of mutual clarification; and *Witness* assumes that religion has a distinctive contribution to offer that could benefit secular society.

Similarly, Carter (1977, 1996) notes four basic models of integration expressed in two different modes. On the secular side, there are Psychology *Against* Religion, Psychology *Of* Religion, Psychology *Parallels* Religion, and Psychology *Integrates* Religion; on the religious side, there are Scripture *Against* Psychology, Scripture *Of* Psychology, Scripture *Parallels* Psychology, and Scripture *Integrates* Psychology. Carter also specifies that simply paralleling or correlating facets of Christian belief with facets of psychology is not yet integration. "Genuine integration involves the discovery and articulation of the common underlying principles of both psychology and the Scripture" (p. 205).

Yet that specification does not tell how integration is to be done nor guarantee that it will happen. In an elaborate example of the very "nature and scope of integration," John D. Carter and Richard J. Mohline (1976) impressively presented a detailed and systematically researched alignment of issues common to psychology and Christianity. For example, Christian belief about the nature of the human, anthropology, supposedly deals with the same issues as do personality theories in psychology. Similarly, Christian doctrine about sin, hamartiology, relates in some way to psychological concern for psychopathology; and Christian concern about salvation, soteriology, relates to developmental psychology. But this presentation is not integration. It is clearly correlation, the paralleling of issues and themes in religion and psychology. To be sure, such an exposition is not without value. It would be very helpful for a psychotherapist attempting to find points of contact between a Christian client's belief and an intended psychotherapeutic intervention. But such usage is more homiletic and ad hoc than scientific or truly interdisciplinary. Even on Carter's (1977) own terms, this exposition is not an example of integration.

That same presentation is also instructive from another point of view. It shows quite clearly that much of the discussion about the integration of Christianity and psychology is not really Christian at all, for this discussion often obscures the very issues that are distinctive to Christianity. The surest example is the suggestion that Christian belief about Jesus, christology, relates to psychology insofar as Jesus becomes the model for the counselor or psychotherapist (Carter & Mohline, 1977, pp. 11–12). By the very nature of things, such treatment must downplay the distinctive features of Christian belief—the divinity of Jesus, the incarnation, the redemption, and the resurrection. These are not matters on which psychology has or could have an opinion. Essentially, the import of these matters is not healthy humanity, which would be common with psychology, but rather the possibility of human participation in divinity, which is distinctive to Christianity. In the terms of this book, they are considerations within the theotic—not the philosophic nor even the theist—viewpoint; though granted these distinctions, one could use contemporary psychology to elaborate Christian belief about Jesus and have this belief also elucidate the concerns of psychology (Helminiak, 1986d). But *virtually all treat-ment of integration overlooks this crucial difference* and claims to be treating Christian issues when only questions of wholesome living or of belief in God are at stake, and these questions are common to most of the world's religions.

Nonetheless, expositions such as those just noted are useful to help clarify what integration is, for specifying an array of models makes clear that most are not models of integration at all but various ways of pitting religion and psychology against one another or of collapsing them into one another. When all is said and done, how exactly integration should proceed is not elaborated.

Even specifying that integration, and not something else, is the task at hand has not removed the ambiguities in this overall project. For there are also different conceptions of integration itself (Bouma-Prediger, 1990). *Interdisciplinary Integration* is the attempt to relate, contrast, and possibly reconcile the conclusions of different disciplines—for example, psychology and religion. *Intra-disciplinary Integration*, or professional integration, aims at coherence between one's theoretical commitments and one's profes-sional practice—for example, in the case of the Freudian or the Jungian or even the Christian psychotherapist. *Faith-Praxis Inte-gration* implies living out in one's daily life what one professes to believe in religious commitment. And *Experiential Integration* en-tails harmony within oneself or between oneself and God as a re-sult of personal, and usually a "religious," experience.

Clearly, *interdisciplinary* integration is the concern of this book. Clearly, too, intradisciplinary integration is closely related to inter-disciplinary integration, even as Bouma-Prediger (1990, p. 26) notes, for one could hardly integrate one's Christian belief with one's counseling practice, for example, unless one had some clear under-standing of how psychology and Christian belief interrelate. By the same token, to some extent those other two types of integration—faith-praxis and experiential integration—also depend on achieved interdisciplinary integration, for both involve matters where psy-chology comes to bear on religious commitment, and one could not live this commitment in any sane way without to some extent being able to articulate the interrelationship. Thus, in practice the latter three types of integration are dependent on the first; inter-disciplinary integration is the heart of the matter. The others may provide applications, provoke questions, and suggest nuances, all inviting elaboration of interdisciplinary integration, but attention to them is really a distraction from the main project, which still awaits completion.

That conclusion about the centrality of interdisciplinary integration weighs against an important position articulated by Farnsworth (1974, 1982). He argued that the mere interrelationship of disciplines, "substantial integration," is insufficient, for such integration needs to become also an "embodied integration." Embodied integration is the living out of truth. Farnsworth's (1982, p. 308) method "is based on *living* truth, not just *knowing about* truth." It emphasizes orthopraxy (right living) in addition to orthodoxy (right thinking). Such integration involves the application of truth to one's life. It is in the living that the truth of the truth becomes real.

No one should doubt the biblical validity nor practical wisdom of Farnsworth's proposal. Religious people, like everyone else, should practice what they preach. Hypocrisy is ever shameful, and in itself personal integrity must always be honored.

But it is a highly dubious proposition that personal integrity, living one's conviction, actually confirms the truth of what one believes. On this basis the Holocaust confirms the truth of Nazi antisemitism, supposedly supported by themes in John and Acts. On this basis parental rejection of children confirms the truth of the evil of homosexuality, supposedly prohibited by Leviticus, Romans, 1 Corinthians, and 1 Timothy. On this basis the scars of a battered wife confirm the truth of the evil of divorce, supposedly always forbidden by Jesus in Matthew, Mark, and Luke. Granted, for the open, questioning, and good-willed person, facing the practical horror of a lived-out personal belief might reveal the factual error of the belief. But the long history of slavery and other social evils does not support so optimistic a prognosis (Helminiak, 1997b).

Faithful living does not confirm the truth of one's beliefs. It is precisely the truth of one's beliefs that must be established before one can responsibly live them. It is precisely the truth of one's beliefs that is challenged when religion encounters the findings of contemporary psychology. And it is precisely the determination of this truth that is the task of integration.

The flaw in the appeal to embodied integration can also be expressed technically. For the scriptural mentality, the truth is something to be done or to be lived. Farnsworth (1974, 1982) is correct in citing this fact, but he is anachronistic in applying it today. The Hebrew mentality, retained in early Christianity, represents a state of undifferentiated consciousness; it expresses itself only in terms of common sense—example, metaphor, suggestive elaboration, inspirational appeal (Lonergan, 1972). But the Western world and Christianity have moved beyond the first century. The paradigmatic example in Christianity is the Council of Nicea (Helminiak, 1986d; Lonergan, 1976). While some at the council requested that its teaching be expressed only in scriptural terms, the bishops insisted on adopting a technical, nonscriptural term *homoousios*. They argued that only such a formulation could answer the objection of Arius, for he had formulated his question in terms that the scriptures never imagined: Was Jesus, the Son of God, a creature or not? To pose this question was to move beyond the Christian practice of worshipping Jesus (orthopraxy), which even Arius allowed, and to ask a purely factual question about the divine status of the Only Begotten of God (orthodoxy).

In its decree the Council of Nicea effected a differentiation of consciousness. It sorted out belief from practice. It distinguished cognition from volition. It is this very kind of differentiation, further refined, that lies behind Lonergan's four-level analysis of consciousness, summarized above. But appeal to embodied integration obscures this hard-won differentiation of consciousness.

Obscuring the difference between belief and living, truth and praxis, precludes the interrelationship of disciplines. For then one is attempting to integrate apples and oranges—theoretically refined disciplines like psychology, on the one hand, and religion as a way of living, on the other. In all fairness to Farnsworth (1982), other aspects of his position do emphatically pair discipline with discipline, theology with psychology, and this is a significant clarification. Overall, Farnsworth's (1996) position is openminded, balanced, and fair. Still, his calling for embodied integration obscures the pairing of disciplines and thus renders coherent integration impossible. Like it or not, the project of integration is a conceptual or intellectual affair, and such a pursuit must not be denigrated. It is a core facet, if only one facet, of the problem of contemporary religion facing the findings of the human sciences.

Principles of Integration

A number of principles commonly govern the integration project, and these do provide important clues for solving the integration puzzle. First, there is the belief that God created all things, so all truth is one (Carter & Mohline, 1976; DeVries, 1982; Dueck, 1989; Farnsworth, 1982; Hill & Kauffmann, 1996; Jeeves, 1969; Vande Kemp, 1996). This presupposition allows that somehow religion and psychology must be fully reconcilable. The beliefs of Christian faith cannot be in opposition to the findings of social science— granted that both are accurate. So the integration project forges ahead.

That commitment to truth, God's truth, one truth, is important to emphasize. That commitment not only grounds the integration project for Evangelical Christians and other religious believers; it also makes this project unavoidable. It is precisely the commitment to truth that forces believers to seek integration of psychology and religion. This commitment is initially a religious affair. It rests on belief in God and in God's revelation. As such, it implies that some statements may enjoy ultimate validity and some may not. Some are true and some are not. There is such a thing as truth, and falsehood and error are real possibilities. Then this religious commitment also spills over into secular pursuits, for commitment to truth becomes a way of life and affects everything that "God-fearing people" do. Thus, religious belief in God introduces important wholesome values into personal living and societal affairs. Admittedly, the result can be both annoying and saving.

The commitment to truth is annoying to those who find religious conviction nothing more than an irritant (granted, of course, that in some of its more strident Fundamentalist forms it is just that). Why always have to be right?! Why always worry about truth?! Why hold so firmly to the Bible and religious faith?! In a basically relativistic culture, in the postmodern world, concern about *the* truth seems peculiar and is sometimes annoying to the more lackadaisical. At the same time, however, this commitment to truth is also a burden to believers. Ongoing agonizing over the integration project is an obvious case in point. Nonetheless, this very same commitment is also saving. It forces people to grapple with important theoretical issues and to grapple until the issues fall into place. To this extent, this commitment is like that of genuine scientists. Not driven by religious faith but by curiosity, personal integrity, and faith in the human capacity to understand, the scientist bears the same burden of relentless thought and research. And this pursuit is not without reward. Through it, understanding is achieved, people find peace of mind, human progress results. Commitment to truth is an engine of human advance.

The similarity between the scientist's dogged research and the religious believer's commitment to God's truth suggests that believer and scientist are more closely related than would first appear. The link, of course, is authentic subjectivity—the human choice to be aware, to question, to understand. Both believer and scientist are living by faith (Van Leeuwen, 1996), and apart from distinctive contents, this faith is formally identical. Indeed, continued insistence on truth in a world that pooh-poohs this "anachronism" also characterizes the position articulated in this book. A thread of concern for the true and the good runs through and links the positivist, philosophic, theist, and theotic viewpoints. The commitment to truth is a most important presupposition for the successful interrelationship of disciplines.

A second common presupposition in the integration project is the insistence on both special and general revelation (Carter & Mohline, 1976; Farnsworth, 1974, 1982, 1996; Jones, 1996; Myers, 1996; Van Leeuwen, 1996). Special revelation refers to what God made known through the inspired Scriptures. General revelation refers to what God makes known through the created world about us. This construal of the matter makes a place within the religious world view for both religion and secular science; it gives religious approbation to, it "baptizes," nonreligious academic disciplines.

That approach is typical of Protestantism, which in Luther and Calvin insisted on the sovereignty of God over and against a fallen and totally depraved humanity. According to such belief taken rigorously and exemplified in the work of Karl Barth (1960), apart from Christ no human pursuits could be of worth. But recognizing the world as an arena of God's revelation and seeing the scientist's pursuit as an attempt to appropriate general revelation can legitimate secular psychology as a facet of a religious project.

Roman Catholicism deals with that matter in a different way. Affirming a weakened but still real rectitude of the human heart even after original sin, Catholicism grants the validity of human pursuits in their own right. As the famous Thomist dictum holds, grace builds on nature. But if this is so, nature retains its integrity. Thus, Catholicism sees the human sciences as elaborating, not general revelation, but natural law, the inherent requirements of wholesome functioning that are built into creation.

In comparison with the Protestant, this Catholic approach, borrowed originally from Stoicism, is more straightforward and direct. It does not require theological constructs like general revelation to legitimate the social sciences. Nonetheless, when deployed within the Catholic Church, this approach also has a liability. It is vulnerable to apodictic claims about the supposedly revealed content of natural law (John Paul II, 1993). In the end, of course, both the Protestant and the Catholic approaches reach the same practical conclusion—that the human sciences can make valid contributions.

Insistence on the validity of natural law theory lies at the heart of the system of four viewpoints, the core structure of this book's interdisciplinary position. This system is but an expansion of the medieval Christian distinction between the "natural" and the "supernatural." Highlighting this fact here serves to point out the compatibility of this book with the integration project of Evangelical Christianity. The overall goal of both is the same, and the approaches have important similarities. This book's position does seem to bypass the impasse that has hampered the integration project. In the end, of course, *acceptance of this book's position would require Christians of every stripe to nuance their claims—* and specifically, in the case of Evangelicalism, about the ultimacy of the Bible. After all, achievement of a global society in the third millennium will require a novel synthesis. Yet the payoff would be a coherent position that does preserve the distinctive in Christianity and also effects its integration with psychology and the secular world.

The third common presupposition of the integration project is Dilthey's distinction between the *Geisteswissenschaften* and the *Naturwissenschaften*, noted above. This presupposition is spoken of in terms of "levels of analysis," and in some form or other, with more or less emphasis, it occurs in Farnsworth (1974), Jeeves (1994), Myers and Jeeves (1987), Gustafson (1990), Myers (1996), and Virkler (1982). However, the integration project has not relied heavily on this approach. As already noted, this approach appears (but only appears) to be useful in relating religion to the *natural* sciences. But since religion and the *human* sciences are all instances of *Geisteswissenschaften*, Dilthey's distinction is not very helpful in relating them. The issue will receive full attention in Chapter Three.

A Most Coherent Model of Integration

The integration project is at an impasse. Criticism of the most coherent of the Evangelical proposals for integration will substantiate this claim.

Lawrence J. Crabb formulated his approach to integration in two books: *Basic Principles of Biblical Counseling* (1975) and *Effective Biblical Counseling* (1977). In many ways Crabb's approach is typical. Reacting to a trend he calls "humanism, a fervent belief in the self-sufficiency of man" (Crabb, 1975, p. 11), Crabb insists that his Christian beliefs are the key to right living and psychological health: "In every instance, the wrong thinking will involve the sinful belief that something more than God (and what he chooses to provide) is necessary for meeting one's needs" (Crabb, 1975, p. 46). In contrast to the self-assertion of humanism and according to Crabb's (1975, p. 110) account of Christianity, health necessarily includes "self-denial and submission." The object of this submission is expressed variably either in terms of God: "God is totally sufficient for me" (Crabb, 1975, p. 46) and "obedience to God (who requires submission)" (p. 108); or in terms of Christ: "to become more like Christ" (p. 110) and "to live in subjection to the Father's will as He [Christ] did" (Crabb, 1977, p. 20); or yet again in terms of the Bible: "committed to a biblical view of man" and "basic biblical beliefs" (Crabb, 1975, p. 11). But in the last analysis the biblical statement is the bottom line; through it one knows the will of God and of Christ. Indeed, as their titles announce, both Crabb's books are about "*biblical* counseling" (emphasis added).

What Crabb (1975, p. 12) was seeking and finally had to articulate for himself was "a substantial understanding of the problems of people and of the best ways to deal with them which could rightfully claim to be thoroughly biblical." The need was for "a solidly biblical approach to counseling, one which draws from secular psychology without betraying its Scriptural premise . . . one which clings passionately and unswervingly to belief in an inerrant Bible and an all-sufficient Christ" (Crabb, 1975, p. 18). Thus, representing Evangelical Christianity in general, Crabb proposed an integration of religion and psychology that respects the Bible as the ultimate authority.

Nuances in Crabb's Position. To be sure, Crabb's position may be more hard-line than those of other Evangelical integrationists

(Myers, 1996; Van Leeuwen, 1996). Crabb (1977, p. 15) surely exaggerates when he writes that "the Scriptures provide the only authoritative information on counseling." More understandable, and probably referring to moral norms, is his still-bold assertion that "only Scripture can provide the needed structure," that is, "a reliable, fixed framework for counseling" (Crabb, 1975, p. 27). Yet like other Evangelicals, Crabb (1975, pp. 109–110) notes the familiar list of ethical issues as the practical focus of his Christian concern: divorce, homosexuality, extramarital sex, a wife's insubordination to her husband, and other "ungodly behavior or attitudes": "resentment, self-pity, immorality, envy, lack of contentment, materialistic strivings, lust, pride, lying, anxiety."

Nonetheless, in his practical advice Crabb is far from an extremist in insistence on biblical principles. He denounces a Christian counseling that would be "something like a witch hunt: locate the sin and burn it" (Crabb, 1975, p. 18). He further insists that biblical counseling, "though often firm and tough, will never be harsh, cynical, sarcastic, or indifferent. It will be characterized by the gentle love of a High Priest who can be touched with the feelings of our infirmities" (p. 108). The allusion is to the compassionate Christ, depicted in Hebrews 4:14–5:10.

Likewise, Crabb is far from one-sided in his treatment of religion and psychology. He denounces a position on integration that he calls Nothing Buttery, whose "basic tenet is Nothing But Grace, Nothing But Christ, Nothing But Faith, Nothing But the Word" (Crabb, 1977, 40). Trained as a clinical psychologist, Crabb cannot but realize that "psychology and its specialized discipline of psychotherapy offer some valid insights about human behavior which in no way contradict Scripture" (Crabb, 1977, p. 15). "Dismissing all secular thinking as profitless denies the obvious fact that all true knowledge comes from God" (Crabb, 1975, p. 26). So Crabb (1977, p. 42) recognizes an expression of God's love in Roger's unconditional positive regard, a help for avoiding self-deception in Freud's discovery of defense mechanisms, and guidelines for dominating the earth and oneself in Skinner's principles of operant conditioning. Indeed, as an uncriticized assumption, Crabb (1977, p. 51–52) seems to accept Albert Ellis's cognitive therapy as *the* biblically approved method, for "Paul [Romans 12:1] taught that transformation comes from renewing neither feelings nor circumstances, but our minds" (Crabb, 1975, p. 44). Thus, Crabb confidently suggests, "The basic interference with the maturing process is unbelief [in the need for submission to God] or, more precisely, wrong belief" (p. 110). "Teaching a new way of thinking, correcting wrong ways of thinking which underlie wrong behavior and wrong feeling is central" (p. 50).

The Hard Line in Crabb's Position. Thus, to some extent Crabb is moderate. He is open to secular psychology and compassionate with unconverted clients. But his position is inconsistent and, it seems, necessarily so. A firm and sometimes harsh commitment to the Bible continues to come through—as, for example, when he writes urging compassion, "When a person is not willing to go God's way . . . the client may have to be told regretfully to come back when he is ready to do business with God" (Crabb, 1975, p. 108).

Doing business with the biblical counselor is equated with doing business with God. Agreeing with what the counselor believes to be God's way is equated with going God's way. There is an offensive self-righteousness, a haughtiness, a triumphalism, a closemindedness here, and it cannot be avoided as long as the "biblical principle" rules. When the presumption is that the Bible contains all truth and when all else must be measured against it, interrelationship with other sources of knowledge is *in principle* excluded. In the end—indeed, from the beginning—the biblical opinion is always deemed right. There is no room for genuine dialogue, no place for real give and take. The Bible ever remains "the final authority" (Crabb, 1977, p. 49).

This same offensive self-righteousness comes through in Crabb's acceptance of findings from secular psychology. He calls his model of integration "Spoiling the Egyptians" (Crabb, 1977, p. 47). The reference is to the behavior of the fleeing ancient Israelites who, "with God's approval," looted from the Egyptians whatever they deemed valuable and useful for their trek to the "promised land." By analogy, the Christian counselor determines, on the basis of his or her biblical belief, what is correct and what is erroneous in psychological findings, and then takes this and leaves that, supposedly infallibly passing judgment in every case.

The Problem of the Biblical Principle. There is an insurmountable problem that dooms this Evangelical project of integration. The problem is the very first principle of the project, the biblical principle, and its unswerving reliance on the teaching of the Bible. Quoting McQuilkin (1975), Crabb formulates this first principle starkly and strikingly as follows: " 'When the teaching of Scripture conflicts with any other idea, the teaching of Scripture will be accepted as truth and the other idea will not be accepted as truth.' . . . The other idea, *regardless of its support from empirical research*, will not be accepted as truth" (Crabb, 1977, p. 49, *emphasis in original*). The problem is insurmountable for a number of reasons.

First, there is the obvious logical reality: when one side of a dialogue is a priori deemed correct, there is no possibility of real dialogue. Integration is but a fiction.

Second, there is the historical reality. Evangelical Christianity does not really rely on the Bible but, more accurately, on a Reformation reading of the Bible. Thus, for example, Crabb's (1977, pp. 23–25) "Christianity" presumes a substitutionary atonement theory and a theory of imputed justification. Already built into what is supposedly biblical teaching are the theological opinions of Luther, Calvin, and a centuries-long Protestant tradition.

Even if it were freely to admit its Protestant heritage, Evangelicalism would not avoid the problem. It would merely admit that it is fudging its claim to reliance on the Bible. By the same token it would admit that, if it would be honest, it must justify its acceptance of classical Protestantism as *the* valid interpretation of the Bible. But in so doing, it shifts the focus of discussion from the Bible to hermeneutics—that is, the principles and processes of correct interpretation. Now the question is no longer, What does the Bible say? but, What does the Bible mean by what it says? and, How does one correctly determine that?

Phrased in terms of fidelity to the biblical principle, the project of integration must inevitably grapple with hermeneutics. And if one grants the importance of hermeneutics, it takes over first place, and the biblical principle is perforce relegated to second place, for the principles of interpretation are now in command. They determine what the Bible actually teaches. Said otherwise, in the late twentieth century there is simply no honest way to maintain the bald biblical principle, for in practice the final authority must become the principles that determine what the Bible means, and "the Scripture is no longer the final authority" (McQuilkin, 1975, as cited in Crabb, 1977, p. 49). The only way to avoid this outcome is to take a fundamentalist stance and at some point or other to insist on a supposed "literal" reading of the Scriptures. Indeed, thoroughgoing fundamentalism is the logical conclusion of the biblical principle.

Nor does Farnsworth's (1982, 1996) clever suggestion avoid this dilemma. Granting the inevitability of interpretation, Farnsworth proposed that interpretations of the Bible may be mistaken, but the Bible itself is inerrant. On this understanding, the Bible in the realm of theology is supposedly an exact parallel to nature in the realm of the natural sciences. The Bible is the locus of special revelation, and the natural world is the locus of general revelation. Just as scientists study nature and propose theories—interpretations—about it, so theologians study the Bible and propose interpretations about it. Thus, theological interpretations are to be reconciled with scientific theories, and in this process the Bible itself can never be wrong, for not it, but only interpretations of it, could ever be shown to have been mistaken in the face of scientific findings.

The flaw in that argument is its first premise, namely, that the Bible and the natural world are parallel realities. Unlike nature, the Bible is the product of human culture. It is a formulation of intentional meaning, rooted in a particular historical time and place. It is comprised of words, phrases, sentences, and these obviously intend to say something. To pretend that the accuracy of their meaning depends only on their interpreter, suggests that in themselves they mean nothing at all. On this construal, there could never be a way of determining whether an interpretation is correct or mistaken because, supposedly, the Bible in itself has no inherent meaning against which to compare the interpretation—or, if it does have a meaning, that meaning could never be known, for every knowing would be but another and supposedly unconstrained interpretation. Farnsworth's proposal saves the inerrancy of the biblical message at the cost of denying that there is any specifically biblical and humanly accessible message at all.

Farnsworth's proposal might be acceptable if it were supposed that the Bible is the word of God and nothing more, that is, a word somehow miraculously written down apart from any particular human language, place, time, or culture. But such a conception is obviously a contradiction in terms: a divine message conveyed to human beings but apart from any specific human conveyance. This saving supposition is untenable.

Therefore, the Bible must be taken as a deliberate and culture-bound formulation of meaning. As such, the biblical word is necessarily subject to assessment of its accuracy. If the Bible does say something, and not just its interpreters, then that something is either correct or it is not. Unlike nature, which is simply there to be investigated and which contains no deliberately formulated message addressed to humankind, discussion of the Bible is inevitably intertwined with issues of hermeneutics. Denial of this fact leaves fundamentalism as the only alternative.

Lest pessimism rule the day, it will be helpful to note here that actually there is another option—the one presented in this book. But it is complex, not straightforward; its reliance on Christianity is differentiated and nuanced. It is to recognize open-mindedness, questioning, honesty, and good will—in a word, human authenticity—as not only a human but also a biblical requirement and to make it supreme, turning it even onto the Bible and Christianity themselves. The end product of such a maneuver will not look like traditional Christianity, and herein lies the crisis for Evangelicalism—and in varying degrees for the other Christian traditions as well (Helminiak, 1997a) and theist religion in general. But this option

- at least builds on some part of Christianity, the requirement of authenticity, although this part is not peculiar to Christianity,

- retains the theism that is another, but not distinctive, part of Christianity, and

- specifies theotics as a realm of distinctive Christian contribution.

This is to say, in these three ways the present option does specify and preserve a Christian perspective. The only other option, inevitably closeminded and incoherent, is various degrees of Christian fundamentalism.

Third, then, numerous contemporary historical-critical biblical studies also show the biblical principle to be an insurmountable problem. By reading the texts in their original historical and cultural contexts, the historical-critical approach calls into question the supposed certainty of long-accepted biblical teachings (Myers, 1996). For example, Jesus' prohibition of divorce seems to have been based on concern for the plight of women in a thoroughly patriarchal society (McKenzie, 1982, pp. 149–160). Applied in today's world, this same mind of Jesus would often support divorce. Again, the biblical condemnation of homosexual acts is seriously challenged (Boswell, 1980; Countryman, 1988; Furnish, 1994; Helminiak, 1994b; Scroggs, 1983). The prohibition of Leviticus 18:22, for example, rests on ancient Hebrew concern about uncleanness, which is irrelevant to contemporary religious considerations. The "unnatural" of Romans 1:26 is simply a mistranslation for "atypical"; the mistranslation reads into Paul a Stoic usage that was obviously not intended. Similarly, in light of contemporary findings regarding how human Jesus really was, Jesus' "subjection to the Father's will" (Crabb, 1977, p. 20) can be accurately rendered in terms of human authenticity: being who he was, the Only Begotten of God, but having become truly human, Jesus' being *true to himself* was his certain and only means of fidelity to his Heavenly Father (Helminiak, 1986d, 1989c). Other examples are myriad. The point is that the "teaching of the Bible" is not so clear as it was once thought to be.

Thus, the "biblical counselor" acts irresponsibly when imposing various requirements on a client in the name of the Bible. To admit more forthrightly that these requirements are merely part of "conservative evangelical beliefs" (Crabb, 1975, p. 108) would, at least, be honest—and less problematic. It would be less problematic from the point of view of biblical interpretation and interdisciplinary methodology. For then, up front, the game would have been called. It would have been admitted that the ethic of a particular social group, and not the Bible nor the will of God, was determining all; and it would have been admitted that openminded interdisciplinary collaboration and integration were really a fiction. Likewise, this admission would be less problematic as regards the care of souls, despite ongoing destructive consequences. People would still be induced to bear burdens that the Bible, understood on its own terms, and so arguably God, simply do not require. Yet, for whatever reasons, they would at least have chosen these unnecessary burdens knowingly. And adherents of this movement would at least no longer be deceived in believing that they are conforming themselves to Christ or the will of God.

But such an outcome is absurd when the topic is a Christian religion. This *reductio ad absurdum* highlights the painful point: in these matters the question of truth cannot be avoided, nor can the truth of a religious teaching be assumed. Attributing religious opinions to the Bible, to Christ, and to God may well be making the unwarranted claim that these opinions are unquestionably true.

Thus, insistence on the biblical principle entails an insurmountable problem that dooms the integration project.

The Prescription of Personal Religious Integrity. It was said above that Crabb's position is the most coherent of the Evangelical proposals. All the criticism presented thus far applies to the integration project in all its formulations. But Crabb's version takes the project one step further. To some extent he already anticipated the problems just laid out, and he prescribed a way of avoiding them. Unfortunately, that way leads to a dead end. Nonetheless, assessment of his further prescription will demonstrate that the integration project based on the biblical principle is, indeed, hopeless.

In describing his model for integration, Spoiling the Egyptians, Crabb (1977) notes the dangers in this operation. The question always remains, How does one buy into secular science without betraying one's biblical commitment? How far can one legitimately go? The remarkable thing in Crabb's suggestion is this: he is well aware that the matter depends on the decisions of individuals and that the only way to ensure legitimate use of psychology is to ensure the religious integrity of the individuals using it. The human subject, the one who makes the judgments and choices, is the key to the matter. Thus, Crabb (1977, pp. 49–50) lays down a list of requirements for "anyone who wants to work toward a truly evangelical integration of Christianity and psychology."

Such a person must submit to the authority of Scripture, must accept the Bible as the infallible, inspired, and inerrant revelation of God, must conform his or her living (and not just believing) to biblical teaching, and must be seriously committed to the content of the Scriptures. This last stipulation entails thorough understanding of the Scriptures and of "basic Bible doctrine" (Crabb, 1977, p. 49), acquired through ongoing regular and systematic study, and participation in an Evangelical community: "regular fellowship in a Bible-believing local church" (p. 50). Compliance with these requirements would form a person who actually embodies the evangelical tradition—a person thoroughly educated in the tradition, thinking like it, living according to it, and committed to it.

That prescription represents a most important safeguard for fidelity to a tradition and ongoing development of the tradition.

Indeed, Crabb's proposal resembles that of the great contemporary German methodologist, Hans Georg Gadamer (1960/1989). Addressing these very problems about correct interpretation in a hermeneutically sophisticated age, Gadamer suggests that truth in best attained through discourse within a long-standing tradition. Profound fidelity to tradition assures validity. Accordingly, the importance of Crabb's suggestion should not be underestimated. When Crabb prescribes characteristics for the Evangelical integrationist, he addresses the heart of the matter.

Nevertheless, that suggestion does not solve the problem. That suggestion might guarantee that one remains faithful to Evangelical Christianity, but it does not necessarily guarantee that one remains faithful to the truth. On this point or that, Evangelical Christianity might be wrong. Of course, the assumption is that Evangelical Christianity is the truth, so fidelity to it would be fidelity to the truth. But this assumption cannot simply be granted. When Christianity confronts differing opinions from the contemporary human sciences (not to mention differences among Christian denominations themselves), the truth of religion is precisely the topic of debate.

Supporting fidelity to a tradition, Crabb's suggestion does not necessarily guarantee fidelity to truth. This is especially so since the tradition in question is defined by commitment to cognitions, beliefs, assertions: "God's infallible, inspired, inerrant revelation in propositional form"; and since being "under the authority of Scripture" means that an idea that conflicts with the Scriptures, "regardless of its support from empirical research, will not be accepted as truth" (Crabb, 1977, p. 49). The matter would be different if the commitment were to perennial virtues: openmindedness, questioning, honesty, good will. These are the virtues associated with the four levels of consciousness and the transcendental precepts in Lonergan's analysis, and all these virtues are also central to the teaching of the Bible. These virtues guarantee that the tradition in question is an authentic tradition. These virtues could guide a person through the maze of contemporary opinion and lead to the affirmation of what more and more obviously, in all honesty, in collaboration with others of good will, must be judged to be true. But in itself, fidelity to a tradition, unless it is an *authentic* tradition, does not necessarily lead to the truth.

Perhaps Crabb had presumed that those virtues lie at the heart of Evangelical Christianity. To some extent they certainly do.

But in matters of methodology, the essential cannot simply be presumed; it must be formulated and stated up front. Besides, an unbending a priori insistence on the "authority of Scripture" and an unswerving allegiance to "revelation in propositional form" effectively discredit this presumption.

The Crisis in Christianity

Crabb elaborates his model for integration further than do most others. Unfortunately, his proposal is still ineffective. Even his further elaboration does not overcome the problems noted above. This failure confirms the assessment that the integration project is inherently doomed, for to some extent or other all its participants accept the biblical principle.

At the same time, it should be noted that this judgment does not fall only on the project of Evangelical Christianity. To some extent, all the Christian denominations labor under the same challenge. Roman Catholicism, for example, needs to contend with the authoritarianism of its hierarchical structure. More liberal denominations—like Episcopalianism and Methodism—need to contend with the conservative elements within their clergy and congregations and within their history. On all fronts, religion faces an almost insurmountable challenge. The case of the Evangelical integrationists is but one, if a very useful, example (Helminiak, 1997a).

But why make a point of Crabb's characterization of the Evangelical integrationist when, in the end, it still leads to a dead end? Because Crabb's focus on the role of the human subject is a move in the right direction. Modern philosophy's "turn to the subject" is now having its effect in religious circles. This very trend, in the work of Bernard Lonergan (1957, 1972) and in terms of authenticity, grounds the interdisciplinary position presented in this book. Thus, a common focus on the subject, though in different forms, provides another point of contact between the integration project and the position of this book.

It hurts to criticize the integration project and to find it, time after time, to be wanting. I do not like being negative, especially about people's religious beliefs. Indeed, the same commitment to truth that drives the Evangelicals also drives me. We are allies in this matter. But I believe I have solved the puzzle that has stumped the integration movement, and I want to share my solution. I offer it in the hope that some consensus may begin to emerge.

The achievement of integration is important—and not just for the religions. We are at a point in history when narrow preoccupation with in-house religious stability is tantamount to sinful abdication of religious responsibility. The responsibility in question is to the world at large. Our world is clamoring for a new spiritual vision, one that will not only touch the heart but also satisfy the mind, for only such a vision will hold in today's highly scientific, critical, and cynical world (Helminiak, 1996a). The kernel of such a vision lies buried in the authentic Christian tradition, but for the vision to emerge the shell of Christianity must be broken and cast aside. If the Christian religions are unwilling to die, to relinquish their structures and prerogatives and religious security, they cannot follow their Master and rise to new life. We are at an unprecedented turning point in history, and turning points can be wrenching. My negative criticisms may seem like the nails of crucifixion that bring death to a beloved religious endeavor. I would rather see them as good-willed reminders of the inevitability of the cross and as invitations to the religions to willingly take it up.

Despite my profound respect for the project of integration, the fact of the matter is that in its present form it is doomed. I point this out forcefully, and I do not hold back at this point, because I also have a positive alternative to offer. I believe the goal of integration is achievable but only with a radical shift of presuppositions. Authentic spirituality needs to be differentiated from the religions that carry it, and spirituality needs to take precedence over religion. Spirituality, in contrast to religion, is the key to the present age. I point out the flaws in the other approaches so that the newer will seem more appealing. Then the new vision might be shared, spiritual renewal might be effected, and all people of good will on this shrinking planet might get on with wholesome living.

Summary Regarding the Evangelical Integration Project

Above, it was noted that there are, perhaps, three general approaches to relating religion and psychology. The first was simply some general insistence on dialogue. The second was the distinction between the *Natur-* and the *Geisteswissenschaften,* and the third, the so-called perennial philosophy. The integration project exemplifies the first general approach, dialogue. As has been shown, this dialogue proceeds without much technical precision, and the results are also dubious. Yet the discussion of "integration" has served a number of purposes: to introduce the matter of relating psychology and religion, to highlight the complexity of the problem, to exemplify suggested responses to the problem, and to honor the endeavors of the Evangelical integration project. In terms of a "revised critical correlation," the analysis of Browning's position in Chapter Three will provide still more detail in the matter of dialogue.

The Nature of Religious Studies

Another debate in academic circles bears on the problem of relating religion and the human sciences. This is the debate about the relationship of theology and religious studies (Bellah, 1970; Brown, 1994, 1997; Gill, 1994; Minor & Baird, 1983; Ogden, 1995; Pals, 1987; Schussler Fiorenze, 1991, 1993, 1994; Segal, 1983, 1997; Segal & Wiebe, 1989; Sharma, 1997; Sharpe, 1997; Wiebe, 1984, 1986, 1994). As in the case of the Evangelical integration project, attention to this other debate will further elucidate the matter.

To characterize this debate in terms of *theology* and *religious studies* does not add much clarity. Even within the debate, these words have ambiguous meanings; the definitions of the terms depend on who is using them. But in general, *theology* refers to the study of religious issues within a particular religious tradition (Smart, 1997). Thus, theology is constrained by the beliefs of the denominations. A key belief is the existence of God. Another way to make the point is to say that the enterprise of theology is "confessional" (Wiebe, 1984). In contrast, *religious studies* represents a broader approach. Not committed to any one religion, this approach attempts to deal with religion in general. A typical methodology is the comparison of religions, the attempt to discern similarities and differences among a variety of religions. Another typical methodology in religious studies is the application of the findings of the human or social sciences. So a sociological or psychological analysis of a religion or of some facet of religion is taken to be part of religious studies.

The matter is actually more complicated (Brown, 1997), but that broad contrast between theology and religious studies shows why the matter is relevant here: in some ways the debate over theology and religious studies is the debate about religion and the human sciences. For religious studies imports the human sciences into itself or even styles itself in the guise of a human science. The question that overshadows the whole matter is the focus of this book: How do denominationally committed religion and supposedly objective human science relate?

Religion as a Sui Generis Phenomenon

When religious studies attempts to explain religion in terms of the human sciences, the accusation comes back that this approach is "explaining away" religion, it is reductionist. Of course, what is meant by "religion" is not even clear—and this is a major problem. But one specific claim lies at the heart of the matter, namely, that religion is a phenomenon sui generis (Pals, 1987; Segal, 1983; Smith, 1997). Any attempt to explain religion in terms other than religious is said to be reductionist.

The core of the supposed uniqueness of religion is the engendering religious experience, and this experience is taken to be an experience of God (or the Ultimate or the noumenal or something similar). So conceived, this experience certainly deserves the status "sui generis." But that the religious experience is really an experience of God, that it cannot be explained in any other way, is precisely the point of dispute. A scientific approach would want to account for the experience in more manageable terms. A confessional or theologically committed approach would protest that the scientific approach precisely misses the point.

The Need for An Alternative Approach

The structure of that debate seems to allow no resolution. The claim for the uniqueness of the religious experience is a priori. From the start, such a claim precludes any treatment in terms other than religious. The question is supposedly answered before the discussion begins, so there is no real possibility for discussion, there is no room for the interrelationship of disciplines. This state of affairs is similar to what we have just seen in the Evangelical Christian integration project. And the response must also be similar: first, to suggest that, as currently conceptualized, this debate has no resolution; and second, to point out another way of conceptualizing the matter.

It has already been stated that this debate, as currently conceptualized, has no possible resolution. The parallel with Evangelicalism explains the rationale. So no more need be said on this first point.

Next, there is an alternative conceptualization that could open the debate to a more positive outcome. This alternative is the one presented in this book. Five considerations will summarize its suggestion as regards the debate about theology and religious studies.

Description versus Explanation

First, the concern of this book is to understand, to explain, religion. Said otherwise, at stake here is science: methodical explanation. This first clarification already excludes from the discussion much of what goes on under the topics of theology and religious studies. These often engage in the elaborate description of a religious phenomenon or provide a coherent rationale for a set of religious beliefs. Such endeavors, though worthwhile in themselves, are not explanation.

An example will help make the point. A group of people may meet in a church and be inspired by the ritual. What is the role of academic religious study vis-à-vis this event? One approach would observe the event, describe in detail what happened, report the accounts of the people involved, and show how the event does or does not, for example, represent the basic tenets of the denomination in question. This approach might even attempt to assess whether these religious practitioners are happier, healthier, better adjusted, or some such thing, in comparison with a control group. This would be a descriptive approach. In contrast, the explanatory approach would take a different tack and ask how exactly the religious service achieves the effect that it does. The goal here is not simply to describe what happened but also to explain how and why it happened. The goal is a scientific account, and the task is to specify the structures, mechanisms, and processes that would explain the functioning of this event as a religious affair (Helminiak, 1986a, 1996a, 1996c).

Inevitably, explaining something means accounting for it in terms of something else (Segal, 1983). Explanation entails collecting things under some general categories. Some would say that as regarding religion such a project is inherently reductionist. For this reason they would reject it. They would protest that this quest for systematic understanding violates the sui generis nature of religion. Be that as it may, the option here is for methodological explanation, science.

Accordingly, from one point of view, it appears that I have already chosen sides in the debate between theology and religious studies. I seem to side with religious studies, the more critical and more liberal stance.

Would that the matter were so simple! Would that it were clear what each of the sides stood for (Sharma, 1997; Brown, 1997)! Then one could express an opinion and at least know on which side he or she stood. But the matter is confused.

The line between description and explanation is never clearly drawn, so two very different kinds of projects get compared. No wonder there is no resolution of the debate. The discussion is often at cross purposes. To highlight this very confusion is the first clarification being made here. Especially in Chapter Three, under the section "Religion and Science: Interpretation and Explanation," more will be said about the nature of science and about the difference between description and explanation.

"Religion" as an Undifferentiated Notion

Second, the debate about theology and religious studies all centers around "religion." This topic is supposed to identify some specific realm of study. But the topic is amorphous. The global term *religion* is unwieldy. It bottles up a whole swath of disparate elements. Like "government" or "civilization" or "maturity" as proposed topics for undergraduate term papers, "religion" is hardly a suitable topic for an incisive and rigorous analysis. No wonder the attempt to deal with "religion" provokes such controversy and confusion.

An alternative approach sorts out the elements within religion and discerns four sets of irreducibly distinct concerns: the positivist, the philosophic, the theist, and the theotic. Most crucial here is the difference between the philosophic and the theist viewpoints, for these distinguish matters that pertain to God and matters that pertain to the human spirit.

Spirituality versus Theology

The third clarification follows immediately. Without appeal to God, most of what is called "religious experience" can be explained on the basis of human spirit. *The Human Core of Spirituality* (Helminiak, 1996a) provides an extended example of the result, which was summarized above. The point is that spiritual matters are highly amenable to rigorous analysis when disentangled from questions of God. Within this analysis, the term *theology* takes on a precise and restricted meaning. Then theology and spirituality are seen as different, though related and still partial, aspects of religion overall.

If this kind of explanation is deemed reductionist, then so be it. However, even under such analysis spirituality remains a phenomenon sui generis, and this fact could rightly be taken as a qualified validation of the insistence, at stake in this debate, on the sui generis nature of religion. Then the only remaining offense is that in this account spirituality is not related ipso facto to God—which brings up the next clarification.

Appeal to the Theist and Theotic Viewpoints

Fourth, then, this analysis does leave room for God. Within the theist viewpoint insistence on the existence of God adds a further dimension of explanation to even an exhaustive humanistic account of spiritual experience. And within the theotic viewpoint, there also emerges a coherent explanation of how it could also rightly be said that one actually experiences God in a "religious experience" and that one shares in divinity (Helminiak, 1982, 1984b, 1987).

Faith within the Positivist and
Philosophic Viewpoints

Fifth and finally, the distinction between the positivist and the philosophic viewpoints clarifies another major point of difference in this debate. On the one hand, the theology emphasis insists that the study of religious phenomena apart from religious commitment is impossible, for the commitment is essential to the phenomena under study. On the other hand, the religious-studies emphasis is more committed to an "objective" study of religion, so this emphasis imitates the human sciences in their claim to neutral and "value-free" analyses.

Now, under the names of positivist viewpoint and philosophic viewpoint, the position presented in this book acknowledges and validates both those emphases and relates them to one another. However, the initial suggestion is that, in fact, neither of these emphases is without some value commitment; value-free science is a human impossibility. The further suggestion is that, while some forms of social science can proceed within the positivist viewpoint, social or human science can be adequate to its subject matter only within the philosophic viewpoint, and within the philosophic viewpoint human science is already spirituality. Accordingly, it becomes clear that human science itself can be of two significantly different kinds, positivist and philosophic, so the importation of the human sciences into religious studies means very different things depending on what notion of human science is in question.

Moreover, the debate about "objective" versus "committed" religious studies is a red herring. Qua human, every scientific endeavor involves some meaning-and-value commitment, some kind of faith. So the goal of objective human science—and of objective religious studies—is not to eliminate faith from the enterprise but to specify the parameters of the faith within which the enterprise moves.

To specify the possible parameters is precisely what the four viewpoints on the human do. So, having initially separated the God question from other facets of religion, the four viewpoints also sort out this other matter of different "faiths" that confounds the debate between theology and religious studies.

Summary on the Debate about Theology and Religious Studies

Taking science to be methodical explanation, this alternative approach sorts out the diverse elements bottled up in the notion *religion*. In a nuanced way, this approach does grant legitimacy to the position that insists that religious experience relates to God. At the same time, this approach also honors the more scientific requirement for actual explanation of religious experience—by envisaging a scientific (and initially nontheist) spirituality. Yet this approach defines spirituality as a kind of human science which, even qua human science, necessarily includes a religion-like commitment to normative meanings and values. Thus, on a range of issues, this alternative approach cuts down the middle through the positions on both sides in this debate.

Nuancing the matter, sorting out the pieces, interrelating them in a coherent and reasonable fashion, the alternative approach reverences the sui generis character of the "religious" and also supports an empirically grounded explanation of it. Attending to what seems valid on either side, perhaps this alternative could help break the logjam in the debate. More detail on these methodological issues is presented below. In light of the full exposition, the suggestive statements here will take on richer meaning.

The overall topic here is the interrelationship of religion and the human sciences. Attention to the debate over theology and religious studies has provided another vantage point on this topic. This brief discussion has highlighted the questions involved and suggested what is at stake in them. Thus, this discussion completes the introduction to these matters.

Outline of the Book

This chapter has introduced the topic of this book, the interrelationship of religion and the human sciences. If this chapter has also raised more questions than it has answered, that may well be to the good. For in the present matter the questions are big, and they are intertwined. They are tangled like worms in a can. Besides, only the mind primed with questions is likely to appreciate answers, and complete answers here require a long and detailed presentation. Such a presentation is what follows in the chapters below.

The core of this book comprises three parts. Each treats a different approach to the interrelationship of religion and psychology. Chapter Two is an extended presentation of the approach proper to this book—a system of higher viewpoints. By highlighting the pivotal role of a coherently conceived spirituality, as in *The Human Core of Spirituality*, this book details an alternative approach to the interrelationship of religion and the human sciences.

The subsequent two chapters summarize the two approaches that currently rule the field. Chapter Three, on critical dialogue, treats Don Browning's (1987) position in *Religion and the Modern Psychologies*. This position combines two broad approaches, as listed above: use of dialogue and appeal to levels of analysis. Though the treatment of Chapter Three focuses on only one book by only one author, the methodological position exemplified there is the standard one in Western religious circles. It has much in common with the approaches of the integration movement introduced above.

Chapter Four, on the perennial philosophy, treats Ken Wilber's (1996) position in *Eye to Eye*. This position also relies on two of the broad approaches listed above: appeal to levels of analysis and application of the perennial philosophy. Likewise, though the treatment of Chapter Four focuses on only one book by only one author, the methodological position exemplified there is the standard one in Eastern thought and has been imported into Western humanistic and transpersonal psychology, New Age Religion, and a host of recent spiritual movements. This position has little in common with the approaches discussed in this introductory chapter. These have their roots in Judeo-Christian soil, this other does not. Championed by Ken Wilber, this other position constitutes a comprehensive and powerful approach in its own right. For this reason, this position deserves extensive and detailed analysis. If the alternative approach of this book is to merit serious consideration, it must be shown to be able to deal more coherently with the issues than does Wilber's approach.

Besides summarizing those two reigning positions, the chapters below also criticize them. Presupposing the alternative introduced here and detailed in Chapter Two, the criticism not only points out the inadequacies in the reigning positions. It also uncovers the source of the problems and suggests correctives to them.

Thus, this other approach appears to be more incisive and more comprehensive than either of the reigning positions. Of course, the reader will have to judge the matter for him- or herself. To be sure, inadequacies in the reigning positions have been noted before—as in the case of the Evangelical integration project—but no coherent alternative approaches have been forthcoming. Here, in addition to criticism, another approach is presented. Granted this alternative, criticism of the reigning positions can be penetrating indeed. Such incisiveness is the novelty in this book.

The hope is that this analysis will further coherent interdisciplinary study. Then the correlation of disciplines might purify religion overall and at the same time enrich the human sciences. Finally, grounded in solid, sane, and widely shared knowledge and committed up front to wholesome values, the whole of humanity might find good-willed cohesion in a global society of the third millennium.

Chapter 2

Higher Viewpoints from Bernard Lonergan

"I think we're on the road to coming up with answers that I don't think any of us in total feel we have the answers to" (Overheard, 1991).

So spoke Kim Anderson, mayor of Naples, Florida, evidently talking about some complicated and profound imponderable: city management.

The topic of this book is also very complicated, the interrelationship of the human sciences and religion. But the suggestion is that this issue is not absolutely imponderable, and the hope here is to give some answers that help set matters in place.

Chapter One has already looked at some attempts to relate psychology and theology. Chapters Three and Four will consider two other attempts in detail. Those approaches have a history, brief though it be, and they are already more or less known. This chapter presents another approach, an alternative to the available ones. This chapter constitutes the core of this book.

The key suggestion is this: religion as such is not a subject matter amenable to scientific study. Religion is a highly varied phenomenon. It is difficult or even impossible to define. It embraces an array of issues, from the mundane to the sublime. The study of religion, globally conceived, allows for elaborate descriptions and provocative comparisons. But religion as such is too diffuse a category to support scientific—explanatory—analysis. Some conceptual breakthrough is needed to sort out and interrelate all the facets of the matter. Then focused analyses can relate an array of religious matters to a parallel array of analyses in the human sciences, as appropriate. Studies in religion and in human science can stand in a precisely defined one-to-one relationship. Then explanation of things religious can advance. Then rigorous and coherent interdisciplinary science can emerge.

This chapter proposes a conceptual system that addresses that interdisciplinary challenge. Central to this system is the delineation of a medium ground between psychology and theology. I have called this tertium quid *spirituality* (Helminiak, 1986b, 1987c, 1989c, 1994a, 1996a, 1996b, 1996c). This term refers both to the lived reality that can be distinguished but hardly separated from religion, and to an academic and research specialization that studies this lived reality. Obviously, the concern here is the latter, the specialized discipline called *spirituality*.

Two theoretical moves allow spirituality to emerge as an academic discipline with its own identity. First, one needs to clearly differentiate the human issues from the divine, and thus specify the difference between the human sciences and theology. Granted that the human mind entails a transcendent dimension that can rightly be called spirit, this move allows spirituality to be seen as a psychological, rather than a theological, specialization. Second, one needs to distinguish two kinds of human science, one that takes human authenticity into account and another that does not. The former would actually be the scientific study of spirituality. The result of these two moves is an array of intricately interrelated disciplines, each dealing with its peculiar focus of concern, yet all dealing with things religious.

This chapter presents that construal of the matter. Discussion will first be about science and what it is and about the notion *higher viewpoint*. Next, the presentation will elaborate a system of four viewpoints, presenting in turn the positivist, the philosophic, the theist, and the theotic viewpoints. These constitute the proposed framework for the interdisciplinary study of religion and the human sciences. Finally, there follows a discussion of the far-reaching implications of this system of higher viewpoints.

The Definition of Science

This chapter is about science and the interrelationship of different sciences. At the outset there is need to clarify what exactly "science" is taken to mean.

Science and Sciences as Currently Understood

What is generally known as "science" today is the rigorous study of the sensible, the measurable, the publicly accessible, and this conception gives birth to a long list of different academic pursuits. Limitation of concern to the sensible is certainly appropriate in the case of the physical sciences and biology, and it can also apply in some forms of human science. Human medicine, for example, could be conceived as mere application of physical, biological, and biochemical principles to human beings. Anthropology, certainly when studying early human history, must be limited to observable, archaeological data. Another classic example is behaviorist psychology, identified with B. F. Skinner (1953, 1971), which claims to be able to explain human beings on the basis only of what is publicly observable. Supposedly, talk of mind is a distraction from the real issues. Yet even Skinner allowed that human speech, as an external production, could be valid behaviorist data.

Consideration of speech begins to open "science" up to the world of human interiority, not publicly available apart from personal report. Thus, going further than behaviorism, cognitive psychology does admit that mind needs to be taken into account. Considering certain externally measured data, this approach attempts to infer what must be going on inside the mind. For example, research concerning imagery measures the time it takes for subjects to rotate letters of the alphabet in their imagination. By comparing the response times, researchers draw conclusions about the internal process of imaging and learn things about the working of the mind unknown even to the subjects doing the imagery experiment (Shepard & Metzler, 1971).

Beyond that methodology of inference from measurable data, psychologists have also long taken the actual content of their subjects' reports as valid evidence about inner experiences, and they also want to call their pursuits "science." Sigmund Freud (1900/ 1968, 1933/1964), for example, listened to his patients and analyzed their statements until he could propose some explanation of their neuroses and, hopefully, help them adjust to a more comfortable way of living.

Notice the differing ranges of data allowed by the sciences in the examples above. The physical sciences and biology certainly allow only the data of sense—the visible, the audible, the palpable. But the physical sciences focus on inanimate things, while biology is concerned with living things, so biology attends to life as well as to motion and chemicals and structures. Behaviorism, though a form of psychology, also limits itself to the sensible, but it is concerned about aspects of living organisms that biology ignores, so it entertains the data associated with conditioned learning. Cognitive psychology also considers only sensible data, but it discovers data the other sciences ignore, and it allows that those data bear on something not sensible, the mind, and it attempts to study that reality. Finally, psychoanalysis elicits and explores the very data of consciousness, accessed through the client's self-presentation, as a valid realm of scientific investigation. According to the prevailing understanding of things, this difference in range of data determines different disciplines or sciences.

Science as the Pursuit of Explanation

Although the range of acceptable data varies in all those sciences, the fundamental question asked remains the same throughout. All those sciences and disciplines want to know, What is actually the case in this matter? What is really happening? How can it be explained?

To give an explanatory account of things is the essence of science. To determine what is happening or how something occurs, actually to explain a given phenomenon, is the goal of science presupposed in the above examples. So physics and chemistry attempt to account for the movement of planets or the emergence of stars or the nature of matter. Biology discerns the processes and mechanisms common to all living things. Behaviorism determines how to induce conditioned responses in living organisms. Psychoanalysis attempts to make sense of the intricacies of a human mind. Yet, despite their specific differences, these sciences all share this common concern: to explain. Thus, they exemplify what science means.

Consideration of that wide range of sciences makes an initial contribution. It suggests what science in general is: the pursuit of understanding (Lonergan, 1957, 1972). This book accepts this understanding of science as a fundamental presupposition. The essence of science is to explain by appeal to appropriate evidence.

Of course there is another much-touted goal of science: to predict and to control. This additional goal follows upon the essential nature of science. Indeed, granted an accurate explanation of a particular phenomenon, one could perhaps predict some future outcome and conceivably control it. But prediction is possible only when it can be guaranteed that the processes in question will continue functioning exactly as they have in the past. Such is the case, for example, in the short-term movement of the solar system, which Newton systematized to give modern science its mesmerizing beginning. So science can accurately predict an eclipse of the moon.

But such predictable regularity in nature seems now almost to be the exception rather than the rule. For the universe is evolving and unfolding, just as people are growing and developing. Indeterminism applies almost everywhere and above all in the human realm. Under these circumstances one might come to understand the process at work in that unfolding, but one could not predict that this or that particular event will certainly occur. The best one could do is give the probability of such an occurrence. So, for example, over the long haul meteorology gets better and better at predicting the likelihood of a thunderstorm. Still, one hardly ever knows exactly what the weather will be when one wakes up the next morning.

Prediction and control are secondary goals for science. They pertain to applied science more than to pure science. This is not to say that they are unimportant. Indeed, science relies on the prediction of outcomes to test proposed explanations. Such testing is intrinsic to the scientific enterprise, and applications are the practical payoff of hard-won explanation. Even in the realm of spirituality, testing and application apply (Feingold, 1994, 1995; Feingold & Helminiak, 1996). Otherwise one is involved in mere speculation, not science, and one is living in an ivory tower, not in the real world. Nonetheless, the essence of science, the key to its nature, is the explanation of things. Science is a specialization on the second level of consciousness; its goal is ever-better understanding of things (Lonergan, 1967b, pp. 259–260; 1972, pp. 94, 129, 315–316).

Obviously, this understanding of science is broader than the usual. "Science" is usually taken to mean study of sensible data that are publicly available. The physical sciences are the best—in fact, the only clean—example. But this narrow understanding of science imposes a major restriction. It allows that only knowledge of what is sensible, physical, and measurable in some way can be science. It gratuitously rules out of court any evidence that is not of this particular kind, and in the process rules out of consideration any realities that are not of this kind. The suggestion here is that physical science is but one example—and, of course, the initial and most impressive example—of science and that the essence of physical science is its achievement of methodically cumulative explanation. But if such explanation could be achieved in other realms beyond the physical, by appeal to appropriate evidence, and by implementation of appropriate methodologies, that explanation would also qualify as science in those other realms. This deeper understanding of science, open to broader application, is the one adopted in this book.

The deeper understanding allows that there can be a science also of the spiritual. For in addition to the data of sense, on which the physical sciences rest, there are also the data of consciousness (Lonergan, 1972, pp. 94–95, 201), the inner experience that people have, and these data constitute legitimate evidence about mental— that is, psychic and spiritual—reality. The challenge for a science of the spiritual is to become methodical and cumulative and thus to achieve real explanation. Presuming this deeper understanding of science, this book hopes to help meet this challenge.

The Differentiation of Different Sciences or Disciplines

That list of different sciences presented above suggests another characteristic of science as currently conceived. According to prevailing usage, sciences differ because of the different ranges of data they consider. So physics and chemistry deal with different aspects of physical matter, while biology investigates living matter, and psychology considers mind according to varying criteria as to what is acceptable evidence. Differing ranges of data determine different sciences.

This book approaches the matter in a different way. Here, not different ranges of data, but different ranges of understanding about the same data, distinguish different sciences. Since the topic of this book is limited to the human sciences, here one and the same reality, the human, is the object of study. But concern brought to this reality can be narrower or broader. Depending on the presuppositions within which one works or, to say the same thing, depending on the questions that one allows, one brings different ranges of understanding to the object of study. One might ask, What really is the case? and so limit concern to the positivist viewpoint. Or one might ask, Is what-really-is-the-case as it ought to be? and so consider the human within the philosophic viewpoint. Or again, one might relate the human to God or Trinity, and so understand the human situation within the theist or theotic viewpoint. In every case, one is still seeking explanation, but the range of explanation is limited by the overarching questions one entertains. Here, different sciences or disciplines depend on different ranges of understanding, determined by different questions, inherent in different presuppositions and commitments. Here, sciences or disciplines are distinguished and interrelated within a system of higher viewpoints.

A System of Higher Viewpoints

The object of study here is one reality, the human being. Yet one could consider this reality from a number of different viewpoints. In relation to one another, some of the viewpoints might be higher than the others, so all together would constitute a system of higher viewpoints.

Let it be clear from the start that to speak of higher or lower viewpoints is not necessarily to speak of what is better or worse, more or less valid. A higher viewpoint is a broader viewpoint, it is more comprehensive than the lower. If one's concern is breadth, then, of course, a higher viewpoint serves one's purpose better than does a lower viewpoint, but even wider breadth confers no more

validity on one viewpoint over another. Each viewpoint is valid in
its own right, and this realization is precisely the point of distinguishing different viewpoints. Moreover, since the system of viewpoints holds together as a whole, the validity of one constrains the
validity of another. The overall concern in positing a system of
viewpoints is scientific: the goal is to achieve comprehensive and
coherent understanding. The system of viewpoints fosters understanding by sorting out the issues to be understood and by interrelating the understandings that are achieved. The relationship of
higher and lower among the viewpoints serves precisely to effect
the interrelationship of understandings—and not to impute worth
to the understandings. The worth of the understandings depends
on whether or not they are correct, and that is a whole other
matter. Clarity should emerge as this chapter unfolds. This initial
section is to introduce the notions *viewpoint* and *higher viewpoint*.

The Bicycle and the Human Being

Let us begin with a suggestive example. Consider the bicycle. To
some people the bicycle is a recreational device. They ride it around
the neighborhood or the local park on the weekend. For others the
bicycle is a serious means of transportation. It is an efficient, or
often their only, way to get around. But again, a mechanic might
view the bicycle as a fascinating convergence of gears and sprock-
ets, balance and motion. The mechanic is concerned about how the
bicycle works. Yet again, a historian might be interested in how the
bicycle was invented, improved, and perfected, and how it affects
life in various societies.

Notice how people can have very different ways of understanding one and the same reality, the bicycle. Similarly, people can bring
different concerns as they consider the human phenomenon.

This chapter presents four viewpoints on the human phenomenon, and the suggestion is that these completely cover the field.
Concern to explain the one and the same human reality could be
positivist, philosophic, theist, or theotic. These terms have technical meanings, and this chapter will explain them. The trick is to
say precisely what these four perspectives entail. But for better or
worse, the terms themselves must already suggest different sets of
concerns. "Positivist" concern might suggest limitation of consider-

ation to the sensible, the palpable. "Philosophic" concern would perhaps ask about what could or should be. And in different ways, "theist" and "theotic" concerns obviously introduce consideration of God and religion into the matter. So different people can be "coming from different places" as they attempt to understand the same human situation.

As conceived here, these four viewpoints do entail different ranges of understanding about the human. But the understandings are not just different; they also relate to one another as ever-increasingly broader. As one moves from the positivist to the philosophic to the theist and to the theotic viewpoint on the human, the wider and wider perspectives and understandings build on one another. Together the four viewpoints constitute a conceptual system that can lock into one coherent and comprehensive account a broad range of concerns. In so doing, this system of viewpoints ties together the input from a wide range of sciences or disciplines. Thus, these four viewpoints comprise an interdisciplinary schema for study of the human.

The Meaning of "Viewpoint"

In its technical sense the term *viewpoint* refers to understanding and to different ways of understanding (Lonergan, 1957, pp. 13–19). Some understandings are broader than others. Broader understandings succeed in combining many narrower understandings. The broader result from an insight that recognizes how all the smaller pieces of a problem fit together. Thus, they raise the whole enterprise of understanding to a new level of generality, a higher viewpoint.

An analogy might be your experience learning your way around a new city. At first, you get familiar with your neighborhood, the area around your work place, and perhaps the downtown area or your regular shopping district. You can plan outings to these areas in your mind. You know them, and you also know how to get from one to the other. But sometimes you come across a new street that connects those familiar areas in a new and easier way. Or visiting a new friend, you learn another area of the city, only to discover that it lies adjacent to your familiar shopping area. As this process of learning continues, you come to know more and more streets and more and more areas of the city and more and more ways of getting from one to another. Now you begin to think of your outings in a new way. No longer do you think of isolated areas connected by one precious route. You think in terms of the whole city. Your growing familiarity with the city allows you to think of all the various areas as connected in one whole, your home town, where you are now quite comfortable getting around. In a sense, you could say you achieved a higher viewpoint on travel around your home town.

That analogy is useful to suggest how higher viewpoints unite the understanding of lower viewpoints and how higher viewpoints entail a more penetrating understanding of things overall. But like all analogies, its usefulness goes only so far. That analogy is not useful insofar as it has more to do with memory and imagination than with understanding. It has to do with being able to picture in your mind more and more streets and their intersections. But imagining is not understanding; psyche is not spirit (Helminiak, 1996a). Moreover, learning to get around town entails only one knowledge. Only one problem, the same question, is at stake throughout. No deeper knowledge, but only more information, is at stake there.

In contrast, the shift from arithmetic to algebra is an example of a higher viewpoint in the strict sense of the term. Arithmetic has to do with addition and subtraction, multiplication and division. Algebra also deals with these things and retains these arithmetical functions. But beyond merely doing these functions, algebra also achieves an understanding of what is at stake when these functions are performed. So algebra becomes a much more abstract, a broader, way of dealing with such functions. It can introduce negative numbers or work with symbols that are not specific numbers at all but represent any number whatsoever. Algebra entails an understanding of the underlying processes that make arithmetic work. So algebra is not limited to dealing with numbers; it deals with the pure relationships in the arithmetical association of numbers. Algebra not only does what arithmetic does and does it in a more comprehensive way. Algebra also achieves a whole new level of mathematical understanding. Algebra is a higher viewpoint in comparison to arithmetic.

Similarly, in relation to algebra, calculus is a higher viewpoint. Or in the field of physics, Einsteinian relativity theory is a higher viewpoint in relation to Newtonian mechanics.

The System of Higher Viewpoints in this Chapter

Perhaps you understand little of mathematics and less of Newton and Einstein. There is still hope for understanding what a system of higher viewpoints means in the strict sense. Another example of higher viewpoints is the one given in this chapter. The meaning of "higher viewpoint" should come clear as this chapter unfolds.

In the meantime, consider another analogy. Suppose there are three different people who are concerned about a new church building. The contractor attends to issues of laying the foundation, setting up the girders, placing the brick and windows and interior walls and structures. The architect is concerned about the effective use of space and about the history of religious buildings and about the impression this structure might make on people. The pastor sees the church as a place for community gatherings and worship and is concerned about the religious meaning of the building as "the house of God." All three consider the same building, but the concerns they bring differ. In some ways the concerns get broader as one shifts from contractor to architect to pastor.

Consider further that the pastor just happens to belong to a family whose business was contracting. Growing up, the pastor learned the business inside and out. Moreover, the pastor studied architecture and worked in that field for years. Only recently did the pastor begin a second career as clergy. Because of these remarkable coincidences, the pastor is able to consider the church building from the perspectives of contracting, architecture, and religion. In one and the same mind, the pastor's, all three understandings cohere. And as is appropriate, the pastor can shift from one to the other. The pastor never thinks of discussing religion with the contractor. Although the building is certainly central to religious concerns, the pastor's concern with the contractor is to ensure quality construction. Similar things must be said about the pastor's discussions with the architect.

Three understandings of church building reside in the pastor's one mind, and the three are not unrelated. These three related understandings in one mind are suggestive of different viewpoints. Indeed, in many ways architecture is a higher viewpoint compared to contracting, for architecture presupposes a knowledge of materials and construction and their possibilities and their limitations. However, religion hardly relates to architecture as a higher viewpoint in any strict sense. A good religious service can happen in a tent. So here the analogy is seriously defective. Nonetheless, the case of the contractor-architect-pastor provides a suggestive example of what a system of higher viewpoints is.

Considering a shift in horizons (Lonergan, 1972, p. 235) is another way of suggesting what higher viewpoints mean. As one's horizon broadens, one can get a broader and broader view of a thing. So the positivist viewpoint might be like examining that church up close and noting the bricks and mortar and the shape of the building. To climb the hill outside the town and see the church in its whole surrounding provides a broader vision that might be like the philosophic viewpoint. Then suppose one were flying overhead in a plane. One's horizon would be broad indeed. One could now get a very different perspective on the same church. It would really be pushing things to speak now of "a God's eye view" of things, but this outlandish suggestion does point to the theist viewpoint. Then what if one could board a rocket and achieve orbit around the earth? One might still, in theory, be able to make out the church below, but now one would have transcended all earthly horizons. The church building would be viewed against the limitless openness of outer space. And pushing the analogy of horizons, one might infer the theotic viewpoint, where human coincidence with the divine surpasses every limitation.

Metaphors of seeing are all very misleading, for higher viewpoints are about understanding, not about looking and seeing. Still, these analogies may provide some insight into the argument of this chapter. Hopefully, the chapter itself will clarify the matter.

The Positivist Viewpoint

As noted above, the question that determines science per se is this: What is actually the case of the matter? What is really happening? How can it be explained? The task of science is to explain things on the basis of relevant evidence; its purpose is to give an ever-more coherent and accurate account of things.

Even when the focus is the human sciences, the same question pertains, though it shows itself in different forms: What is it that people do? How is it that people function? Why do they act as they do? Part of the answer will turn on objective factors: biology, heredity, training, and environment. And part of the answer will turn on subjective factors: beliefs, values, motives, and attitudes. But whether the factors are objective or subjective, the same concern prevails: to explain the human in terms of definable factors as they actually happen to be. Said otherwise, the concern is to explain "the way things are."

Further consideration of the wide range of sciences noted under the section, "The Definition of Science," makes another contribution. It suggests what "the positivist viewpoint" means.

Concern to Explain a Phenomenon as Given

The presupposition of all the sciences is that the goal is to explain. But a second presupposition is also at work in the sciences as currently conceived: concern is limited to what is now in fact the case. All those sciences, natural and human, despite the difference in the breadth of data they allow, deal only with the status quo. They do not consider what could or should or would or might be the case. They deal with what actually is. In the words of Detective Friday, the sciences want "The facts, Ma'am. Just the facts."

Of course, there is bias as to what might fall under the category "Facts." This is an important point. Science as depicted thus far deals only with what actually is the case. The telling difference, the contrast with the philosophic viewpoint to be noted below, is this: these sciences do not consider whether what happens to be the case ought to be the case. They do not consider whether it is best that things be as they are. Their concern is simply to explain things correctly, not to determine the correctness of things. Even when focus is on human beings and the meanings and values that determine them and their societies, the positivist viewpoint limits its concern to correctly determining the meanings and values that people in fact hold. In every case, the concern is "merely" to give a coherent and comprehensive account of things as they are.

Such limitation of scientific concerns defines the positivist viewpoint. The concern of the positivist viewpoint is the de facto. *Pursuit of systematic explanation that takes only the status quo into account is science within the positivist viewpoint.*

For example, consider the kinds of studies generally done as human science. These studies tend to be only descriptive. With elaborate experimental designs and sophisticated statistical analyses, these studies accurately determine the way things are. Left alone unobserved, so and so many people are likely to take what is not theirs if given the opportunity. People alone are much more likely than people in groups to intervene when another person is being attacked. Physiological arousal that is unexplained will easily be associated with a particular emotion if the suggestion is made. Once people have made an investment in some enterprise or other, they are more likely than others not so invested to defend the worth of that enterprise. The life expectancy for men and women in our society is such and such. So and so many people continue to smoke. They have such and such reasons for smoking. One's life expectancy is likely to be decreased by such and such as a result of smoking. People who exercise so and so much per week tend to live such and such longer than others who do not exercise regularly or who exercise more. So and so percentage of the population claims to believe in God. People who belong to a religious congregation tend to report more happiness than people who do not. Such and such proportion of the population agrees that the president is doing a good job. These results compare favorably or unfavorably with those of six months ago. And so on and so on.

The social sciences determine the present facts of the matter. They do not consider whether the facts ought to be as they are. Is the president right in current public policy? Are the happy churchgoers really living better lives than non-churchgoers? Is living longer an ultimate value in life? Ought people to defend enterprises in which they are personally involved? Does the widespread acceptance of a dishonest practice make the practice innocuous? These questions transcend the positivist viewpoint. They open onto another level of pressing human concern. They reveal inadequacies that call for another stance, one that I call the philosophic viewpoint.

In his criticism of the methodology of the social sciences, Richard Bernstein (1976, p. xix) presents a parallel analysis summarized as follows:

For all the sharp disagreements between "tough-minded" empiricists, their analytic critics, and phenomenologists, there are certain framework assumptions that they shared. They advocated a conception of theory and the role of the theorist that would approximate the ideal of the disinterested observer who explains, understands, interprets, or simply describes what is. But their understanding of theory and the theorist harbored difficulties and unresolved problems that were not brought out into the open. These very problems and their ramifications are the *fons et origo* of the critical theory of society.

Bernstein focuses the central concern of science—to understand and explain what is. In my terms, this concern defines the positivist viewpoint. Yet this conception of science is narrow, especially when human studies are in question. This conception of science contains inherent flaws and provokes further questions. The need to address these further questions calls for a shift to another perspective or, in my terms, the philosophic viewpoint.

Adequacy of the Term "Positivist"

I use the term *positivist* in the sense just defined. General usage of the term does support such a meaning (Abbagnano, 1967), though there could certainly be squabbles over whether or not the term *positivist* is completely accurate. For example, whether the term *positivism* really applies to science that does allow, and attempts to explain, mental phenomena could be debated. So one might allow that two kinds of positivism are at stake: hard positivism, which limits concern to sensible data; and soft positivism, which allows the validity also of internal, mental, experience.

Despite possible debate, because the underlying concern in both cases is the same—to explain things as they are—according to the present usage, the term *positivism* applies in both cases. My problem is simply to find a name, more or less appropriate, for a particular understanding of things. Here the term *positivist* is being used to name an approach to explaining things that limits its concern to determining as precisely as possible what happens to be the case with a given phenomenon. Contrast with the philosophic viewpoint will highlight the significance of this limitation.

The Positivist Viewpoint as Only One Form of Science

In an earlier version of this system of four viewpoints (Helminiak, 1979), I used the term *scientific* to name the viewpoint under discussion. The term *scientific* is valuable insofar as it readily suggests the best-known instances of what is meant by the positivist viewpoint. When people think of "science," they generally think of physics, chemistry, biology, and perhaps sociology and psychology; they have in mind the kind of concerns that define the positivist viewpoint: supposed "value-free" rigorous explanation.

However, use of the term *scientific* to name this viewpoint would be misleading. It would suggest that here the issue is scientific but concerns in the further viewpoints to be introduced below are not scientific. Such an understanding would reflect the bias of hard positivism or narrow empiricism—the "scientistic mentality"—which claims for itself alone validity in explaining things. What is not of that kind is said to be not scientific at all, not valid in any objective sense, but mere opinion, belief, superstition, piety, speculation.

In contrast, the contention here is that the whole of this system of four viewpoints is scientific (Kukla, 1989). That is, this system entails interlocking perspectives that together envisage a coherent and comprehensive account of things. This system envisages complete explanation. Accordingly, insofar as the concern of science is explanation, the viewpoints beyond the positivist are also scientific. If their specific concerns do not square with those of positivism, it is not because they are not scientific but because they introduce broader questions that positivism cannot address or has chosen to ignore or tends to deprecate. But answer to those broader questions is still part of the complete explanation of things—especially when the things in question, as in the present case, are human beings. Pursuit of such answer is part of the scientific enterprise.

The claim is that psychology, philosophy, and even theology, both theist and theotic, can be rigorously scientific—methodical, dependent on evidence, producing cumulative results (Hedges, 1987), and, cohering with the findings of other disciplines, tending toward complete explanation. There is, however, no claim that those disciplines are at present scientific. Indeed, the "scientific" criticism of psychology, philosophy, and religion is correct: these fields are often examples of no more than opinion, belief, or speculation in highly elaborated metaphor, carrying strong emotional appeal. Yet the possibility of a scientific transformation of these fields is precisely the thesis of this book. The very point to be made here is that an understanding of human mind as spiritual clarifies the scope of psychology, legitimates scientific and non-sectarian treatment of the spiritual, extricates the spiritual from the theological, and delimits the realm of theology in relation to the human sciences. All of this fosters comprehensive and coherent understanding, so all of this is thought to be scientific.

So the term *scientific* has connotations useful to suggest the meaning of *positivist*. But the term *scientific* is not an accurate substitute for *positivist*. The whole present enterprise, the disciplines it entails, and the four viewpoints under consideration, are all conceived as science.

The Arational Mentality

There is another intellectual position that stands apart from the positivist and all viewpoints. It could be called the arational mentality. Consideration of it highlights the meaning of *scientific*.

This mentality is prescientific or, in recent history, post-scientific. In either case, it is a rejection of commitment to critical thinking as a means of understanding. Its ultimate base is the hypothesis that humans cannot really understand or explain anything.

At times I have suggested that this mentality is prior to or beneath the positivist, and I have referred to it as the chaotic or anarchic or magical or ascientific "viewpoint." But to the extent that it is of this kind, it is not really a viewpoint at all. On the contrary, it is the absence of a coherent viewpoint and even the rejection of all viewpoints.

No argument is possible within the arational mentality, nor can one argue with someone who operates out of this mentality. As Whitehead, I believe, exemplified the matter, arationality leaves one facing the man who thought he was a fried egg: what can one say? There can be no corrective response. For arationality rejects the validity of argument, coherence, consistency, logic. It is arational because it entails the outright disqualification of rationality. It is not merely irrational, for irrationality implies offense against rationality, which is itself still considered valid. Arationality rejects the validity, the use, the relevance of rationality altogether.

The arational mentality occurs in a number of forms. In the prescientific era, it occurs as a commitment to magic, superstition, and various religio-cultural beliefs. In this naive form it would be found in presocratic Greek society, before the sophists raised questions and introduced critical thinking and in the process "raised consciousness." Such arationality is also found in primitive societies and cultures. It is widespread in preenlightenment Western society in most realms of religion and daily life, and it is found in isolated pockets to this day in most people's everyday living. It shows itself in beliefs and practices—superstitions—that can have no reasonable justification or may even be known, from a scientific perspective, to be foolish, mistaken, or harmful.

Arationality also shows itself in precritical cultures in their passive approach toward life. The supposition is that things are the way they are because that is just the way they are. There is little awareness that one could do something to produce certain effects. Hope for control is invested in magic and prescribed rituals. Otherwise, one trusts and hopes that things will get better. When they do not, blame is attributed to the cosmic forces that be. But there is no commitment to understanding, explaining, and acting in order to introduce change and control. Such a maneuver would be inconceivable. The mentality is arational.

In the scientific and postscientific era, arationality is found in an overt form and in a latent form. The overt form is deliberate and self-conscious. It represents the outright and argued rejection of rationality. It is exemplified in philosophical skepticism, nihilism, or relativism. It is also the position underlying contemporary postmodernism (Lyotard, 1988; Mohr, 1995; Rosenau, 1992; Spretnak, 1991, Van Leeuwen, 1996). Disillusioned by the recently discovered complexity of the universe, both physical and social, people have argued for the abandonment of the attempt to understand. Supposedly, there is no objective truth or objective good, so it makes no sense to pursue them. All things are relative, nothing is absolute. Of course, this position is blatantly self-contradictory. It stands on an absolute claim that there are no absolutes; it expects respect and feigns validity while it grants only qualified validity, only social validation, to any position. But for this position logical coherence and self-contradiction do not matter, for at the core of this position is the denial of any reality apart from a social construction, so there is nothing that constrains the human mind and requires the principle of contradiction. To this extent overt arationality represents a deliberate return to a prescientific worldview, to a world of magic, superstition, whim, power politics, and personal preference, all supposedly beyond the possibility of any adjudication.

The latent form of the arational mentality is arationality in disguise. In practice it is a rejection of rationality, but in words it claims to be fully legitimate. Its disguise is usually an appeal to the unknowable: ultimate reality, mystery, God. It does not insist on the rejection, but rather on the transcendence, of rationality. Rather than being arational or irrational, this position claims to be beyond reason.

Latent arationality is common in spiritual and religious circles, so the present considerations are central to the interdisciplinary problematic of this book. Indeed, sometimes "religion" and "science" are said to be irreconcilable precisely because the religious supposedly surpasses reason—as if science does not also face mysteries of its own. Then again, facing the mysteries of science leads others to conclude that the religious stance was not only correct but needs to be expanded to include all things (Jones, 1996). Then trust in reasonableness is abandoned across the board.

Latent arationality is the elaborated position that, in the end, denies that a coherent position on reality is possible. According to it, supposedly any talk of ultimates must involve paradox. Or alternatively, in the ultimate, in the really real, all is one, and there are no distinctions: the requirements of rational discourse—the relevance of Yes-No judgments: "dualisms"—are transcended. The criticism that paradox is just self-contradiction by another name is rejected as dullness, lack of wisdom, obtuseness. Appeal to spiritual wisdom or enlightenment supposedly legitimates this latent arationality. This form of arationality appears the most legitimate of all since it is cloaked in lofty terminology and moves in rarified realms. This is the position that denies the possibility of true scientific treatment of things spiritual. This is the position in contrast to which this book argues at its core. The discussion of Ken Wilber's perennial philosophy in Chapter Four engages this matter in detail.

Now, obviously, matters of religion and spirituality *are* subtle and complex. In this discussion mystery lurks at every turning. Paradox seems inevitable. Half-truths abound. Sorting out the matter is a Herculean task. Most despair of doing it, and many have reached the studied conclusion that it cannot be done (Bracken, 1997). In contrast, this book argues a minority opinion. Its claim is that coherent explanation is possible even regarding things spiritual. Flagging a supposed latent arationality within spiritual circles is but another way of announcing this claim. It is a way of calling our age to a renewed patient and humble effort to seek understanding. It is a way of holding off our age's growing dark cloud of intellectual despair.

Another version of the latent form of arationality is nonphilsophical. It is the position of the crass hedonist or egoist, who allows no principles for living, no morality, but lives by whim and for pleasure and self-satisfaction. Pushed to justify itself, this position moves into the explicit philosophical form either by actually attempting to justify its stance or by rejecting the objection as an attempt at being logical or consistent or responsible, all of which it holds to be irrelevant. The name *anarchic* is illuminating in this case.

Across the board I make a deliberate commitment to the possibility of human understanding and explanation, so I reject the arational mentality, even in its latent and religious formulations, as obscurantism. But let it be clear what is at stake in this commitment. It is not a claim that all things are rationalizable—and paramount among these "all things" and in the present discussion is God. The insistence is only that even regarding God one must be reasonable (Helminiak, 1986d, pp. 29–32). Not every belief about God is as valid as every other. Some are more reasonable than others. Some make more honest appeal to the evidence and make more sense of the evidence. Some are more logical; their statements are coherent. These differences matter. Precisely these differences are at stake in the contrast between the arational mentality and the commitment to science as I am using these terms.

Said otherwise, the commitment to scientific explanation is not a rejection of mystery, but mystery is not the same thing as paradox. Paradox entails supposed seeming contradictions, and so the appeal to paradox begs off seeking understanding. Mystery entails a surplus of meaning (Ricoeur, 1967), and so appeal to it allows for some understanding but pleads inability to achieve comprehensive understanding, even while granting that such understanding does exist in the ideal. For a position that accepts mystery, all does somehow make sense, though human efforts to understand may prove inadequate. For hard-core insistence on paradox, inconsistencies are said to be inherent in the matter itself and unable to be eliminated. The one approach allows for the transcendence of reason without needing to opt for arationality. The other approach opines that in the ultimate case rationality becomes irrelevant.

Thus, the arational mentality actually stands outside the field of the pursuit of scientific explanation. The arational mentality is an intellectual stance that is completely incompatible with the system of four viewpoints.

The Philosophic Viewpoint

The positivist viewpoint has been defined by its concern to determine accurately what happens to be the case. Such a scientific attitude appears to be adequate in physics, chemistry, biology, and even animal psychology. In all these cases, the object of study is more or less fixed; it is given apart from the scientists studying it. The task, then, is "merely" to explain the object.

To say that is not to deny that the intrusion of the observer does have an impact on any object of observation. The serious epistemological questions raised by quantum mechanics are not to be blithely dismissed. To say that is only to highlight a significant contrast with the human phenomenon—people—whose reality depends on the self-determining objects of study themselves: people form themselves.

People change. They change especially through interaction with other people, including interaction with researchers who are studying them. But the most important source of change in people is their own self-determination. People make themselves what they are. Furthermore, what people are and what they are able to become depends on what they believe and what they value. And within certain broad limits, they are free to believe and value what they wish.

Definition of the Philosophic Viewpoint

That set of affairs introduces a scientific concern not present else-where. Now the question is not merely, What happens to be the case? Or said with focus on the human: What do these people actually believe? Why do they structure themselves and their society this way? What are the values they actually hold? Now further considerations must also be taken into account: Is what they believe correct? Is what they value good? And are they faithful to their beliefs and values? In a word, *authenticity* (Lonergan, 1972) is an essential consideration when people are the topic.

Chapter One summarized a technical definition of authenticity, which I have elaborated elsewhere (Helminiak, 1987c, 1996a). Here, the general discussion makes clear enough what is meant. At issue is simply human goodness, that people be of good will: open, honest, concerned.

Being human inherently entails those further considerations, so one cannot adequately treat human beings apart from concern for authenticity. Whether or not humans are acting in accord with what they believe and value and whether or not what they believe and value is actually correct and worthwhile—these considerations have a lot to say about what the people in question will be. For example, if people suffering in a drought believe quenching their thirst, even with polluted water, is the most urgent goal, this belief will determine what they will be—dead. Or again, if people believe that getting the most for themselves is the supreme measure of success in life, their society will eventually crumble in deceit, mistrust, vicious competition, and various forms of covert self-loathing.

A major presupposition here is that there are objective truth and goodness and that the true and the good are built into the structure of the universe. More about that below. But granted that, to follow the true and the good would lead to further developmental possibilities, to solidly based growth, to lasting expansion. But to follow what is false and wrong would inevitably lead to dead ends, to self-contradiction, to self-debilitation, and to some form of self-destruction. Though in the short run recreational drugs will help allay the "ordinary" stress of living, for example, a society that needs drugs just so people can face another day must eventually collapse in disarray.

Another major presupposition here is that the human being is inherently geared toward the true and the good. More on that below, as well. But again, granted that, to act in accord with what one believes and values, even if one may be mistaken in those beliefs and values, is at least to establish integrity within oneself. It is to set up harmony within oneself and so to nurture and encourage, to reverence and foster one's inherent being. Then the human system, with its inherent desire to know correctly and to love honestly, is more likely at least eventually to discover the true and to embrace the good. But to betray one's own beliefs and values is to set up opposition within oneself, to war against oneself, and so to doom oneself to unresolvable conflict, frustration, and self-repression.

Moreover, those same considerations apply to scientific researchers: Are they authentic people? Do they conduct their studies carefully? Do they analyze their results intelligently? Do they report their findings honestly? Do they change their opinions as new evidence requires? Whether they are authentic or not has a lot to say about what they will advance as the best available opinion of the day. So this specifically human concern about authenticity is essential to the human sciences.

Concern for the further question about human authenticity determines a viewpoint higher than the positivist viewpoint. Universal concern for the true and the good determines the philosophic viewpoint. Within the philosophic viewpoint, the truth or falseness of what people think and the goodness or evil of what they value are essential. If concern within the positivist viewpoint can be said to be descriptive, concern within the philosophic viewpoint can be said to be prescriptive or normative. The prescriptions or norms rest on a thoroughgoing critical realism (Helminiak, 1996a; Lonergan, 1957, 1972).

The shift from a lower to any higher viewpoint entails a major new presupposition and a commitment to it. The fundamental presupposition in the case of the philosophic viewpoint is this: concern about truth and goodness matters, authenticity is of the essence. *Pursuit of systematic explanation whose focus is authenticity is science within the philosophic viewpoint.*

The Peculiarity of the Philosophic Viewpoint Today

Such a concern may seem strange in our day. Whether stated this starkly or not, the more prevalent attitude is that all things are relative: "What is good for you may not be good for me. So who is to say what is good or right?" The same relativist thinking holds with regard to the truth: "What you call 'truth' is what is true for you; but what is true for you is not necessarily true for me. So you hold your truth, and let me hold mine." The popular adage runs, "You do your thing; I'll do mine." The point is that the true and the good are supposedly not objective things that can be discerned and shared. Rather, *true* and *good* are just terms for what people hold very dear. *True* means meaningful or significant, and *good* means pleasurable or satisfying. "It's all subjective." Supposedly, there is no way to determine objective truth or objective morality. Cross-cultural studies and historical-critical studies can offer support to this supposition (Helminiak, 1986d, pp. 2–5). They show that across time and across cultures people differ radically in their basic beliefs and values. Then to argue even that there is a common human nature seems problematic. So we live in a world where belief in truth and goodness has become quaint. On the popular level, talk of objectivity is not popular.

The same thinking holds sway also on the professional level. Since Locke, Berkeley, Hume, and especially Immanuel Kant, philosophers have been unable to give a coherent account of human knowing. According to Kant, we can know only "phenomena," that is, appearances; we cannot know things in themselves, the "noumena." Supposedly, our knowing is locked into ourselves in such a way that we can only know what things are for us; we can never know what things are in themselves. Such a line of thinking, in highly elaborate forms, rules and bedevils philosophical circles. Under the name of "postmodern," such thinking constitutes a school of thought in itself. No one seems able to explain what knowing is; no one seems able to show how human knowing is valid. So even modern science, once thought to be able to give us the truth about things, cannot account for its own validity. The waves of postmodernism begin to move in. Karl Popper (1985), a leading philosopher of science, optimistically allows that we might be able to come up with a correct explanation of things but we could never know that we had. And the arguments are persuasive—but not definitive.

Of course, I would not suggest that determining the truth is easy in any case or that we ever do possess the full truth. The shift from the Aristotelian to the modern understanding of science highlights the matter (Lonergan, 1967b, pp. 259–260; 1972, pp. 94, 129, 315–316). We no longer speak of scientific truth but of the best available opinion of the day. The pursuit of understanding is an ongoing process. At best, we are on the path toward the truth. Still, there is a difference between being on or off the path.

It is clear that we learn as we go and that subsequent insight fills in gaps and even corrects previous oversight. We all make mistakes. Yet the very detection of a mistake suggests that there is a serious difference between what I or we happen to hold and what in fact is so. What we believe and what is the fact, may not be the same thing. Once I realize this difference, I have the option either to seek to know the true and the good or to rest content with what I think and feel. The option is quite clear. The analysis almost begs me to choose the higher ground. And to do so would not be at all unreasonable.

So there is an answer to the popular relativism that rules our age. Despite the unpopularity of the position and the difficulty it entails, one can set oneself on the pursuit of what is really true and truly good. One can become a "truth-seeker." One may not always be certain if one is correct, but one can always act only as one is reasonably sure one ought. With deliberate commitment to this enterprise, one can always be ready to rethink the matter, to seek out new evidence, to listen to discussion, to change one's mind, to revise one's theory, to correct one's mistake, to admit one's fault— in regard to all matters. Thus, one lives within the philosophic viewpoint.

There is an answer on the professional level, too. Or, at least, this book presupposes that there is. That supposed answer is the position of Bernard Lonergan. His major work, *Insight*, addresses three issues: What do we do when we know? Why is that knowing? and What do we know when we do that? His responses provide in turn a cognitional theory, an epistemology, and a metaphysics. In other words, Lonergan responds to the dilemma that has hung up Western philosophy and Western civilization since Immanuel Kant. Lonergan gives an account of human knowing, of the meaning of *true*, of objectivity, of reality, and of ethics. In his second major work, *Method in Theology*, he expands his treatment of value and the good and elaborates his account of the self-constitutive nature of the human being. Lonergan proposes an elaborate, comprehensive, and coherent answer to the questions about correct meaning and wholesome value that plague modernity and confound the human sciences. The reader will have to judge for her- or himself whether Lonergan's position is correct. This book will help by elaborating the implications of Lonergan's thought for psychology and the human sciences in relation to religion. Succinct statements of Lonergan's answer occur in Chapter One in the three subsections beginning with "The Inherent Normativity of Consciousness" and in Chapter Four under the title "Objectivity in 'Subjective' Domains." It is hoped that in the end, like the author, the reader will come to believe that Lonergan's position may be the breakthrough that can bring order to the epistemological chaos of our world and methodical coherence to the pursuits of the human sciences, including theology. In the meantime, the present exposition continues, presupposing the philosophical viewpoint and committed to it.

The Validity of the Philosophic Viewpoint

It was stated that concern for the true and the good is inherent in being human. This assertion can be defended in a number of ways.

Consider that people need to believe that they are correct in what they think and do. We expend tremendous energy wondering about things or keeping ourselves from wondering about things. We wonder because we want to be sure; we keep ourselves from wondering because we do not want to disturb our security. In either case, the point is the same. We need to believe we are right. We are very disturbed when it appears that we are mistaken in some belief or wrong in some action. If we cannot bring ourselves to admit a mistake or right a wrong, we convince ourselves that there is nothing to correct. We rationalize our position, and only then are we able to go on our way. Concern for what is true and good is not the uncomfortable luxury of the conscientious. In one way or another, it is the poignant burden of every human being.

Do you agree with what I just said? Why or why not? If you think I am wrong, have you reasons for that? Your reasons address the rightness or wrongness of what I have just said. Evidently, then, what I said is correct! Or correct, at least, in your case. You are concerned about being correct, for you argue your case.

But why be concerned at all about being correct? In fact, we have little option. Either we are concerned and so we enter into discussion to determine what really is correct, or else we insist that being concerned about being correct is pointless. But if we insist that it is pointless, do we think we are correct about that? And if being correct were pointless, why do we bother to make an issue of it? In either case, then, the assertion stands: people need to believe they are correct. Even to deny that people are concerned to be correct is to take a stand for what one believes to be correct. To do so is to affirm with one's deeds what one wants to deny with one's words. One argues that being correct about things is pointless, yet one's arguing argues that being correct matters. The argument is inconsistent; it falls in self-contradiction.

The only other option is to dismiss this whole discussion—either by explicitly dismissing it, by adopting the arational mentality, and this maneuver will entail self-contradiction; or by retreating into silence, by withdrawing from this and all discussion. For as Socrates pointed out, once the skeptic begins to speak, self-contradiction is inevitable. On this issue, one must either agree or appear foolish or be silent. And to recede into silence, to stop inquiry, is to cease being human. So the claim stands firm: people need to believe they are correct.

The all-important implication is this. When some conflicting opinion arises, people will need to rethink and perhaps revise their own stand. Human mind is such that it impels us to rest at ease only with what is true and good, as best we can determine.

The argument just made is philosophical, and it arrives at a universal conclusion. Social scientists might be uncomfortable with that and prefer to go out and count noses—and from one point of view, they are right. In fact, there is really no need to push the issue of universality here. The matter under discussion is interior to each separate individual. Each one knows his or her own experience in this regard, and only the individual knows whether she or he is telling the truth when reporting that experience. The matter at stake here is not open to public observation. But this does not mean that the issue is not real nor that there is no evidence on the matter. Let each one search her or his own soul; let all be honest in their response. The evidence is found in oneself; it is not available to the scrutiny of others. In the last analysis here, talk of people in general is really beyond the point, and it can become a distraction. No abstract humankind, but only you and I are at stake in the present discussion. Others stand out there, but the matter in question stands within oneself. Argument will not settle the matter, cogent though the argument be. People cannot be convinced unless they are willing to be. And even if others cannot agree, one still needs to live with oneself. It is precisely oneself, and not a universal conclusion, that is at stake in this discussion. So the issue is really addressed to each individual in his or her own conscience, in his or her own soul.

Where does that leave us in practice? Those who find validity in what is written here are most welcome fellow travellers. What more could one desire than to find such worthy company? Together let us pursue the issues with all rigor and integrity.

Those who cannot go along may still find interest in categorizing this position among the human curiosities to be studied within the positivist viewpoint, adding it to the list of the wide range of human phenomena that actually occur. But they miss the point and do violence to the analysis, for the question about authenticity remains real, and it is different from the positivist question about what really happens to be the case. What happens to be the case is that I am insisting on the validity of the notion of authenticity. Whether or not I am correct is a valid, further question. This question deserves its due. Merely to list it as one some people continue to ask is not to address the question; it is to miss the point.

Unfortunately, in any matter whatever, there is no way to convince those who do not agree. Affirmative judgment and responsible decision cannot be coerced; they must be freely given, on the basis of sufficient evidence and good will. Let this book serve as an invitation to further consideration that, with openness on all sides, may lead to eventual consensus.

As for the social scientists concerned about counting noses: any social scientist qua human could certainly join the present company of fellow travelers. But if the social scientist qua scientist cannot go along, one must begin to wonder about the adequacy of social science (Bernstein, 1976; Habermas, 1991; Taylor, 1989). How can it claim to treat people when it ignores the core of the person? It appears that the philosophic viewpoint is a requisite of adequate human science.

Nor is the approach offered here really much different from the empiricism of current science. The experimental task is to test a hypothesis against the relevant data. In the present experiment each one finds an experimental subject in him- or herself. It can be no other way, for subjectivity is the matter in question. That all cannot analyze the very same subject is no argument against the validity of this experiment. In no scientific enterprise do all the experimenters study the very same subjects. Rather, the very point of science is to show that the hypothesis does apply to any of the subjects within a specified class. So let each use her- or himself as the subject of this human experiment. If you determine that the analysis presented here does find verification in your own self, yet another instance of replication adds to the credibility of the present account. Add one more nose to the list—a very important one, your own. And realize that what is unfolding here is but the empirical method, generalized to apply also to the peculiar case of human subjectivity (Lonergan, 1957, pp. 72, 243).

Another (more standard) empirical approach also supports the assertion that concern for the true and the good is inherent in being human. When a person lies, respiration increases, pulse goes up, muscles tense, and palms perspire. These physiological reactions are the basis for the polygraph or lie detector test (Saxe, 1991). Evidently, lying causes stress. Dishonesty disrupts the human organism. The implication is that lying is not good for a human being. Lying introduces some kind of incompatibility within the person, and the effect shows in taxing physical changes.

William Perry's developmental study of college-aged youth suggests another source of empirical evidence on the question at hand. Using an interview technique, he was able to discern the impact of inauthenticity. He writes, "Those whom we perceived as standing still, or stepping to one side, or reaching back, acknowledged that they were avoiding something or denying something or fighting something, and they regularly remarked on an uneasiness or dissatisfaction akin to shame" (Perry, 1970, p. 50).

Again, Marjorie Lowenthal concluded her landmark study on mental health among the elderly with this hypothesis: "the failure to reach their goals—or lack of self-actualization in one's own unique terms—is conducive to illness in old age (mental, physical, or both)" (Lowenthal, Berkman, et al., 1967, p. 270). That is to say, some form of inauthenticity is often the root of mental disorders. Lowenthal explains in more direct terms: mental illness in old age "may constitute escapes from an insupportable realization that self-actualization, in terms of one's own life goals, has not been achieved and is not likely to be, and that it is one's own fault. (Self-blame . . . tends to characterize the elderly who are hospitalized for mental illness in old age)" (p. 270).

Erik Erikson's (1963, 1978) well-known stage theory of human development entails a similar suggestion—not only in the "crisis" of old age, integrity versus despair, but in each of life's turning points. For each calls for a particular strength or virtue: hope, will, purpose, competence, fidelity, love, care, wisdom (Erikson, 1978, pp. 19–30). Especially those in the latter stages obviously imply something of authenticity.

Or again, in *To Thine Own Self Be True* Lewis M. Andrews (1987) collected evidence on the impact of honesty on mental health. Andrews proposes a counseling approach called "ethical" psychotherapy. His solution may be a bit too simple, ignoring the complexities of psyche and focusing one-sidedly on spirit, but his overall argument is similar to the one being made here. Concern for truth and goodness is healthy; its opposite is a source of psychological dysfunction. More recently and most importantly, in *Soul Searching* William J. Doherty (1995) argues in the same direction, though his argument is often couched in terms of that old bugaboo, self-interest versus altruism (Helminiak, 1996a, pp. 108–109). Nontheless, relying on the analyses of Wolfe (1989) and Taylor (1992), Doherty comes close to outright insistence that moral living is essential to psychological health. Using the theological term *sin* (Helminiak, 1987c, p. 119) as perhaps the only way still left in our society to point to real wrongdoing, Karl Menninger (1973) made a similar argument about wrongdoing and mental health. So accepting the philosophic viewpoint appears to be the wholesome, healthy—the human—thing to do.

The Term *Philosophic*

According to the etymology of the term, the philosopher is the lover of wisdom. Concern for the true and the good is precisely the love of wisdom, so a stance that takes that concern is rightly called *philosophic*.

It should be clear that to accept the philosophic viewpoint does not necessarily mean to become a philosopher. Neither is the philosophic viewpoint to be understood as the domain of academic philosophy. Rather, the term *philosophic* points to the kind of concerns that govern this viewpoint. They are the concerns associated with classical philosophy: the love of wisdom. Yet those concerns are essential to being human, period. So any science that would adequately study human beings must take those concerns into account. The matter is not one just for philosophers; it is one for anyone truly concerned about the human situation.

There is also a technical reason for the term *philosophic* here. According to Bernard Lonergan (1957, pp. xxix, 387–390, 399–401, 568, 602–604, 618; 1972, p. 95), the task of philosophy today is to analyze human consciousness—certainly a debatable proposition among contemporary professional philosophers. Formerly, philosophy concerned itself with everything: art, music, mathematics, poetry, physics, biology, anthropology, religion, metaphysics. Whatever fell under the category of being, whatever existed, supposedly fell to philosophy to explicate. But as independent disciplines branched off and found their autonomy, and especially with the rise of modern science and the emancipation of art in secular society, the domain of philosophy shrunk. That is as it should be. Various methodologies, more appropriate to their various objects of study than was "philosophical" armchair speculation, now govern those other fields. But still left to be treated is the one phenomenon not amenable to other methodologies and available for analysis only to the inquiring human subject him- or herself: human subjectivity, human consciousness, human spirit. According to Lonergan, this phenomenon remains the proper domain of philosophy, which comprises cognitional theory, epistemology, and metaphysics. These, of course, are the very things at stake in the philosophic viewpoint. In this sense, the term *philosophic* is technical. It implicates the whole theoretical structure borrowed from Lonergan and undergirding the present enterprise.

The Pivotal Role of the Philosophic Viewpoint in Interdisciplinary Human Studies

The philosophic viewpoint is determined by concern for authenticity. Said otherwise, it is determined by universal commitment to pursuit of the true and the good. Or again, its distinctive domain is the unrestricted unfolding of consciousness; its focus is relentlessly dynamic human spirit. It follows that the study of the human within the philosophic viewpoint is the study of spirituality. It follows further that differentiation of the philosophic viewpoint—from the positivist viewpoint on the one hand and from the theist, on the other—determines the distinction and the link between the human sciences and theology.

The argument moves very fast in the above paragraph, for it is a summary statement of much of this book. Exactly how an analysis of human subjectivity or consciousness or spirit entails a theory of spirituality and how the philosophic viewpoint and the authenticity of human spirit are linked has been suggested already and elaborated elsewhere (Helminiak, 1996a) and will become clearer as this book unfolds. At this point we stand dead center at the intersection of the two fundamental conceptions that undergird this book, the system of four viewpoints and an account of human mind as spiritual (Figure 1.4). The interrelationship of all these issues makes it difficult to present any one without involving the others at the same time. The author begs the reader's patience and relies on mutual good will.

Here it should already be clear that differentiation of the philosophic viewpoint casts the human sciences into two types: those limited to the positivist viewpoint and those governed also by the philosophic. The concerns that determine the philosophic viewpoint seem essential to being human. So the contention here is that only human science within the philosophic viewpoint is adequate to the human being, and psychology of that type is already spirituality.

Nonetheless, many will continue doing human science solely within the positivist viewpoint, and such science can make valuable contributions to understanding the human phenomenon—as, for example, in biology, medicine, physiological psychology, and behaviorism (Bufford, 1981; Miller & Martin, 1988). For though the human is self-determining, the scope of our self-determination is circumscribed. We are not as free as we might like to believe. So the sciences that study people as fixed and determinate do have something to offer. If behaviorism makes the mistake of wanting to explain everything about people on the basis of conditioning, to suppose that conditioning explains nothing would be equally mistaken. Yet it remains that psychology restricted to the positivist viewpoint ignores the distinctive essence of the human.

In contrast, psychology within the philosophic viewpoint already attends to that distinctiveness. Then, is there anything to be gained by shifting to an even higher viewpoint in theism? Does God really have to be brought into the picture? The answer is, Yes, and some detail on the matter will be given later in this chapter. However, that Yes is quite qualified, and here the more important point needs to be made: the philosophic viewpoint is the key to the human enterprise, and analytically it is the most significant.

As will be shown presently, a theoretical account of theism is an extrapolation from authenticity. Buried in the understanding of inherent, human, spiritual dynamism, is the seed of a conception of God. So the criteria of human authenticity determine and constrain all possible statement even about God. The direction of inference is that way, and not the inverse. Authenticity is the major premise. On it all else depends.

Even in the concrete believer—and here the discussion shifts from theory to practice—whatever advantage belief in God may offer, it is a difference in degree, not a difference in kind. The believer in God does not cease being human, does not become a different species, but the believer is human more intensely, human more humanly. For granted that God exists, belief in God must entail an augment in authenticity, a broader and more risky commitment to the true and the good. But unless belief in God so surpasses as to discredit human commitment to all that can be humanly known as true and good, belief in God does not disqualify human authenticity but rather somehow merely perfects it (Helminiak, 1986d, pp. 33–36, 1987c).

Or again, even in commitment to God, human authenticity retains a priority. One might claim revelation from God to justify a certain belief, and one would be right in so doing if, indeed, the revelation was of God. Still, one would be bound by the demands of human authenticity in determining precisely this issue: Is the revelation really from God? What reason is there for believing so? Belief in God, if that "God" be true, can never excuse inauthenticity—close-mindedness, silliness, dishonesty, and irresponsibility.

So the heart of the matter, theoretical and practical, is authenticity and the philosophic viewpoint. In comparison, and while we remain in this world, theism is a refinement—a valid refinement, mind you, but nonetheless a refinement.

On the opposite front, the comparison between the positivist and the philosophic viewpoint entails more complexity. As understood here, there is real continuity between these two viewpoints, just as there is between the philosophic and the theist viewpoints. Indeed, such continuity is essential to this unfolding system of four viewpoints on the human phenomenon. For the argument is that this system provides a coherent and comprehensive approach to interdisciplinary study of the human. So some kind of coherence among all four viewpoints and some kind of continuity between every lower and every next higher viewpoint, must be discernible.

The continuity between the positivist and the philosophic viewpoints shows in both meanings and values. On the one hand, to wonder what is really the case, as positivist science does, is to be committed to correct meanings, to be committed to truth. Such limited commitment could lead one to realize that it makes no sense to pursue correct understanding in particular cases unless there is a human capacity ultimately to attain objective truth in general. Otherwise one would have to be able to specify why correct understanding were possible in the one case but not in another. And if one were able to do that, one must have some understanding of correct understanding in general, some understanding of truth. So there is continuity between the positivist and the philosophic viewpoints. The continuity entails the inherent human possibility of ever-broader understanding and the actual human commitment to such broader understanding.

On the other hand, there is also the issue of values. Now, despite the supposed "value-free" status of positivist science as generally understood, the question about the good is indeed at stake in positivist science (Bernstein, 1976; Habermas, 1991; Myrdal, 1958; Weber, 1949). For the value of pursuing correct understanding is the presupposition of such science. That value is real, and positivist scientists do embrace it. Moreover, decisions about which topic of research is worthy of pursuit, about which methodologies and designs are appropriate to specific projects, about how carefully data will be collected, analyzed, and interpreted, about how results will be publicized and applied—these are all matters of value. Commitment to these questions of value opens onto the question about value in general, about objective good. Again, there is discernible continuity between the positivist and the philosophic viewpoints.

The complexity arises because of current misunderstanding about the nature of positivist science. Specifically, the "value-free" claim projects a wholly different understanding of things. If this claim were granted, the difference between the positivist and philosophic viewpoints would be a difference in kind, not merely one in degree. On this understanding, my present point would be all the more easy to make. The shift from the positivist to the philosophic viewpoint would be a switch to another track, and only there would continuity with the theist and theotic viewpoints begin. Then the pivotal nature of the philosophic viewpoint would stand out in stark relief.

Of course, I do not accept the value-free claim of positivist science. Nonetheless, the pivotal position of the philosophic viewpoint is still easy enough to expose. If questions of truth and value are inherent in positivist science and if universal concern for the true and the good defines the philosophic viewpoint, then science within the positivist viewpoint is but a limited instance of science within the philosophic viewpoint. The philosophic viewpoint is the center point around which all human explanation, all science, revolves. Surely, this assertion holds for the human sciences, insofar as only the philosophic viewpoint allows an adequate treatment of the human. Similarly, this assertion holds even as regards the natural sciences, insofar as the scientists in question are pursuing correct—true—understanding and insofar as they are themselves human beings. For unless the work of these scientists flows from authentic human beings, the science in question is specious.

The philosophic viewpoint is pivotal in the analysis at stake in this book. In contrast with the positivist, only the philosophic viewpoint allows adequate treatment of the human. Besides, from the philosophic viewpoint, theist and theotic considerations can follow as needed. And even natural science, unless it be done authentically, is not really science at all. The key to the matter, when the matter is human, is human authenticity.

No amount of theology, on the one hand, or positivist science, on the other, can substitute for an adequate treatment of the human being and of human society. These topics as such are simply disparate. Not God nor supposed value-free science but authentic humanity is what needs to be addressed, especially today. And precisely that—the general question about truth, about the good, and about the possibility of determining them—has had Western civilization hung up for three centuries as modern science went its own way. Whether because of historical accident or theoretical necessity—or, undoubtedly, some combination of the two—in today's situation among the sciences and religions the philosophic viewpoint is pivotal.

The Theist Viewpoint

Within the positivist viewpoint, the concern is to know what is really going on, to know the correct explanation of what happens to be the case. Said otherwise, the concern is to know the truth of the matter, as best as can be determined.

Concern for truth in a limited, particular case within the positivist viewpoint raises the question about truth in a broad sense and about the value of pursuing the truth. Is there objective truth in general to be sought? Is there objective value in general to be pursued? Are human beings really able to know reality? Can humans determine what is objectively good? Response in the affirmative to these questions and the concomitant commitment to that affirmative, determine the philosophic viewpoint.

Of course, pursuit of the true and the good in the human situation is always an ongoing affair. We learn as we go, we refine our position. We grow in truth as we grow also in virtue. What we knew as certain may have been certain—and indeed so—only within yesterday's limited understanding, and what we affirm as good today may change tomorrow as we understand more about the case. We are well aware, sometimes painfully aware, that no one is in possession of full truth and full goodness. In all honesty, we are wary to insist that we definitively know the objective truth and good in any particular case.

Emergence of the Theist Viewpoint

Nonetheless, committed to the philosophic viewpoint, we live in relentless pursuit of the true and the good. So the further question arises, Is there full and objective truth? Is there absolute goodness?

Is there a terminus of the authentic human pursuit of all that is true and good? And if not, what validity could the human pursuit of the true and the good possibly have?

Thus, from within the philosophic viewpoint a legitimate question arises, a question that cannot be answered within that viewpoint. An invitation emerges that asks one to consider a still higher viewpoint.

To that further question and its invitation may be added one's own experience—experience of the incessant emergence of questions from a curiosity that will not be satisfied but that on occasion does recognize a satisfactory answer; experience of an inner need for reasonableness that on its own criteria assesses what is indeed sufficient reason; experience of what here and now is good, implying recognized fulfillment of some universal criteria of what would qualify as good. Within the course of daily living is buried some awareness of absolutes, some exercise of criteria of objective validity. The commitment to the pursuit of the true and the good seems to entail some inkling of an absolute truth and goodness. Judgments of fact and judgments of value seem actually to apply those criteria of objective validity in limited cases and thus in some sense express an absolute.

Now, one may recognize that experience of an absolute as somehow connected with the emergent question about full truth and absolute goodness. Thus, the combination, question and experience (Lonergan, 1972, pp. 101–103), bids one make a further commitment to the terminus implied in one's present quest.

To make that commitment to the fullness of truth and goodness is to affirm the existence of that terminus. It is to acknowledge that somewhere there is Complete Truth and Perfect Goodness. It is to admit that there does exist Explanation of Everything about Everything. It is to believe in "God." The affirmative answer to the further question about the fullness of truth and goodness determines the theist viewpoint. *Pursuit of systematic explanation whose focus is the Creator-God of the Universe is science within the theist viewpoint.*

Talk of God in terms of Truth and Goodness follows the tradition exemplified so well by Thomas Aquinas, who wrote in his *Summa Theologica*: "Not only is there truth in God, but God is the highest and first truth itself" (I, q. 16, a. 5). And again, "God is the highest good," for "good is in God as in its first cause and so is

there in the most excellent way" (I, q. 6, a. 2). Moreover, Thomas
continues, it is "absolutely true" that "the good which is good by
nature is God, from whom all other things are said to be good by
means of participation" (I, q. 6, a. 4).

The Priority of the Philosophic Viewpoint

The theist viewpoint emerges out of the philosophic viewpoint. This
is not to suggest that people come to believe in God by means of an
elaborate theoretical analysis, such as was just presented. In fact,
people generally believe in God—in some fashion or other—before
they turn to questions about truth and goodness, and they often
resolve those questions on the basis of their belief in God. It is no
accident that concern about objective truth and goodness is a particular preoccupation of Western civilization, where belief in a God
who stands in contrast to creation is a pervasive cultural influence.

That state of affairs suggests that it is important to sort out
the God question from the truth-goodness question—something that
popular religion is not wont to do and for the most part has no need
to do, but something that scientific treatment of religious questions
cannot omit doing. This very sorting out is what is at stake in the
present differentiation of viewpoints.

To say that the theist viewpoint emerges out of the philosophic viewpoint is not to suggest that one reasons oneself into
belief in God. For belief in God is a choice, and though reason can
support a choice, it can never necessitate one. Nor is this to say
that God is secondary and the human primary. For if God is what
believers profess, in every matter God is first ontologically and
logically (if not, strictly speaking, however, chronologically, for before creation there is no time). Nor is this to say that God is merely
a projection of human aspirations, as many assailants of theist
belief suggest. For, as classical and contemporary theologians and
philosophers point out, unavoidable logical constraints surround
the affirmation of the existence of God. And though these constraints do not constitute a formal proof for the existence of God,
they show that belief in God is a reasonable choice.

To say that the theist viewpoint emerges out of the philosophic
viewpoint is only to suggest that, in a theoretical analysis of the
matter, the philosophic viewpoint holds the priority of a presupposi-

tion; it is pivotal, as noted above. When human explanation is at stake, explanation is constrained by the human. This is so even when God is the object of concern. Humans are capable of treating of God only insofar as humans are capable of treating of anything. The same human desire to understand and the same human capacity to explain are at stake in every case. A statement about God, simply because it is about God or because it occurs in a supposedly inspired book, has in itself no greater validity than that attributable to any other human statement. On the contrary, a statement about God, because God so surpasses the capacities of human understanding, should be more suspect than a statement about any other thing.

The point is that God-talk, like all talk, is conditioned by human capacity. As Thomas Aquinas repeated often in the beginning of his *Summa Theologica*, if we must admit *that* God is, we certainly do not know *what* God is. Experience and question may lead us to the point of positing the intimated Self-explanatory Terminus of our unending stream of questions seeking explanation of all things. True to the demands of our own intelligence and reason, we may even be able logically to outline in heuristic fashion what that Terminus must be like to fulfill its function as terminus (Helminiak, 1987c, pp. 101–122; Lonergan, 1957, pp. 657–669). But we would be wrong to suppose that we comprehend the meaning of our own valid statements.

We may legitimately talk about God, but all legitimate talk about God is constrained by the demands of human authenticity. Said otherwise, the theist viewpoint emerges from the philosophic viewpoint.

A Revolutionary Shift of Emphasis

This heavy emphasis on the priority of the philosophic viewpoint as presuppositional, even in the face of treatment of God, may be offensive to religious believers. Indeed, it is revolutionary (Crowe, 1980; Tracy, 1970). It entails a profound challenge to religion. Whereas formerly religious belief was to determine what life meant and how it should be lived, here human authenticity is the locus from which all else proceeds. Whereas formerly appeal to revelation was to have settled the questions, here intelligent questioning and reasonable argument must first legitimate even that appeal to revelation.

This important shift of emphasis derives from Lonergan's analysis of consciousness and his understanding of theological Foundations (Lonergan, 1972). The shift is visible, for example, in a comparison of Aquinas's theology in the *Summa Theologica* and Lonergan's understanding of systematic theology. Whereas Aquinas presupposes the metaphysical categories of Aristotle and begins with the question of God, from which all else flows, Lonergan begins with an analysis of human consciousness and from there derives the categories of metaphysics and theology (Helminiak, 1986d, pp. 303–305, n. 53). Again, Lonergan describes this shift in his retrieval and reformulation of Aquinas's theology of grace, transposed from Aristotelian categories into the categories of consciousness (Lonergan, 1971, 1972, pp. 165–166, 352).

Lonergan has shifted the basis of discussion to a deeper level. Since human consciousness is operative in any intellectual pursuit whatsoever, consciousness must be the common factor that interrelates and constrains all disciplines and sciences. So, on Lonergan's analysis, even theology jogs down one notch to a new and firmer basis, and since this basis is the presupposition of all scientific pursuit, it must be the ultimate foundation, it is rock bottom. The implication is that human authenticity, and no simple appeal to religious revelation or conviction, is now definitive.

No Threat to Religion but Clarification of "Religion"

This approach is not an attack on religion; it is a clarification of religion. In fact, authenticity is a central concern of all the great religions. If theist religions also include belief in God, often God-talk is but a way of furthering human authenticity. For instance, to insist on "God's commandments" is a way of insisting on what *we believe* to be right. Or to speak of "God's will"—when this is not an outright manipulation enforcing the merely conventional—is a way of talking about what ought to be done as best *we* can *honestly* determine. But in addition, theism contains something over and above ethical concerns about human authenticity. It contains affirmations about God. The present analysis differentiates these matters, the theist and the philosophic, and so preserves both of them. Moreover, as will be seen below, the differentiation of theotic concerns from theist concerns again highlights a uniqueness too often obscured when the specifically Christian dimension of Christian religion is not kept in focus.

Besides, all religions also carry merely positivist content— that one kneel or bow or stand while praying, that one wear a certain color for a certain occasion, that one cut one's hair or not, that one dress this way or that, that one eat or not eat certain foods, that one hold particular days as holy. These are traditions and practices that are as they are simply because that is the way they happened to develop. They are accidents of history or culture; in themselves they have no objective validity. They are very different, for example, from the philosophic concern to be honest and loving. This matter claims universal validity and in one way or another is common to every great religion. Or again, they are different from theist insistence that one reverence the God of the Universe or from Christian belief in the divinity of Jesus and a Trinity in God. These latter matters are in no way optional in those religions.

Religion includes a whole swath of concerns. The present analysis sorts them out. Christianity includes specifically theotic concerns in addition to theist, philosophic, and positivist elements. Theist religions include only the latter three, and non-theist religions include only philosophic and positivist elements. Possibly other religions, some mix of magic, superstition, and inherited beliefs and rituals, entail only positivist elements. But it is unlikely that any religion or culture could contain no objective truth and no wholesome values whatsoever. The present system of four viewpoints applies to religion itself and shows that significantly diverse and irreducible elements may be bundled up in one religion. Sorting out these elements makes it clear that *religion* is not a useful category for interdisciplinary studies. *Religion* is too imprecise. Like charity, it covers a multitude of sins (1 Peter 4:8)—in this case, sins of fuzzy thinking.

When the analysis is complete, religion may seem to have lost out. But that is only because of misunderstanding, only because of the Western penchant to identify religious concerns with theist concerns. Then when it is said that even theological statement must submit to the demands of human authenticity, it may appear that religion is subordinated to humanism. But human authenticity is also a part of religion, so nothing at all has been lost to religion.

Higher Viewpoints Sublate Lower Viewpoints

This exposition has presented the positivist, the philosophic, and now the theist viewpoints. The resultant picture is sufficiently broad that some comments about these viewpoints as a system can now be made. These comments will exemplify how this system of higher viewpoints sorts out and interrelates issues that determine different sciences or academic disciplines. The present and the following three subsections treat these methodological considerations. Only then does the presentation return to further clarification of the theist viewpoint.

Since the theist viewpoint emerges from the philosophic viewpoint, the theist viewpoint loses nothing from within the philosophic viewpoint. Rather, the theist viewpoint retains all that is within the philosophic viewpoint and spells out a further implication.

For example, theism continues to pursue the true and the good; the shift to the theist viewpoint does not free one from the constraints of human authenticity. Yet theism raises that pursuit to a new perfection when in God it envisages the ideal fulfillment of the human pursuit of the true and the good, that is, Absolute Truth and Goodness. Within the theist viewpoint, the philosophic pursuit of the true and the good takes on a new and broader meaning: the unending quest of the human heart is understood to be really a search for God, and when the quest is pursued authentically, its ideal termination is known to be God. Thus, only the theist believer could say with Saint Augustine, "Lord, you have made us for Yourself, and our hearts are restless till they rest in You." Yet both the authentic humanist and the theist believer are on the very same quest.

In a word, the theist viewpoint *sublates* the philosophic viewpoint.

More generally, within this system of four viewpoints, each higher viewpoint sublates the lower viewpoints. This same effect is obvious in the example of calculus, algebra, and arithmetic, given above. This effect is obvious here when one considers the questions that determine each of the viewpoints. The positivist viewpoint asks, What really happens to be the case? The philosophic viewpoint goes on to ask, Is what happens really to be the case—is it as it ought to be? Are beliefs there true? Are values there really good? The philosophic viewpoint accepts the valid conclusions of the positivist viewpoint and even accepts the limited validity of the questioning that determines the positivist viewpoint; for that questioning is about correct understanding, the very concern of the philosophic viewpoint. Yet the philosophic viewpoint envisages a broader question. But the theist viewpoint proposes an even broader question when it asks, Is there a fullness of truth and goodness? The affirmative answer here still allows the validity of the philosophic pursuit of the true and the good and perforce the validity of the positivist concern to determine what really is the case in limited instances. Yet the theist viewpoint situates the human concern for truth and goodness in a broader context. Finally, as will be noted below, the theotic viewpoint goes on to ask, Is there human participation in that Fullness of Truth and Goodness? Again answering in the affirmative and with Jesus Christ as the paradigm, for example, Christianity envisages some possible coincidence of the human and the divine. Yet once again, Christian considerations within the theotic viewpoint retain the validity of the concerns and valid conclusions of the theist, philosophic, and positivist viewpoints.

By way of example, consider the scientific study of spirituality. The guiding question here is this: When studying spirituality, how does psychology function within the theist and theotic viewpoints? The direct answer is that, strictly speaking, psychology does not function within those higher viewpoints. Rather, psychology is sublated into a broader horizon of concern.

Psychological questions are proper, in the first place, to the positivist viewpoint, and within that horizon of concern the task is to spell out the structures, mechanisms, and processes that explain the ordinary functioning and integration of the tripartite human being: organism, psyche, and spirit. But more appropriately, since *human* psychology is in question, psychological questions are proper to the philosophic viewpoint. It introduces explicit attention to authenticity and looks toward that human functioning and integration that alone fosters and represents ongoing self-transcendent growth. Such psychological treatment is spirituality (Helminiak, 1996a). So psychology functions within the positivist and philosophic viewpoints but not within the theist and theotic viewpoints.

Then what happens when one looks to understand spirituality from within the theist viewpoint? First of all, everything that is understood psychologically about spirituality—about the authentic functioning of the human being—from within the positivist and philosophic viewpoints remains valid. After all, if that psychological explanation accounts for things spiritual within human experience and if that psychological explanation is really accurate, why should anything in the account be changed? Introducing into the matter the further concern of the theist viewpoint, namely God, will not make what was true psychologically and spiritually now no longer be true. The valid conclusions of the human sciences stand firm even before God and before authentic belief in God. The epistemological presuppositions behind the system of viewpoints necessitate this insistence. Secondly, then, what the theist believer does is to take those human-science explanations and understand them within a broader horizon of concern. But the explanatory contribution of the theist viewpoint is narrow and quite specific. This broader horizon introduces the realization that the human functioning that the human sciences may accurately explain is none other than the handiwork of the Creator-God. In other words, within the theist viewpoint the understanding of the human sciences takes on a further dimension of meaning, but nothing of that human-science understanding changes. It is not the role of the theologian to propose psychological explanations. It is the role of the theologian rather to account for God's relationship to the human functioning that the psychologist explains, and God's relationship is that of Creator (Helminiak, 1987c, Part II).

Something similar must be said about the still further shift to the theotic viewpoint. Again, all that is valid within the lower viewpoints is retained intact. What the theotic viewpoint adds is merely the further realization that at stake in the created human process of spiritual growth is actually an inchoate process of deification. Speaking more graphically, a Christian might say that human spiritual growth is actually the work of the Holy Spirit within the human heart, and the suggestion is not only that God created the human process but also that God has further intervened to facilitate that human process so that it might attain a specifically divine end. The theotic viewpoint considers the effect of God's deifying intervention in the created human process. This consideration is delicate and subtle, for it must both propose an explanation of how God's deifying intervention does actually make a difference in the human process and at the same time preserve intact the psychological explanation of this process (Helminiak, 1987c, Part III). But once again, like the theologian, the theotician is not doing psychology but is simply making her or his proper contribution by adding another further dimension of understanding to what has been achieved within the lower viewpoints.

Theist and theotic believers might be uncomfortable with this approach. They would likely object that it limits the scope of God's working within the spiritual process. They would insist that admitting God's involvement in the process adds something "more" that cannot be understood by merely human efforts. The effect of this objection is to make spirituality impervious to rigorous and coherent explanation. Moreover, this objection might imagine that, when treating spirituality, theist and theotic believers as such do in some way function as psychologists. For supposedly the believers bring further data to bear on the matter of human spiritual process. Now, this analysis within the four viewpoints has already allowed that theologians and theoticians do have a specific contribution to make, but their contribution is not psychological, and their contribution will not change the valid explanations of positivist and philosophic psychology. The challenge that this analysis poses to the believers is this: specify what that supposed "more" is and how it has not already been accounted for by analysis within the theist and theotic viewpoints (Helminiak, 1987c, Chapter 6).

Surely, there may be legitimate differences of opinion on these matters. The suggestion here is that the four-viewpoint analysis already represents a possible coherent treatment and that the structure of this treatment both focuses the differences of opinion and specifies the discussion needed to resolve them. So this analysis stands as an invitation to further discussion.

These considerations about spirituality exemplify how the higher viewpoints sublate the valid conclusions of the lower viewpoints. Analysis within the system of viewpoints sorts out various disciplines and their realms of competence and also interrelates their conclusions in a comprehensive whole, all the while respecting the proper competence and autonomy of the respective disciplines. At stake is an overall process of coherent and comprehensive explanation—science.

The Elimination of Reductionism and Fideism

The interlocking series of ever-broader questions that determine the four viewpoints both coherently relates the viewpoints to one another and irreducibly distinguishes them from one another.

On the one hand, each of the successively higher viewpoints represents a broader understanding of one and the same set of data, so the viewpoints are *intelligently* related to one another. But from the bottom up they are not *logically* related to one another (Lonergan, 1954, pp. 637–638). Only from the higher viewpoint, granting its broader range of presuppositions, can the logical consistency between the lower and the higher viewpoints be shown. From the lower viewpoint, coherence with the higher depends not on logical deduction but on question, insight, and ultimately on responsible decision. One moves from a lower to a higher viewpoint not by logical argument but by reasonable choice grounded in deeper understanding. The point is that the four viewpoints constitute a coherent whole. The coherence is intelligent, not in the first instance logical. The coherence depends on understanding and on ever-further ranges of understanding, not, from the bottom up, on deduction or necessary implication.

On the other hand, the questions that determine the viewpoints are different, so the viewpoints are irreducibly distinct from one another. The philosophic question about truth and value in general is not the same as the positivist question about accurate understanding about particular, limited topics. The theist question about a Fullness of Truth and Value is not the same as the philosophic question about the ongoing human pursuit of the true and the good. The theotic question about human participation in that Fullness is not the same as the theist question about the existence of that Fullness. The error of reductionism is precisely to obscure the validity and the distinctiveness of these separate questions.

On this understanding, from within any higher viewpoint, a valid conclusion within the lower viewpoint appears to be but a particular limited application of the broader understanding that determines the higher viewpoint. Within algebra, arithmetic appears to be a valid but limited application of algebra, and then again within calculus, algebra now appears to be the limited but valid application. Similarly, within Einsteinian relativity, Newtonian mechanics appear to be a limited but valid application of a broader understanding. So it is, too, within the system of higher viewpoints under discussion here. Thus, a comprehensive system that interrelates diverse human sciences and disciplines results.

In that arrangement, the lower viewpoints impose certain constraints on the higher viewpoints: the higher must preserve what is valid within the lower. Thus, just like reductionism, fideism is also eliminated.

Fideism is the attitude that simply says, "Take it on faith," whenever a question arises. More specifically, fideism is appeal to the presuppositions of a higher viewpoint in response to empirical questions proper to a lower viewpoint. As such, fideism entails the unwarranted disqualification of input from the lower viewpoints.

For example, creationism claims to explain the origins of the universe by simple appeal to the "Word of God" in the Bible. Such an approach rejects all positivist scientific evidence as if such evidence had no validity in the face of contrary belief. On the present understanding, though creationism claims to find its authority in God, creationism is not a theist-viewpoint position at all. Rejecting critical questioning and the unbounded pursuit of human understanding, creationism is not open to honest human curiosity and so does not even meet the criteria of the philosophic viewpoint. If the position is not compatible with the philosophic viewpoint, perforce it cannot be legitimate within the even higher theist viewpoint. In fact, then, creationism is a positivist-viewpoint position, an assertion made by a particular sociological group, an item on the list of the different things that different peoples, in fact, happen to hold. Creationism is an ideology (cf. Smart, 1997). The fact that the position is presented in terms of divine revelation and of God does not place it in the theist viewpoint. The meaning of one's terms is what determines a matter, and the meaning of *revelation* and *God* in the case of creationism is bald appeal to religious authority. Thus, creationism is an example of fideism.

Belief in God supplies no ready-made answers to the vast array of questions in the physical and human sciences. Nonetheless, theist believers working in secular fields can make a unique contribution. That contribution is not a simple-minded quoting of religious belief nor naming God nor bearing witness to Christ. That contribution is to keep the secular field open to a broader horizon of legitimate concerns.

Theist believers who are also practitioners in secular fields bring to their scholarship presuppositions not shared by their non-believing colleagues and so may rightly be said to be working within a higher viewpoint. Nonetheless, in their scientific or scholarly work the believing practitioners must meet the current valid requirements of their secular fields (Myers, 1996), and on these bases they must be able to show that their conclusions are reasonable, even though their questions and conclusions may have been provoked by broader faith. If within a lower viewpoint the believing practitioners do advance a reasonable argument influenced by their commitment to a higher viewpoint, they will likely raise questions that disturb the secular field—and ultimately advance it. Those questions would highlight the inadequacies of the lower viewpoint. Those questions, though legitimate within that lower viewpoint, might be unanswerable apart from a higher viewpoint. So such faith-filled scholarship would point to the need for being open to a higher viewpoint. All the while, however, such faith-filled scholarship would do no violence to the legitimate requirements of scholarship within the lower viewpoint (Helminiak, 1986d, pp. 19–36). The insistence of this book, that the human sciences must be open to issues of authenticity if they would be adequate to human beings, is an example of a higher-viewpoint concern challenging the adequacy of a lower-viewpoint analysis. This book challenges a human science limited to the positivist viewpoint by raising legitimate questions that can only be answered within the philosophic viewpoint.

Openness to the "little" as well as the "big questions" keeps all the disciplines and their practitioners honest. Mere openness to the legitimacy of higher-viewpoint questions—one need not have an answer to those questions—is enough to keep lower-viewpoint analyses authentic. And fidelity to the valid requirements of the lower-viewpoint discipline is enough to make its conclusions valid. No discipline needs actually to answer all questions to prove itself a legitimate enterprise. Neither reductionism nor fideism is an acceptable approach.

All that is simply to say that the disciplines on all fronts need to be aware of their own limitations and need to acknowledge the validity of other specialized disciplines. Within such a framework collaborative and cumulative understanding will flourish. The diverse specialized disciplines will enrich one another. Comprehensive science will progress.

The Resolution of Conflicts Between Disciplines

Of course, the important question arises as to how one determines just what is valid within the conclusions of a lower viewpoint. Simply by focusing the specific kinds of questions proper to each viewpoint, the present system of viewpoints already goes a long way toward answering this question. In the present case, for example, whether or not the universe is created by God is a question proper to the theist viewpoint; but exactly what that created universe is and how it unfolds is a different question. This question is proper to the positivist viewpoint as regards non-human reality and to the philosophic viewpoint as regards human beings. The theist viewpoint legitimately holds that God created the universe, but how God chose to do that is a question for empirical study of what God created, a question proper to the lower viewpoints. An answer to this question that emerges from appeal to divine revelation but that cannot meet the criteria of pertinent lower viewpoints has no validity.

Still, uncertainty often remains. Often seemingly reasonable religious tradition and seemingly valid scientific findings do differ. In this case the present approach shifts the locus of debate from between disciplines to within a discipline. The debate is not about which discipline, for example, theology or geology, has the right to pronounce on the matter of the age of the earth. The debate is about the sufficiency of the evidence and the adequacy of the theories within the appropriate discipline, in this case, geology.

Religious tradition, though it tends to phrase everything in terms of God, contains much that is properly philosophic and also positivist, as noted above. So let religious believers isolate the philosophic and the positivist aspects of their religion from the strictly theist issues and, with others who share the pertinent viewpoints, discuss their philosophic and positivist beliefs on the basis of the criteria of these lower viewpoints. On such an approach, religion still has its say—except now it must legitimate its position rather than merely assert it, and when legitimation becomes tenuous, it must consider the possibility that it has been mistaken. But continued assertion without legitimation is fideism.

To disallow any input from psychology on questions of spirituality is likewise an example of fideism. On the other hand, to insist that the "spiritual" is *merely* a matter of neurons, neurotransmitters, brain waves, and their patterns is an example of reductionism.

God and Images or Concepts of God

The conception of God in the theist viewpoint is not free to be whatever one might want. As constrained by the philosophic viewpoint, only the true God is pertinent to the theist viewpoint. So simple affirmation of some god or other does not qualify as the theist viewpoint. All conceptions of god but one are pertinent not to the theist viewpoint but to the positivist viewpoint. Within the positivist viewpoint one could catalogue a list of conceptions proposed as god, and with contemporary positivist sociologists and anthropologists one could determine that there are many different kinds of "belief in God." But all those so catalogued within the positivist viewpoint would not ipso facto pertain to the theist viewpoint. The present system of viewpoints allows only one, and a very specific, understanding of God.

Similarly, one may study various images that people have of God, study the emergence and evolution of these images, and study the part that these different images play in people's personalities and development (Heller, 1986; McDargh, 1983; Rizutto, 1979). For example, people of high self-esteem tend to image God as loving and kindly, whereas people of low self-esteem tend to conceive God as controlling, vindictive, and impersonal (Benson & Spilka, 1973). As part of the psychology of religion (Fuller, 1994; Malony, 1991; Meadows & Kahoe, 1984; Paloutzian, 1996; Wulff, 1997), such study makes a very valuable contribution. It analyzes the formation and function of deep psychic symbols pertinent to the human need for a coherent, meaningful, and valued world. And because the symbols in question are associated with God, the Ultimate Transcendent, they can also express the human need for, and facilitate the human process of, ongoing self-transcendence.

Images of God can be studied within the positivist viewpoint. Such study catalogues the diversity of images and determines the correlations of such images with other aspects of human experience (cf. Smart, 1997). But images of God can also be studied within the philosophic viewpoint. Then concern is to understand how various images or concepts of God foster or hinder the open-ended unfolding of human spiritual capacity along the lines of human authenticity. This is to say, such study of God-images can be an important aspect of the study of spirituality both as a theoretical and as a practical or pastoral discipline. Understood in this way, religion is not necessarily about God, but mostly about fostering positive human relationships, wholesome human communities and societies, and ongoing human growth (Murray & Morgan, 1945)—in a word, about authenticity.

To speak of God images is not necessarily to speak of God. For God-talk often serves the societal status quo or, more importantly, serves to foster human authenticity. And all the while such God-talk may prescind from the further question about God as a distinct reality. Only when discussion turns to God as a distinct reality and when this reality is the one true God of the Universe, has discussion really shifted into the theist viewpoint and is one really doing theology, as understood here. So psychologists of religion may treat questions of belief in God within the merely positivist viewpoint. Further, they may also treat questions of God insofar as they relate to human self-transcendence and spiritual development, that is, they may do psychology within the philosophic viewpoint, or spirituality. Yet all the while they may themselves not be theist believers; or, being theist believers, they may nonetheless not be working within the theist viewpoint.

Those considerations have important practical implications for religion (Helminiak, 1982, 1984b, 1986c, 1992, 1994a). The main point is that talk of God does not necessarily deal with the Creator-God of the Universe but may be only a convenient shorthand language for talk of what is humanly known to be true, right, good, and beautiful. In the face of this fact, religionists need to be careful. Speaking too freely of God and God's will, they risk, on the one hand, granting divine authority to mere cultural and societal norms. Such a maneuver cannot but inhibit human questioning, social change, and personal integration—the very goal religion is to foster: spiritual growth. Current virulent discussion about gender and sexual mores is an obvious case in point. On the other hand, religionists also risk losing the proper meaning of talk about God. When talk of God is only a solemn way of talking about important aspects of human affairs, belief in the God of the Universe never really gets addressed. Religion becomes another venue for psychotherapy. This may, in general, be to the good. But the specific task of theist religion is neglected—to the detriment of believers and non-believers alike. Specification of the theist viewpoint, in contrast to the philosophic, is a way of securing the legitimacy of talk of the true God.

This matter also has practical implications for psychotherapists. More and more they realize the impossibility of helping people without eventually delving into spiritual issues (Butler, 1990; Chandler, Holden, & Kolander, 1992; Dan, 1990; Shafranske & Gorsuch,

1984; Shafranske & Malony, 1990). Yet, if spiritual wisdom is phrased only in terms of theist belief, psychotherapists may feel unqualified to deal with spirituality or may appear to others to have no such competence. Still, God-talk is often merely religiously coded talk of human authenticity. Understanding this fact, psychotherapists can go about their work of healing people even in spiritual realms without overstepping the bounds of their professional competence. In fact, a whole list of issues central to psychotherapy can be expressed in either religious or non-religious terms: ultimate meaning, hope, vocation and career, suffering and death, resentment, forgiveness, ethics, self-love, sexuality (Helminiak, 1995; Patterson, 1992). Discerning these basic human issues underneath religious talk, psychotherapists may legitimately attend to these issues without pretending to pontificate on questions of God and religion as such. The distinction between God and images of God and the differentiation of the positivist, philosophic, and theist viewpoints sort out these matters.

Treatment of images or concepts of God is not necessarily treatment of God. Only treatment of the true God of the Universe, the Explanation of Everything about Everything, is a genuine theist-viewpoint enterprise.

The Creator-God of the Theist Viewpoint

What, then, is that one, true God of the Universe?

This is not the place for a full exposition on that question (Helminiak, 1987c, pp. 101–122; Lonergan, 1957, pp. 657–669). Here suffice it to say that "God" is to be the terminus of the human quest for understanding. So "God" must be the Explanation of Everything about Everything. This Everything includes all meaning and all value, so this "God" is all Truth and all Goodness.

More importantly, however, this "God" must explain not only every particular thing that exists but also the fact of each thing's existence. So it is commonly and correctly said that God is the source of all things. This same common wisdom could be stated more accurately if the statement were inverted as follows: Whatever it is that ultimately accounts for the existence of things, that is "God." In the latter formulation, while affirming God, one does not appear really to understand what "God" is. For, in fact, "God" is the shorthand name for the expected answer to a legitimate question about the existence of things.

Talk of existence introduces a heretofore unmentioned issue. Already at stake within the positivist viewpoint was some notion of truth, and within the philosophic viewpoint, generalized notions of truth and goodness. But the scientific pursuit of understanding within those lower viewpoints always presupposed the givenness of the things to be explained. Here, not the matter of what something is but the matter that it is, comes to the fore. Nonetheless, the existence of things was part of the data from the beginning. Positivist and philosophic pursuits of understanding presuppose that existence. There would be no inquiry about things did they not exist to be questioned. Yet insofar as existence is real, it itself is open to question. Here the question about existence finally emerges. This question is the distinctive issue at stake in theism.

Thus, the question about existence is the key to an understanding of the true God. The fundamental conception of God is self-explanatory being. Said otherwise, God is Creator.

The Theist Viewpoint as Scientific

At stake in the notion of God as Creator is the scientific commitment to explanation. It is possible that all we know in this world could not be. The universe is contingent. It does in fact exist, but it could just as well not exist. The fact is that our world just happens to be. The merely contingent existence of all things has awed philosophers through the ages as they pondered the key question, Why is there something rather than nothing? This is a legitimate question, and it deserves an answer. The existence of things in this world must be explained. Ultimately it can be explained only by appeal to something that exists necessarily. Only something whose existence is not dependent on anything else can account for contingent existence. The only other option would be to posit some infinite regress, contingent explaining contingent. But this approach avoids the real question. If something is contingent, whether it exists infinitely long or only briefly, it still needs something else to explain its existence. Chronology is not the issue here; explanation is. So the question about existence is real, and it needs an answer. The matter necessitates an inviolable distinction between contingent being and self-explanatory being. If explanation is to be coherent, the one cannot be the other. And if explanation is to be had at all, granted that contingent being does exist, self-explanatory being must likewise exist. So positing self-explanatory being satisfies the scientific need to explain.

There is continuity between the theist viewpoint's emphasis on the question about existence and the lower viewpoints' emphasis on truth and goodness. The link is the search for explanation. The argument is that "God" must be self-explanatory being; for if there is no self-explanatory being, there is no explanation for contingent existence. But if there is, indeed, no explanation for contingent existence, then philosophic pursuit of truth loses its validity, for there is a reasonable question—How is it that things exist?—that has no possible answer. Then who could say what other perfectly reasonable questions also have no answer? By the same token, then, the limited pursuit of correct explanation within the positivist viewpoint also loses its validity. For, except by arbitrary decree, how does one determine which seemingly reasonable questions do and which do not have answers?

On this analysis, scientific commitment to explanation entails commitment to the possibility of ultimate explanation of all things. Then when the question about existence arises, it, too, must have an answer. The inherent rationale of the analysis demands positing self-explanatory being. Thus, acceptance of the concern of the theist viewpoint appears to be as scientific as acceptance of any other concern for explanation.

That the treatment here depends primarily on sheer reasoning and only tangentially on empirical evidence, does not disqualify this treatment of "God" as unscientific. If explanation is the determinant of science, this treatment is indeed scientific. And it does rest on important empirical evidence, the simple fact of the existence of things. That this empirical evidence is not more arcane or specialized, results from the nature of the particular subject matter, existence and God. Within the universally valid demands of explanation, each particular science requires its own appropriate methodology. Treatment of subjectivity within the philosophic viewpoint, for example, must rely on the evidence every person can find but only within her- or himself, so such treatment can claim "public availability" only in this modified sense. Likewise, treatment of theism again requires an adjustment of the standard expectation of "science" designed to apply only to physical reality. But granted the legitimacy of its own peculiarity, inherent in the subject matter as such, treatment of God can also be explanatory. It can also be legitimately empirical and scientific.

Creation as the Key Theist Issue

Until now, the theist viewpoint was presented in terms of "the Fullness of Truth and Goodness." In contrast, here emphasis is on self-explanatory being and the difference between Creator and creatures. The shift from the one understanding to the other calls for explanation.

This shift is legitimate because "Fullness of Truth" includes the truth about existence. Among the questions that need to be answered before complete explanation, the fullness of truth, is had, is the question about existence: How is it that things exist at all? Attention to this question provides a supplement of explanation not envisaged in the philosophic or positivist viewpoints. Highlighting the new issue is a valuable addition. Further, the argument here revolves around truth, rather than goodness, because the overall concern is science, correct understanding, explanation. The concern at this point is not ethics—a concern proper to the philosophic viewpoint where understanding of the human is at stake. Besides, in the Fullness, truth and goodness coincide. In the classical theology of Thomas Aquinas, as noted above, God is Truth and God is Goodness. In summary, then, the present, more pertinent, and more convenient attention to the Fullness of Truth is a legitimate tack. And the further focus on only one aspect of that Fullness of Truth, the truth about existence—that is, the focus on God as Creator—is also legitimate.

Keeping those clarifications in mind, one could conceive God as Fullness of Truth or as Fullness of Good rather than as Self-explanatory Being, Creator, and one would be correct. Indeed, emphasis on God as Truth and Goodness is integral to the overall coherence of the four analytic viewpoints insofar as these, including the theist and theotic viewpoints, are a tool for understanding human—and not divine—reality. For the theist viewpoint can say something about people, that they are created and are or are not committed to the God of the Universe, as well as say something about God as a distinct reality.

However, there is a possible ambiguity in that emphasis on God as Fullness of Truth and Goodness. This concept of God is not entirely safe. On the one hand, understood from within the theist viewpoint, the presupposition of the philosophic quest for the true and the good is that there is continuity between what humans correctly know to be true and what God knows to be true. Since objective truth is at stake, how could it be otherwise? It does violence to the notion *true* and to the notion *God* to suppose that something is true for us but not also true for God. The same kind of reasoning holds for the notion *good*. And this reasoning is valid, even granted the analogous nature of all statements about God (treated in Chapter Four). So, as human pursuit of the true and the good asymptotically approaches its terminus, there is continuity between human truth and goodness, on the one hand, and God, Explanation of Everything about Everything, on the other. In a limited way humans can know and love what God also knows and loves.

But on the other hand, precisely that possible continuity entails a danger. It might incline one to suppose that human knowledge and human love are per se participations in divinity or, more broadly, that human spirit is a participation in divinity. This supposition suggests that in some way to be human is to be divine. Such reasoning seems to be operative in ancient Gnosticism, Neo-Platonism—and so perhaps in some of Augustine's thought on divine illumination—Hinduism, contemporary New Age religion, and here and there in contemporary "Christian" approaches to spirituality. Conceiving God as Fullness of Truth or Fullness of Love or imagining God as Infinite Light easily allows a blurring of the distinction between the human and the divine. Then the divine is merely the fullness of humanity or, vice versa, the human is merely a dull form of the divine. This is a serious problem. The mistake is that picture-thinking and not clear conceptualization is at work. Unlike concepts expressed through propositions, which are governed by the principle of contradiction, images can represent any combination of things whatsoever. So, for example, a dream image might be both one's mother and one's father, and the unicorn represents both stalwart beast and blithe, magical spirit.

Conceiving God as Creator allows no such ambiguity. The distinction between creator and creature, between the self-explanatory and the contingent, is inviolable. The terms are defined in contrast to one another. The conception expresses pure intelligibility. It cannot be imagined or "imaged"; it must be understood. Once understood and affirmed, by dint of mere logic, it precludes all possibility of ambiguity. It cannot be fudged. So the heart of the matter when talk is of God is creation. Creation is the determinative intelligibility of the theist viewpoint. Thus, the theist viewpoint highlights an issue irreducible to the philosophic or positivist viewpoints.

The Limitations of Theological Competence

By the same token, the range of valid explanatory value within the theist viewpoint is remarkably small. Legitimate talk there is about the Creator-God and nothing else. Within this system of four viewpoints, the task of the theologian, strictly defined, is specific and narrow—to explicate by reasonable argument the created nature of the universe; to sketch heuristically what God, Explanation of Everything about Everything, must be like; to highlight the analogous nature of such statement; and to explain the compatibility of such a self-explanatory being with a contingent, temporal, nondeterminate world.

Those are the matters that in divinity studies formerly fell within the tract *De Deo Uno*, About God as One—in contrast to study of the Christian Trinity, *De Deo Trino*, God as Three. Those are also the matters that in the *Summa Theologica* (I, q. 1, a. 7) fall under Thomas Aquinas's definition of theology. In contrast to current usage, his definition is remarkably narrow. For Thomas, theology is the study of God and of all things insofar as they are related to God, their source and final end. (Thomas himself, of course, also included a broad range of other issues pertinent only to Christianity in his "theological" discourses, never distinguishing a theotic viewpoint.)

The current prevalent understanding of "theology" is quite different. Now "theology" refers broadly to the rational treatment of religious beliefs or, again, to the studies proper to professional training in ministry or, even more generally, to the reasoned treatment of any and every issue pertinent to a particular community of faith (Brown, 1997; Rahner, 1970; Sykes, 1983). More incisively, Lonergan (1972, pp. 138–140, 170, 267, 331, 355) understood "theology" to be reflection on religion, for lived religion is one thing, and reflection on it is another. But the present analysis shows that such reflection may be positivist, philosophic, theist, and theotic. If the term "theology" is to apply to the whole lot, the matter tends to be muddled. Or again, Lonergan (1972, p. xi) has said that the task of "theology" is to mediate between a culture and a religion. But as the culture develops and as differentiations of consciousness emerge, theology must meet the new situation by becoming itself more differentiated. When differentiations within a culture and the specialization of disciplines become sufficiently elaborate, mediating religion to the culture may demand narrower specification of the very term *theology*. For the continued usage of a broad, ill-defined, umbrella term works against the effective mediation between religion and culture in the sophisticated, contemporary, scientific world.

Accordingly, here I take the term *theology* in the very limited sense defined by the theist viewpoint and explicated in the third last paragraph. If the term is given this strict meaning, namely, treatment of the Creator-God, nothing other than this is really theology. And within this analysis of four viewpoints, the broader and prevalent meaning of theology—namely, faith-committed study of religion and whatever relates to religion—now seems quite confusing.

As it is, books continue to appear on the "theology" of work and the "theology" of play (which is to say, the psychology of leisure), moral "theology" (which is to say, ethics), liberation "theology" and feminist "theology" (which is to say, social ethics and history), black "theology" and Hispanic "theology" (which is to say, ethnic perspectives on religion), and more. Some of these "theologies" have perfectly good, accurate, and current secular names, as the above parentheses suggest. But the term *theology* is used to indicate that the analyses are done within a particular religious perspective, according to a particular set of beliefs and values. On the present analysis, one must wonder how this religious perspective could really make a difference if the conclusions are actually correct and if to be correct is the concern. For acknowledgment that the universe is created by God, the sole legitimate concern within the theist viewpoint, offers no content-specific help in sorting out questions about work, play, and leisure, or about ethics, history, and sociology. And the name *theology* then really implies no guarantee that opinions expressed on these other matters are correct.

Perhaps the term *theology* is used to suggest that the analyses in question are done with an eye toward objective truth and value. These studies purport to tell us what God would say about this or that matter. To be sure, in our pluralistic and relativistic society, the claim does have to be made explicit when the concern is for normative meanings and values in the realm of human affairs. Positivist secular society does not generally believe in the possibility of such statement. Secular society has branded that concern a quaint curiosity of a former age and has relegated it to the religions. And religion is usually assumed to be identical with theism. So, indeed, perhaps the only way for anyone to claim objective validity for such statement is to call it "theology."

But for theist believers to accept that warped understanding of things is to acquiesce to the current interdisciplinary confusion. It is to collapse the philosophic and the theist viewpoints into one. It is mistakenly to identify honest and loving living with belief in the Creator-God of the Universe. Then claims to divine revelation and inspired opinion readily enter the picture, and sectarian debate muddles any possible hope of achieving widespread consensus on issues important to the whole of society (Helminiak, 1997b). For now what should be society-wide discussion is seen as "theology," the specialized concern of religious believers, and the attempt to clarify issues is seen as imposing religious standards on secular society.

Is the claim to objective validity really the issue? Then, in the long run, it would be more useful and more accurate for believers to stop speaking in terms of God—and to start speaking in terms of human beings and human community and the authenticity they require implicitly. If the believers' argument is valid, it should be able to be made apart from appeal to God and religious tradition. It should have an inherent validity that believers can spell out and that any people of good will could appreciate. In fact, the American Catholic Bishops have adopted such an approach in their statements on nuclear war and on the American economy (National Conference of Catholic Bishops, 1983, 1986). Recently, the same bishops show increased openness to public reasoning about even the red-hot topic, abortion (Feuerherd, 1991; Gahr, 1991; Holewa, 1991; McManus, 1991). Though the bishops admit holding the values they hold because of the religious tradition they represent, they advance those values in the marketplace by appeal to a rationale intrinsic to their topic and not by appeal to the authority of a religious tradition. Then the discussion is not "moral theology" but much more simply ethics, a concern that every human being and every society must address. And the conclusion, if correct, is not only binding on religious believers but also relevant to every human being and every human community.

But perhaps use of the term *theology* has another meaning. Perhaps the implication is not concern to be really correct but rather the desire to advance a sectarian position and the naivete to suppose it correct simply because of its religious affiliation. Perhaps there is the desire to speak authoritatively on diverse topics, which used to be within the domain of religion, without needing to be accountable to the demanding criteria of the relevant and highly controverted secular disciplines. In this case, the name may be *theology*, but the argument is hardly theological. The argument moves not within the theist viewpoint nor even within the philosophic viewpoint. The argument moves merely within the positivist viewpoint. The presentation is the mere explicated opinion proper to a certain religious leader or a particular religious group. The presentation, then, is not what really is true and good but rather simply what happens to be the case, what happen to be the beliefs and values, among certain religious believers. The position is simply an ideology, advanced in the name of God (cf. Smart, 1997). But the weight of the position depends not on God nor even on an intrinsic rationale but merely on the social authority of a religious group or "theologian."

Society at large does not generally acknowledge objective truth and value; making a case for them is certainly difficult; and the burning questions of the day are indeed complex. So, in desperation many religious believers seem to have abandoned even the stance of the philosophic viewpoint. On what, according to the present analysis, is clearly an illegitimate appeal to God and revelation, they are content to take their stand and insist, "This is what we believe. This is what our tradition has always held." Religions today too easily slip into a positivist position, adopt a legalistic, authoritarian stance, and simplistically proclaim it as "God's Word" or "God's will." Fundamentalism is rampant. For the task of authentic religion is difficult. It is difficult to foster an open

and questioning, an honest and loving, attitude. And such an attitude, if fostered, inevitably challenges the authority and power of
the status quo, including that of the religions themselves. It is
easier to fall back on the past, to advocate the clear and the simple,
to guide by appeal to the bald authority of religious belief, and to
control by guilt and fear in the face of the mysterious or complex.
But such obfuscation and manipulation are not even humanly
authentic. How could they possibly be theologically correct?

Or perhaps those diverse studies are called "theology" simply
because that is how they have come to be named and no one has
thought to make a change. Perhaps sufficient awareness of the
specialization of disciplines has not yet had its impact in religious
circles and beyond. Then it simply ought to, and quickly. Otherwise, the religions will continue to lose their influence in secular
and multi-religious societies.

That having been said, some positive assessment of those
religious contributions is also in order. The religions do have contributions to make to secular society, for they carry concerns and
commitments that too often get overlooked. Precisely the humanistic issues—like work and play, ethics, art, women, and culture—
are more likely to arise in circles of religious believers. Such topics
are not unrelated to strictly theist belief. Indeed, since the Creator-
God of the Universe is the Fullness of Truth and Goodness, commitment to God does entail pursuit of the true and the good in all
human affairs: the theist viewpoint subsumes and expands the
philosophic viewpoint. But more generally, most of us learn our
value systems through some kind of religious upbringing or other,
so in our thinking and living those systems are tied to, and even
identified with, belief in God. And, thank God, there are still people
somewhere who passionately grapple with those issues of humanity and justice. If people of religion did not attend to those issues—
even if under the technically inaccurate name *theology*—one wonders
whether those issues would ever be addressed at all.

My concern here is theoretical—to distinguish and interrelate
the intrinsic intelligibilities of the various issues at stake: positivist,
philosophic, theist. Of course, in the living, in the human subjects
involved, these distinguishable issues all cohere. They are the presuppositions and commitments, the beliefs and values, that make
these subjects who they are, for meanings and values are constitutive of human beings. The system of higher viewpoints, a theoretical

analytic tool, posits distinctions within unities or wholes and thus allows coherent discussion about them. In contrast, this analytic system does not suggest separations among these issues in their real-life, concrete occurrences. Intelligently discerned distinctions are not space-time separations, as will be explained in detail below. This rigorous attention to theory may seem to demean or deny the contributions of the religions. But my intention is precisely to preserve the force of those contributions by locating them in their appropriate arena. Though people certainly and correctly associate with theist belief many other issues besides the nature of the Creator-God, I wish only to indicate that these other issues are not inherently theist. Then, in a multi-cultural, religiously pluralistic, and secular world, those other issues would be more effectively treated apart from relationship with God. And treated apart from God, they lose nothing of their inherent validity.

"Theology" as a Christian Enterprise

The question of the meaning of "theology" is further complicated because, over and above theism in the West, there is also Christianity. And Christianity also calls its scholarship "theology." Patently, the term is ambiguous. As will be shown presently, the content of Christian "theology" includes other distinct elements beyond simple theism. So there really should be another term for the distinctively Christian enterprise of reflection on Christianity's constitutive beliefs. I use the term *theotics* to meet this need.

Moreover, because of Christianity's historical nature, much of its scholarly activity is but specialized application of interpretative and historical methodology to specifically Christian themes. Happily, names like "biblical exegesis or interpretation" or "bible history" or "church history" readily reflect the disciplinary communality that these fields share with the parallel secular specializations. Biblical exegetes and church historians must first of all be respectable historians. And for the most part this is simply what they are. The name *Christian theotics* must be reserved for the specific task of determining, formulating, and explicating the distinctively Christian message.

Certainly, it is no easy matter to define exactly what the widely used and abused term *theology* means. The term does have a history of its own. Luckily, the intent here is far less ambitious. The main point is simply that, as within the theist viewpoint, so also within the theotic viewpoint, the realm of specific disciplinary competence is rather circumscribed. The theist and the philosophic viewpoints have already accounted for all ethical and all theist matters. So only the distinctive Christian beliefs fall within the theotic viewpoint. In practice this means that on other matters Christians cannot legitimately settle the discussion by simple claim to special revelation, to special insight, or to special authority. Granted, the Roman Catholic First Vatican Council taught that some things that could be known naturally have also been revealed so that they could be known more easily, surely, and without error (Denzinger & Schonmetzer, 1965, par. 3005). But things that could be known apart from revelation should, once known, also be able to be explicated apart from revelation. If they cannot be, the claim to divine revelation in their case loses credibility.

These considerations relate directly to the Roman Catholic belief that the Church may infallibly define all matters of faith and morals. Within the present analysis, the legitimacy of this teaching may stand without question as regards specifically Christian beliefs, strictly Christian matters of faith. For these beliefs are the property of the Christian community. Who else but that community and its leaders could or should define them? Moreover, as long as these beliefs do not offend reasonableness and logic—and even trinitarian belief has been shown to meet these criteria (Lonergan, 1964)—there can be no legitimate external objection to them.

But morality—ethics—falls within the competence of the philosophic viewpoint. There, not theist belief nor Christian belief nor ecclesiastical definition but human authenticity is determinative (Curran & McCormick, 1980; Gula, 1989; Wogaman, 1989). Although there may be variations in the way different religious traditions go about treating ethical questions and in the emphases they place on certain values over others, there cannot be any specifically Christian ethics. Ethics is about the specification of objective right and wrong, so what is ethical for one must be ethical for all (Van Leeuwen, 1996, p. 157). Different religions cannot correctly hold different opinions on these matters. So if some religious teaching on ethics is proposed as correct, acceptance of its correctness could not depend solely on its being "revealed" or "infallibly taught." It would need to be arguable also apart from appeal to church authority.

Despite the appearance of current practice, the Roman Catholic Church has never declared any of its ethical teachings infallible. So discussion of supposedly infallible ethical teaching remains purely hypothetical. It is also instructive to realize that in the last analysis the core of Roman Catholic ethical thinking is natural law theory and not the Bible nor tradition (John Paul II, 1993). Now, as the reader may have already discerned, talk of a philosophic viewpoint is but a refined and nuanced version of natural law theory. This fact is even more apparent in my full treatment of spirituality as a psychological concern (Helminiak, 1996a). My whole argument rests on a philosophical anthropology, an understanding of the nature of the human being. So, in the end, there appears to be no conflict at all between the present position and even the awesome Roman Catholic claim to infallibility.

Focus on the Relationship between Theology and the Human Sciences

This exposition has given considerable attention to the theist viewpoint and its relationship to the philosophic and positivist viewpoints. The treatment has even anticipated some specifically Christian concerns, which pertain to the theotic viewpoint, and subsumed them under discussion of theology. Why such emphasis on the theist viewpoint?

First, the interface of theology (not theotics) and the human sciences is the topic here. On this score, theology already implies all the relevant questions. Belief in God, revealed knowledge, ethical prescriptions, religious authority, conflict between faith and "science"—discussion of all these typically religious topics is already at stake with the emergence of the theist viewpoint. In contrast, specifically theotic concerns may appear to be but a subtle refinement or even an unnecessary complication.

Moreover, Christian spokespersons themselves seldom make an issue of the difference between Christianity and theism. Because Jesus Christ is believed to be God, in practice their preaching Jesus usually appears to be but another way of preaching fidelity to God. In fact, "God," "Jesus," "Holy Spirit," "Father"—all often appear to be but different names for the same thing. The subtle but important implications of accurate trinitarian theology is all but lost in contemporary Christianity, certainly on the popular level and almost as certainly even among religious professionals (Armstrong, 1993, pp. 107–131; Helminiak, 1989a). In the least, subtle doctrinal matters are not at stake in the conflicts among Christian religions, "science," and secular interests in today's society. Even for the Christian religions, the specifically Christian issues are not at stake in the religion-science debate. So the focus is rightly on the interface of theology and the human sciences.

Christians who rally around what are really merely theist issues act on a correct intuition. The specifically Christian issues seem pretty irrelevant to the interdisciplinary problem at hand. Nonetheless, the specifically Christian issues do need to be highlighted so that their difference from theism will show forth and so that the important theoretical contribution of Christianity will not be lost. As things stand, Christianity is usually collapsed into theism, and theism and the philosophic are likewise collapsed. There results a grossly oversimplified conception of Western "religion" standing over and against an equally grossly oversimplified conception of "science." Actually, however, religion (if it is Christian) and science (broadly conceived) both operate legitimately within all four, the positivist, the philosophic, the theist, and the theotic viewpoints. So completion of this analytic system now requires exposition of the theotic concerns.

The Theotic Viewpoint

The philosophic viewpoint entails a commitment to pursuit of the true and the good. There, the questions at stake are, Is it true? Is it really good? A further question defines the theist viewpoint: Is there a Fullness of Truth and Goodness? And the more incisive question is, Is there self-explanatory being? An affirmative answer founds the theist viewpoint and makes one a theist, a believer in the Creator-God of the Universe.

Within the theist viewpoint, "God" has a very particular meaning. "God" is the Explanation of Everything about Everything. "God" appears to be the ideal terminus of the human pursuit of the true and the good. So the further question may arise, Do humans ever attain that terminus? Can humans ever understand everything about everything? But given the analysis thus far, it is obvious that this further question can be rephrased. Indeed, if analysis is to progress accurately and honestly, the question must be rephrased. The further question is really asking, Can humans attain to "God"? Can we share in divinity?

The Issue of Human Deification

This analysis has led to a peculiar and startling juncture. We are now asking whether humans can participate in divinity. Consideration of commitment to the true and the good inherent in positivist science, explicit in philosophic concern, and extrapolated in theist reflection, leads to the seemingly far-distant question about human deification.[1] Yet at this point in the discussion, the emergence of this question is completely reasonable. The question is legitimate. Unless obscurantism be tolerated at this late stage of the analysis, the question deserves serious consideration. This is not to say that everybody will or even should find this question personally relevant. It is only to say that in itself the question is absolutely legitimate.

Theism recognizes that there is a terminus of the human pursuit of the true and the good and acknowledges that terminus as the Explanation of Everything about Everything, the Creator-God of the Universe. Human spiritual striving does move toward that terminus, and that terminus must somehow be operative in the dynamic unfolding of human consciousness, somehow drawing it along. Nonetheless, theism also recognizes that human consciousness is not itself that terminus. For the contingent cannot be the

---

1. Formerly in this context I used the term *divinization*. I am grateful to Richard Woods of Loyola University in Chicago for alerting me to this matter and to Bishop Maximos of the Greek Orthodox Diocese of Pittsburgh for clarifying it for me. According to Greek Orthodox usage, *divinization* refers to the idolatrous process of making a human being into a god. For example, Alexander the Great was divinized. In contrast, *deification* refers to the process of human participation in divinity. *Deification* is the standard English translation of the Greek term *theosis*. It was used by the Greek Fathers to name this very process, and from it I coined the term *theotic viewpoint*. In deference to the Greek Orthodox tradition, I henceforth use the term *deification* rather than *divinization*.

self-explanatory. The created cannot be the Creator. So if the creature in question is human spirit, the spiritual is not the divine.

Moreover, there is no reason to suspect that human pursuit in itself will ever attain its ideal terminus. The human spirit does, indeed, long for the divine. People want to understand everything about everything. But they never have. And, given the analysis thus far, there is no reason to suspect they ever will. The human pursuit is conditioned by time and space. Granted, to some extent human understanding does transcend space and time. Computation within Einstein's theory of relativity is the striking example here. Still, Explanation of Everything about Everything must fully transcend space and time and yet fully account for every particularity of the spatial and the temporal manifolds. Thus, the very physical and psychic, spatio-temporal, constitution of the human seems to militate against attainment of ultimate, complete explanation. It does not appear natural for humans to attain to the divine, though the human inclination is precisely that (Lonergan, 1967d).

So theism is content to acknowledge the Creator-God of the Universe, who it knows must exist but who it also knows it cannot grasp. It worships, petitions, praises, and thanks. It is grateful for the joys and beauty of the human experience. It trusts in the midst of human sorrow, loss, and pain. It rightly believes that humans must pursue the path proper to them in all authenticity but live nonetheless in mystery, live by faith. For theism this is enough. The authenticity that is still part of theism realizes there can be nothing more.

I understand the above paragraph to be a summary of the basic theist insights of the Hebrew Testament. But the Christian Testament and subsequent Christian thought focus on the coincidence of the human and the divine in Jesus Christ. More than that, with the resurrected Jesus as the paradigm, Christianity envisages participation in divinity as a universal human possibility. Thus, a higher viewpoint emerges. To the question, Can humans share in the Fullness that is "God"? Can humans be deified? Christianity answers, Yes.

Christianity legitimates its vision of human deification by appeal to the early Christian experience of Jesus Christ and to the historically documented understanding of a new possibility for human fulfillment that emerged in that experience. In theological terms, Christianity bases its vision on "revelation." But this claim of revelation rests on empirical grounds. It points to historical events in particular places at particular times, and it appeals to historical documents (the Christian or "New" Testament) for support. Christian belief claims to rest on verifiable evidence. To this extent, scholarly treatment of even specifically Christian beliefs may fall under the category of science as understood throughout this book. Thus, even matters of the theotic viewpoint pertain to the scientific enterprise, the pursuit of coherent and comprehensive explanation by appeal to relevant evidence.

In its focus on human participation in divinity, Christianity appears to be unique among the world's religions. I have looked into the matter and have thus far found nothing similar to Christianity in this regard. For that reason, until recently (Helminiak, 1996a, 1996c), I consistently referred to matters of human deification as proper to the *Christian* viewpoint. But I want to leave the question open. Perhaps some other religion, about which I am ignorant, does propose a genuine account of human deification. Besides, my purpose here is not to advance any specific religion. Rather, with a concern for interdisciplinary method, my purpose is to highlight what appears to be a universally valid question about the possibility of human deification. Therefore, I now use the more generic term, the *theotic* viewpoint. *Theotic* is the adjectival form of the noun *theosis*, used by the Greek Christian Fathers to refer to human deification. Literally, it means the process of becoming godlike. The study or treatment of this process would be called *theotics* and a person engaged in such treatment would be a *theotician*. I use the term *theotics* in contrast to *theology*. Working within the theist viewpoint, theology limits its concern to God as Creator and to the universe as created. In my differentiated usage theology does not concern itself with the further question about the possibility of human participation in qualities proper only to the Creator-God of the Universe. *The pursuit of systematic explanation whose focus is human deification is science within the theotic viewpoint.*

The Christian Account of Human Deification

I know of no other coherent theotics apart from traditional orthodox Christianity. Accordingly, I must rely on it to illustrate explanation within the theotic viewpoint. I repeat that by "Christian" I do not mean Fundamentalist. As Buddhism developed from Hinduism, as Christianity arose out of Judaism, and as Islam branched off from Judaism and Christianity, I believe that Biblical Fundamentalism has become an independent religion. It is a theistically formulated moralism that departs from the defining core of the Christian tradition. This departure is obvious in Biblical Fundamentalism's inattention to history, which is central to Judaism and to Christianity. Human deification entails some coincidence of the human and the divine, that is to say, a coincidence of the historical and the eternal. The christological doctrines of Incarnation and Resurrection entail a similar coincidence. By ignoring history Biblical Fundamentalism disrupts this critical tension between the human and the divine and precludes any meaningful coincidence. Thus, Biblical Fundamentalism ceases to be Christian (Helminiak, 1997a).

This is not the place to present a full exposition of Christian theotics and so to legitimate the understanding of Christianity just proposed. Elsewhere I have treated the specifically Christian issues at length (Helminiak, 1979, 1986d, 1987c). I have argued the reasonableness of classical Christian belief about Jesus and the redemption he effected, emphasized the complementary role of the Holy Spirit in human salvation, and showed the continuity and distinctiveness among Christianity, theism, and human authenticity. Here a brief and popularized summary of this material must suffice.

According to Christian belief as understood here, Jesus Christ is the Eternally-Begotten of God who became human and was born of Mary. As human, he made no use of divine prerogatives but lived his earthly life within all the limitations proper to the human state. A contemporary critical reading of the Christian Testament supports such an understanding. But though human, because of who he was, the Eternally-Begotten, his human life represented a unique possibility. Just by being true to himself, he would necessarily be faithful also to God, his "Father," and would live sinlessly; he would live his earthly life as a perfect "child of God." At the same time, such virtuous living provoked opposition that led eventually to Jesus' being executed as a criminal. But even in the face of death, he remained faithful to himself—wholly authentic!—and so faithful to God. His death confirmed his life as a life of perfect fidelity, lived in full trust and surrender to all that is right and good, and so in surrender to God. Thus, Jesus expressed as perfectly as humanly possible on earth what he is eternally in God: Of-the-Father.

Again because of who he was and also because of his fidelity even unto death, God raised Jesus from the dead. In his resurrection, Jesus was deified. This does not mean that he became God. The inviolable distinction between Creator and creature implies that "becoming God" is a logical and ontological impossibility, a self-contradictory notion like "square circle." Besides, as Only-Begotten of God the Parent, Jesus already is God eternally. Rather, Jesus' deification does mean that through the resurrection and *in his humanity* Jesus came to share in qualities that are proper to God alone. The fullest ideal potential of his human spirit was released. Even in his human mind he came to understand everything about everything, and in his human "heart" he loved everything and everyone insofar as they are loveable. Surely his resurrection also entailed some transformation of his human psyche and physiological organism as well. The Christian Testament testifies to some such transformation, and critical reflection on deification also suggests the necessity of such a release from the limitations of time and space. But what exactly such a transformation might be remains unclear. The point is that Jesus Christ did attain to the ideal terminus of his dynamic human spirit and so shared in certain qualities that are properly divine. He was deified.

Deification is a created participation in divinity. It entails divinity because it depends on qualities proper only to God. Examples of such qualities would be perfect and complete knowledge and love. However, divine qualities like eternity, omnipotence, or aseity could not be shared with creatures, for they are definitive of divinity. So deification is but a participation in divinity, not an identification with it. This participation is created because God effects it in other beings, in human beings, creatures, which are not God.

Jesus' deification represented not only a change in himself but also a change in the meaning of human history. Because of the solidarity that binds the human race as one, Jesus' achievement of deification introduced into human affairs a new concrete possibility for human fulfillment (Helminiak, 1979, 1988a). What has happened is certainly possible. If the human Jesus attained deification, then under certain conditions deification must be a human possibility—a concrete human possibility, not merely an ideal possibility.

Opening a path of perfect fidelity to God and so reversing the course of sinful human history and, then, also introducing into human history the concrete possibility of deification, Jesus "redeemed" the human race. Here *redemption* becomes a technical term to name the saving work proper to Jesus.

But the new possibility for human fulfillment that Jesus introduced into history depends on certain conditions. The conditions in Jesus' own life were that he be the Eternally-Begotten of God and that he be faithful to himself and so to God even unto death.

The conditions in the case of other human beings are three. First, there must be a real possibility of human deification. This first condition for others, Jesus himself fulfilled by his life of fidelity even unto death and by his resurrection from the dead. Jesus made human deification a historical reality. Hence, Christians reverence and love Jesus not simply as God but especially as a remarkable human being whose human virtue even in the face of death transformed the meaning of human life (Helminiak, 1986d, 1989b).

Second, Jesus was destined for deification because of who he was. From the beginning there was a divine principle within him, his own self, that called for divine fulfillment. If others could likewise be destined for deification because of a divine principle within them, deification could follow for them, too. But unlike Jesus, the others are not eternally begotten children of God; and because of the nature of the matter, they could not become eternally begotten. Instead, God determined to make humankind adopted children of God and sent the uncreated, divine Holy Spirit to dwell in human hearts. Because the Holy Spirit is sent to humankind, God transforms the human spirit, opening it to the Holy Spirit and so to an end that fulfills its own ideal possibility. The Christian treatise on sanctifying grace, uncreated and created, explains this transformation. This transformation does not change or add to the structure of human spirit or consciousness (Helminiak, 1996a, pp. 94–99). It does not reroute the dynamism nor disqualify the exigencies inherent in human spirit. Rather, it perfects these, bringing them to a new level of intensity and opening them to ideal, and so to divine, fulfillment.

Now just by being true to their own selves in the Holy Spirit, all human beings follow the path that Jesus first trod and move toward deification, which he first experienced. Their fidelity to themselves and so to God is the third condition for deification. Because of the gift of the Holy Spirit, which posits a divine principle within redeemed humanity, this condition in others is analogous to the condition of fidelity to himself that Jesus, a human being, also had to fulfill. Thus, even within the Christian version of the theotic viewpoint, human authenticity remains the key to human fulfillment, though the gift of the Holy Spirit and the possibility of human deification add new meaning and implications to that authenticity.

I know of no other coherent theotics apart from the account provided by traditional Christian orthodoxy, which I have just summarized. Nonetheless, I also know that, within current "Christian" circles, many would question or even deny the key Christian presuppositions in that account—namely, the resurrection and the divinity of Jesus and the Trinity in God. For many, these core Christian doctrines are to be taken metaphorically or symbolically but surely not literally: "Father/Mother," "Son/Offspring," and "Holy Spirit" are but different names or symbols for God but hardly different Persons or Identities who are God, and resurrection merely means that Jesus could still be a real force in people's lives.

However, apart from the Christian presuppositions, can a coherent account of human deification be made? Could the ripened fruit, an account of human deification, be plucked from the tree of the Christian tradition and still be kept fresh and even grown again apart from its engendering roots and branches? I have argued strenuously that it could not (Helminiak, 1986d, pp. 245–252). Still, now that the defining issues of a theotics have been clarified, might it not be possible to somehow elaborate a non-Christian theism into a coherent theotics?

I raise this question to clear a space for contemporary (and supposedly Christian) theologians who, on the impressive grounds of careful historical scholarship, are questioning the evidence that has traditionally supported the core Christian beliefs (Armstrong, 1993; Borg, 1995; Crossan, 1993; Mackey, 1979; Sheehan, 1986). Whatever the eventual answer to this question, the question makes clear what is at stake in this enterprise. Howsoever elaborated, theotics is not theology. Very different but equally important issues are at stake in each. Scholars need to be aware that, in questioning traditional Christian orthodoxy, they are also subverting its theotics. It may well be possible to do the one without doing the other. But in whatever case, the challenge stands: provide a coherent account of human deification. Christianity has already made its suggestion. No one should easily reject this suggestion without at least addressing this challenge.

The Essence of Christianity

The above account of Christianity focuses a content that is distinct from theism and, as far as I have been able to determine, distinct from every other religion. A new question, Is human deification possible? is at the heart of Christianity. Christianity gives an affirmative answer to this question and offers a coherent explanation. Only this affirmation and its explanation are distinctive to Christianity. Then, not a particular ethics nor belief in God but an understanding of human life as an inchoate process of deification is the essence of Christianity (Beauchesne, 1990, p. 550; Helminiak, 1979, 1986d, 1987c, 1997a).

The three distinctive core doctrines of Christianity all bear on the issue of deification and accordingly implicate one another. Those three are

* Trinity: an understanding of God as Three Subjects in one divine nature;

* Christ: a belief in redemption effected by the incarnation, life, death, and resurrection of Jesus, the Eternally-Begotten of God become human; and

* Grace: a belief in the divine Holy Spirit poured out into human hearts.

There is a fourth Christian matter that is distinctive in content but not in form—Church: the community of Christian believers, which holds and proclaims these distinctive understandings. Church is distinctive in content because of its commitment to the distinctive essence of Christianity, but church is not distinctive in form because in one way or another every religion entails a community of adherents. So with one concept, deification, the present understanding integrates all the peculiarly Christian doctrines and shows them to have important implications. This fact argues for the validity of the present interpretation of Christianity. Deification is the essential and the only distinctive Christian issue.

The Uniqueness of Christianity

In its own way, of course, Hinduism, among others, also gives an affirmative answer to the question about human participation in divinity. Then are there other equally valid ways of approaching this issue? It does not seem so. The Hindu problematic is significantly different from the Christian.

Emerging from Judaism and endorsing its theism, Christianity accepts as inviolable the distinction between Creator and creature. In the face of this distinction, Christianity accounts for the possibility of human deification. In contrast, Hinduism is ambiguous about the distinction between God and humankind: Atman is Brahman. Such a position is already incompatible with the theist viewpoint, as defined here. So this position can offer no alternative to the Christian version of the theotic viewpoint, which presupposes the theist.

To say that Hinduism offers no alternative to the Christian version of the theotic viewpoint is not to state the obvious, that Hinduism and Christianity differ as religions. It is to suggest that Hinduism does not provide a coherent treatment of the question about human deification. So that position is not likely to be very helpful in resolving the interdisciplinary questions behind this book. On the present analysis, if Brahman is Atman, if the Ultimate-God is the human spirit, then the theotic, theist, and philosophic viewpoints collapse into one. The distinction between theology and an adequate human psychology, which entails spirituality, dissolves. The discussion about what the human actually is and what it should be, reverts back to religious opinions about God. The standoff between positivist science and "religion," in the global, undifferentiated, unmanageable sense, continues with no hope of a breakthrough.

The present line of reasoning is not presented as an attack on Hinduism. This same analysis and criticism applies to a long strain of religious thought, not unique to Hinduism. Neo-platonism, ancient Gnosticism, and contemporary New Age Religion all blur the distinction between the spiritual and the divine, and all entail the same interdisciplinary consequences just spelled out. And the same line of thought now also colors much of supposedly Christian religion and spirituality. The critique of Ken Wilber's position in Chapter Four is a full discussion of this intricate matter.

I do propose deification as the essence of Christianity, yet it is not to be supposed that the many Christian churches are explicitly aware of the distinctive essence. History has but recently begun to require such a clarification. Nor is it to be assumed that all church groups would concur in this depiction of the essence of Christianity—and especially as regards its very limited practical implications. Indeed, on the present analysis, much of contemporary Christianity is not Christian at all but is some form of Western moralistic theism. This is especially so in the case of the contemporary Biblical Fundamentalist movement. It has effectively appropriated the name *Christian* and modified it to mean *Fundamentalist*—which, according to the present analysis, is not Christian at all (Helminiak, 1997a).

So the present line of reasoning challenges all religions, even those defined sociologically as Christian. Far from derogating the religions, the intent here is to highlight important and irreducible questions that concern the religions and all humankind. If the religions—or likewise, the sciences—decline from addressing these questions, they themselves undermine their credibility before any who are willing to think.

I am well aware that the understanding of Christianity that I present here is novel. Moreover, the formulation of the system of four viewpoints, an overall interrelationship of pivotal issues, is original. And because of the nature of higher viewpoints, these matters of psychology, epistemology, ethics, theology, and theotics all constrain one another. Still, within this system and despite its interlocking constraints, it appears that each of its disparate elements is respected. The claims about Christianity are solidly grounded in the Christian tradition (Helminiak, 1979). The theist understanding—though at variance with Eastern thought, and herein lies a key issue—is consistent with classical Western theology, as exemplified in Thomas Aquinas. The ethical and epistemological emphases of the philosophic viewpoint echo perennial Western philosophical themes. And the notion of human science reflected in the positivist viewpoint squares with the prevalent contemporary understanding. Only acceptance of Lonergan's (1957, 1972) epistemological position is required to clarify all these issues and lock them into one coherent conceptualization. The coherence of the whole constitutes in itself an argument for its validity. But does this coherence imply bias or breakthrough? This is the question that calls for discussion. So I present this matter for public adjudication. I invite others of honest mind and good-willed heart to consider and assess it. Though this overall position challenges understandings on numerous fronts and calls for refinements in a range of current opinions, might it not be a basis on which some consensus might begin to emerge? Could not, then, our postmodern world, combining classic and modern concerns, attend collaboratively once again to the necessary human task of structuring a society for wholesome living?

The Religious Motivation behind This System of Viewpoints

It must be obvious that the present system of viewpoints overall is conceived from within the horizon of Christian belief. There could have been no other way. The rationale of the analysis constrains the matter. Only within the theotic viewpoint does the whole system hold together. And only grappling with questions proper to Christian belief (Helminiak, 1979, 1986d, 1987c) was I forced to elaborate this system of higher viewpoints.

More specifically, it is also true that among the many Christian churches the long-standing Roman Catholic tradition has massively influenced the present analysis. I speak of the Roman Catholic tradition—and not of the fundamentalist-like authoritarian emphases within current official Catholicism nor of the pieties so salient in popular notions of Catholicism and its practice. I speak of Catholicism with its reliance on natural law theory, its insistence in the face of classical Protestantism on both faith and reason, its continued affirmation of objective truth and goodness (John Paul II, 1993), its infallibly defined teaching that religion and science are reconcilable (Denzinger & Schonmetzer, 1965, par. 3017, 3042), its official understanding of God as Creator in the classical sense of the term, its continued adherence to classical Christian orthodoxy about Trinity, Christ, and Grace, and its long and profound treatment of religious and human questions.

The present system of viewpoints emerges from Catholic Christianity. Still, my critical concern is not commitment to a religion but commitment to human authenticity and perforce to coherent explanation: science. One can arrive at important insights from within a religious tradition and then present those insights apart from religious faith as such. As the religious source of insights does not automatically validate them, nor does it automatically discredit them. Religion does have valid contributions to make. But the validity of the insights must now stand on the reasonableness of the overall presentation, not on the authority of their religious origins. Such is my emphasis here, both in statement and in fact. Here, concern for scientific explanation of important human issues—not reliance on religious belief—motivates the questions and constrains the answers. Reassuring to me is the fact that the answers do not come down far from those of the religious tradition in which I have been formed. But if this fact also evinces bias in my presentation, I need the help of other honest and good-willed people to point that bias out to me. Thus, together we can all shift to a more adequate position and stand more in accord with our common commitment to the true and the good. Then even in this new position I could rest assured that I had not abandoned, but rather had approached more closely, the requirements of my religious upbringing and my present commitment.

Different Opinions about the Universality of Grace

But within Christianity itself there are important differences. Despite the Catholic Christian origin of the present conceptualization, some churches that call themselves Christian would reject this assessment of Christianity. This conceptualization presupposes that, as one moves up the system of viewpoints, the data to be explained do not change; only the questions to be addressed change. This understanding implies that the positivist scientist and the Christian theotician are both trying to explain the same human reality. The key methodological difference is only that the one asks broader questions than the other.

According to unanimous Christian belief, through Jesus Christ Christians are graced, gifted with the Holy Spirit. But the present analysis presumes that this grace is given to all people, whether they know and believe in Jesus Christ or not. So the data to be explained, the human situation to be understood, is one and the same for every kind of scientist. The object of study for all is in fact the one and the same graced human being, although a treatment of grace is completely irrelevant, for example, to human cardiology. But especially the Evangelical strains of Christianity insist that without explicit faith in Jesus one is not graced and so cannot be "saved," deified. This difference in belief has implications not only for Christian ecumenism but also for the structure of this system of higher viewpoints.

If only Christian believers are graced, their ontological status is different from that of other people. Two categories of people result, the graced and the ungraced. The data to be explained in each case differ and not just the questions about a supposed one and the same reality. The structure of the system of four viewpoints breaks down and falls apart.

Given the nature of the hypothesized difference between the graced and the ungraced, one must question even the human adequacy of the supposedly ungraced. Such questioning touches the philosophic viewpoint, for it asks whether human capacity is capable of knowing the true and the good. The Evangelical answer is, No. Appeal is to the "Fall," and emphasis is on the classical Protestant doctrine of the "total depravity" of the sinful human being. Through the Fall, sin has supposedly vitiated humanity's spiritual capacity, and from the Fall only explicit belief in Jesus can supposedly save. So supposedly, apart from Christian faith, humans are incapable of knowing the true and the good. Or alternatively, Christ must be proclaimed the only valid norm. To speak of truth and goodness apart from Christ is said to be sheer nonsense. On this understanding, only Christian believers could know what authentic humanity entails. As the giant of a Protestant theologian, Karl Barth (1960), argued at length, Jesus is the only valid measure of the human, and "human" can be defined only in relation to Jesus. There is no valid account of humanity apart from explicit belief in Jesus Christ.

The methodological result of such a position is already familiar. The theotic, the theist, and the philosophic viewpoints collapse into one, and as a unity they stand in contrast to the positivist viewpoint. The old antinomy reemerges. Science and religion, reason and faith, are pitted against one another in unresolvable conflict. Then coherent interdisciplinary study becomes impossible. The conflict is unresolvable because there is no common ground: the mind of Christian faith completely disqualifies the mind of human science. The graced mind is thought to be simply different from, simply superior to, the ungraced. How could coherent understanding be possible when the minds, the source of understanding, on either side of the question are deemed incompatible?

That unhappy interdisciplinary implication already suggests the inadequacy of the hard-core Evangelical position. But the argument can be carried further. There is a self-contradiction within this position itself. The telling question is, How does one know that this supposed Christian position is correct? If, as an unbeliever, one cannot trust one's own mind, how would one ever responsibly become a believer? One could become one only by whim! Of course, believers would apply more noble terms here: inspiration, election, faith, call, the work of the Holy Spirit. But these remain fully immune to assessment, for, supposedly, no valid human reason can be given for them. So this position is also essentially unreasonable, or at least its reasonableness is intrinsically undemonstrable. At this point it relies on the arational mentality.

Religious appeals to "grace" or "God's call" carry no weight in this discussion. The issue is reasonableness, coherent argument, cogent account, scientific explanation, not religion or feeling or choice or devotion or belief. At the same time, to be reasonable is not the same as to be proven. There is no insistence here that religious faith be fully provable. In fact, nothing is provable apart from a shared set of presuppositions, apart from some shared faith (Lonergan, 1972, p. 338). Nonetheless, religious faith can be reasonable. That is, one need not be a fool to believe; one can have good reasons for religious belief. Indeed, religious belief must be reasonable lest it be an insult to thinking, self-responsible human beings—and to the God who created them. But the ultimate logical implication of the Evangelical position is the rejection of this requirement.

That position claims to be the truth when it appeals for acceptance as God's revelation. But it implicitly denies the possibility of knowing the truth when it disqualifies human endeavor apart from that acceptance. If the truth cannot be humanly known, how could anyone ever recognize that position as true? How could that position know that it itself is true? It could know itself as true only because the position itself says that it is. So the ultimate argument is this: the position is true because it claims that it is, but there is no human way of knowing the truth of a claim. Here, truth is affirmed as a valid notion and simultaneously denied as a valid notion. The word *truth* is used, but it has no meaning. Authority and blind faith, not truth, is the real appeal. The position is incoherent. It inevitably founders on an inadequate epistemology.

"In-house" Christian arguments can make the same point. The Christian Testament does teach, "Very truly, I tell you, no one can see the kingdom of God without being born of water and Spirit" (John 3:5). This text has been taken to mean that apart from faith in Jesus and Baptism, a person cannot be saved, graced. But this or any text can be taken literally, or it can be interpreted according to historical-critical method (Helminiak, 1986d, pp. 1–17; 1994b). This method is accepted among all mainline Christian churches. It requires that the primary meaning of a text be determined within its original historical and cultural context. Interpreted critically, this Johannine text, addressed to a specific Christian community, does not seem to be treating the question of universal salvation that has emerged only in relatively recent history. The intent of that text must be something else.

Or again, 1 Timothy 2:3–6 declares that God "desires everyone to be saved. . . . For there is one God; there is one mediator between God and humankind, Christ Jesus, himself human, who gave himself a ransom for all." There is no reason to interpret this text restrictively, insisting that it applies only to those who explicitly know and reverence Jesus Christ. So in its 1965 "Pastoral Constitution on the Church in the Modern World," article 22, the clearest such statement in the history of Christianity, the Second Vatican Council of Roman Catholicism argued,

> All this [conformity to the image of the Son through reception of the Holy Spirit and the experience of death and resurrection in Christ] holds true not for Christians only but also for all men [and women] of good will in whose hearts grace is active invisibly. For since Christ died for all, and since all men [and women] are in fact called to one and the same destiny, which is divine, we must hold that the Holy Spirit offers to all the possibility of being made partners, in a way known to God, in the paschal mystery. (Flannery, 1975, p. 924)

In one way or another, this position is more and more commonly shared among all mainline Christian churches.

Thus, both on the basis of reasonable argument and on the basis of religious authority, one can mount a convincing argument that the Evangelical position is inadequate. Then the alternative position may stand: grace, the Holy Spirit, is given to all humankind. Therefore, human scientists working within the positivist, the philosophic, the theist, or the theotic viewpoints all study one and the same reality, the graced human being.

Of course, that the human being is graced is of no interest to any explanatory pursuit apart from Christian theotics. Still, as understood here, the grace that Christian belief presupposes is known to be operative even where it is not recognized. Thus, only within Christian theotics does the matter of the universality of grace have any relevance, but within Christian theotics, that universality is granted. So Christian belief in deifying grace poses no problem for scientific pursuit within any of the viewpoints.

Whether or not the human mind is capable of knowing the true and the good apart from grace becomes a moot question. The question arises only as a Christian concern. Apart from Christian concern, the question is irrelevant. When the question does arise within Christian concern, the question is purely hypothetical, for according to Christian belief grace is in fact given.

To some extent this understanding of the matter also addresses the Evangelical concerns, for it allows that any human pursuit of the true and the good does presume grace in Christ. That is, relying on Christian belief, one may understand that every good-willed human endeavor is under the guidance of the Holy Spirit; one believes that there is no human authenticity apart from Christ. On this understanding the Lordship of Christ and the requirement of divine grace are fully preserved. However, on this understanding one need not insist that others accept these Christian beliefs. The graced human reality that these beliefs bespeak, if it indeed be reality and not just a construct in the mind of believers, does not depend on explicit human belief. This graced reality is rather the already achieved result of the saving work of Christ and the Holy Spirit, now built into the human situation, whether acknowledged or not.

So Christians may freely and trustingly collaborate with all others of good will who may not, however, believe in Christ nor even in God. These Christians know that they are indeed collaborating in Christ and the Holy Spirit, though their collaborators do not share the same awareness. Nor need they share that awareness to be collaborating in graced human reality, for through Christ and the Holy Spirit grace is a universal condition of the human situation. Moreover, such collaboration is not patronizing or demeaning to the nonbelievers. On the present understanding there is no valid Christianity apart from human authenticity, and patronization precludes authenticity.

This understanding of the matter also addresses the more common and valid Christian concern about the sinfulness of the human situation. According to Christian belief, humankind is fallen and sinful, but humankind has also been redeemed by Christ and sanctified by the Holy Spirit. If the positive half of this belief is really true, there is no need for preoccupation about human sinfulness. More trust can be given to human good will and more hope placed in human promise. The thrust of humanistic psychology and the efforts of non-religious humanitarianism must be granted their validity, and concern for self-actualization must not be demeaned as if self were always selfish. Such thinking does not mean to endorse a naive oblivion to bias, dishonesty, and evil intent, which too often do color human activities. It merely means to suggest that Christian preoccupation with sin belies Christian belief in redemption.

The Core Presupposition of This Analysis

One can coherently construct the present approach only by initially allowing the validity of human intellectual capacity. This constraint should not be surprising. The presupposition, spoken or unspoken, of any theoretically coherent account is the validity of the theorizing instrument, the human mind. This requirement holds even when the account is about God. Granted the validity of the human mind, one can construct a coherent presentation that preserves and integrates even the central doctrines of Christian belief. Then these beliefs, integrated into the overall picture, themselves confirm the validity of the human mind by insistence on the universal gift of the Holy Spirit and the ontological reality of redemption in Christ.

Of course, one could insist that the argument here is circular. The coherent explanatory account is but the unfolding of its presupposition that the human mind can know. And one would be correct. Lonergan's critical realism, the optimistic analysis of human consciousness as capable of objectively valid knowledge, is the presupposition of this entire study. But what of it? Every position is but the unfolding of its presuppositions.

The more telling issue is whether the presupposition here is correct. One criterion must certainly be avoidance of self-contradiction; and another must be effectiveness in dealing with the issues. On both scores, the Evangelical position fails, as do, for similar reasons, the supposed theism of Eastern philosophy that blurs the distinction between creature and Creator, the philosophical relativism and epistemological skepticism that despair of actually knowing truth and goodness, and the narrow empiricism or positivism that neglects the real human (spiritual) issues. These other positions ultimately pit faith against reason; they ultimately require an option between religion and science. The present position suggests that such a construal of the matter is mistaken, for an option for correct knowing—an option that is itself a kind of faith—opts for both science and religion. So the present account recommends itself and invites consensus among the churches as well as among the religions and the sciences. For in their own way, the issues that wreak havoc among the Christian churches are also at stake in the overall interdisciplinary problematic of this book. Besides, if one were to deny the particular presupposition in question here—namely, that the human mind is capable of objectively valid knowledge—this denial would invalidate the very mind of the denier. So the contrary argument is inevitably self-contradictory.

The Qualified Validity of the Theotic Viewpoint

The theotic viewpoint is presented as a viewpoint higher than the theist, philosophic, and positivist viewpoints. Moreover, its content implies that it is the highest viewpoint possible, for what could be beyond participation in divinity? The theotic viewpoint is a higher viewpoint because it addresses a broader question, but it still presupposes and retains all that is valid within the lower viewpoints. That means, of course, as noted above, that the lower viewpoints constrain the possibilities for the theotic viewpoint. So its position of highest viewpoint grants it no autonomy. Nor does it grant it increased validity. "Higher" does not mean "better" in any absolute sense. As with all the viewpoints, the theotic has validity only insofar as it coheres with the other viewpoints, and it has unique authority only with regard to the narrow range of issues that define it. These issues regard only the specific question of human union with God. This matter concerns those who want to clarify the possibility of human deification (including Christians who think it important to specify the distinctive core of Christianity). Granted that deification or union with God is a critical issue in both Western and Eastern spirituality, the very delineation of the theotic viewpoint represents a major clarification. Still, this clarification remains illuminating only with the overall structure of the system of higher viewpoints.

Summary

Treatment of the theotic viewpoint completes the respective exposition of the four viewpoints on the human. Each of the four represents a different stance on possible explanation of the human phenomenon, for each entails different presuppositions, determined by the kind of questioning each allows. Asking what is in fact the case, the positivist viewpoint limits explanatory concern to the de facto status quo of the human. Asking what ought to be the case, the philosophic viewpoint allows the broader question about human authenticity and its role in human being and becoming. Asking about the fullness of understanding that accounts even for existence, the theist viewpoint adds the still-broader concern about the created status of the human. And asking about the possibility of human participation in that fullness, the theotic viewpoint envisages the ideal fulfillment of humanity in some coincidence with divinity.

All four theoretical stances regard one and the same human reality. Yet each entails a different way of understanding this single reality. Each represents a broader horizon within which further understanding of the human is possible. Moreover, the different ways of understanding, like expanding horizons, presuppose and supplement one another. For the questions that determine the presuppositions of each of the viewpoints both irreducibly distinguish the viewpoints from one another and intelligently interlock them in a coherent whole. Thus, these four viewpoints provide an approach to comprehensive and coherent explanation of the human. They provide an elaborated context for the interrelationship of religion and the human sciences.

Further Clarifications

The purpose of this book is to specify a way of precisely and coherently interrelating religious concerns and the human sciences. The system of four viewpoints is the central structure of this alternative approach. This system is presented as a conceptual analytical tool. It sorts out and interrelates different explanatory issues. By the same token, it interrelates different disciplines that can be called human sciences. Similar to other approaches in some ways but different in still other and sometimes subtle ways, this alternative approach needs to be presented as clearly as possible. Its exact significance needs to be stated explicitly.

The present section is a reflection on the implications of the system of four viewpoints. This complex conceptual system has implications that cut in three different directions. It has theoretical implications, existential implications, and ontological implications. These different sets of implications are inextricably interrelated in the interdisciplinary problematic, and they are often confounded. Just calling attention to them and thus sorting them out is important in itself. Sorting them out is also important for clarifying the meaning of the system of four viewpoints.

Theoretical Implications

Most obviously, the system of four viewpoints has theoretical import. That is to say, this system is a conceptual tool for furthering understanding and explanation.

The differentiation of higher viewpoints makes a contribution by offering distinctions of a purely theoretical kind. An example is the difference between Christianity as a religion and Christianity as a version of the theotic viewpoint. As a higher viewpoint, the core Christian doctrines are but one aspect of Christianity as a religion. For Christianity also includes elements that are theist, philosophic, and positivist. The differentiation of these four is an intellectual affair, an attempt to make coherent sense of a very complex phenomenon. Indeed, at times one would be hard pressed to separate those dimensions in the concrete.

For example, Catholics sign themselves with a cross. This sign is to associate them publicly with the mysteries of Christ's death and resurrection, so this Catholic gesture has obvious theotic-viewpoint meaning. Yet Eastern Catholics sign themselves from right to left while Western (Latin) Catholics sign themselves from left to right, and, because of differences rooted in the Protestant Reformation, other Christians tend not to sign themselves at all. Besides, that a sign of the cross is used and not some other sign, depends on the contingent fact of Jesus' having been executed in the Roman style of his day. So this central Catholic sign also carries positivist-viewpoint elements, aspects of the matter that just happen to be as they are and that carry no intrinsic validity in themselves. Moreover, Catholics making the sign of the cross express a commitment to Jesus, a commitment to living a life of honesty and virtue as he did, despite all costs. This commitment to authenticity is a philosophic-viewpoint implication of the sign of the cross. Finally, Catholics understand God's will for them to be that they be good people, as Jesus was, even if the cost be death, so strictly theist considerations also determine this same sign of the cross.

Accurately analyzing this Catholic symbol would require sorting out those various dimensions of the matter. Those dimensions really are distinct, each carries very different significance, and treatment of each would require very different presuppositions. Yet all cohere in the real-life, concrete sign of the cross. Sorting out the positivist, philosophic, theist, and theotic dimensions of the matter is an important theoretical task. Sorting them out contributes to accurate understanding of the matter.

Another example is the overall concern behind this book: the possibility of a coherent and comprehensive account of the human itself. The suggestion is that the distinction of positivist, philosophic, theist, and theotic issues allows intelligent treatment of this very complex matter; yet nowhere is there the suggestion that the human being is cut up in pieces. The differentiation of four viewpoints on the human serves a strictly theoretical purpose. These distinctions are in the service of correct understanding, explanation. Far from positing time-space separations within the human, the four viewpoints merely suggest intelligent distinctions. The system of viewpoints suggests that, if one wants to achieve incisive understanding of the human, one would do well to make these fundamental distinctions; one would do well to sort out the critical dimensions of the matter, and to treat each within its own right. The concern is theoretical. It touches on the intellectual analysis of things.

The differentiation of higher viewpoints serves an even more obvious theoretical function. As already noted, it distinguishes and interrelates different disciplines. But as a shift in viewpoint presumes a shift in presuppositions, disciplines within the various viewpoints will require their own methodology. So treating Christianity as science within the theotic viewpoint, for example, will be largely a matter of studying the empirical evidence on Jesus and early Christianity, available in texts and other historical sources, and of proposing a reasonable account of core Christian belief about union with God in Christ through the Holy Spirit. In contrast, the theist viewpoint requires application of metaphysics, the study of being. Its empirical starting point is the very existence of contingent reality. Again, the concern of the philosophic viewpoint, human authenticity, depends on one's sensitivity to one's own self and specifically to one's inherent (spiritual) dynamism toward the universe of being. Other empirical evidence could be the real-world and measurable consequences of authentic versus inauthentic living. Finally, study within the positivist viewpoint attends to de facto human reality and in the natural sciences restricts itself to fully sensible evidence. Thus, particular disciplines retain their autonomy and must develop their own methodologies, yet within the system of higher viewpoints they all cohere as diverse instances of empirically grounded explanation, science.

That differentiation of sciences within a unity depends on sublation, whereby a higher viewpoint preserves yet expands what is valid within a lower. This state of affairs discredits all reductionism, for the questions that determine the higher viewpoints are distinct and are not amenable to treatment in the lower viewpoints. Contrariwise, this system eschews all fideism, for higher viewpoints are not autonomous. They are constrained by the lower viewpoints out of which they emerge. So specialization becomes the rule of the day, and the discipline appropriate to each particular matter is to address the correlative questions.

Of course, this system as presented is geared to human studies, so it hardly touches the unification of the "hard sciences," as generally understood. But there the coherence of disciplines is already well appreciated as physics moves into chemistry and chemistry, into biology, and biology gives way to psychology. These disciplines all fall within the positivist viewpoint, and their nonreductive interrelationship can be specified as further instances of "sublation" (Lonergan, 1972, p. 241) or "emergent probability" (Lonergan, 1957, pp. 123–128, 171–172, *et passim*; 1972, p. 288).

Finally, this system of viewpoints itself envisages a comprehensive and integral account of the human phenomenon. So this is a heuristic system. By discerning pivotal issues within the human phenomenon, this system not only sorts but also anticipates knowledge about the human. As a heuristic system, Mendeleev's periodic table both systematized available chemical knowledge and successfully anticipated the discovery of elements yet unknown. Likewise, this system of viewpoints both systematizes a wide array of knowledge about the human and opens a treasure of further questions that need to be addressed. If the pivotal determinations are indeed on target, pursuit of these questions will be fruitful (Feingold, 1994, 1995; Feingold & Helminiak, 1996; Helminiak, 1994a), as are methodically derived questions in the established sciences. Thus, this system is itself an important contribution to human science. It is the framework for a comprehensive science of the human.

In contrast to the formulae of physics, the periodic table of chemical elements provides a relatively non-mathematical example of implicitly defined scientific formulation (Lonergan, 1957, pp. 12–13). The evolutionary theory of biology provides an even less mathematical example, though this theory does not yet enjoy the rigor found in chemistry and physics. In any case, the fully conceptual (non-mathematical) nature of the present system for interdisciplinary human science does not discredit this system of higher viewpoints from being real science (Helminiak, 1996a, pp. 78–79). The task of science is to discern the necessary and sufficient to explain a phenomenon—and not necessarily to express itself in numbers. Indeed, even within the natural sciences numbers serve a conceptual function. They serve as appropriate expressions of relationships that human intelligence has discerned. So the present conceptual enterprise does qualify as real science.

Of course, questions do remain. Yet in broad strokes this present system of viewpoints envisages an integration of human knowledge. The integration depends on understanding, on insight into ever-broader coherences. Not always logic, not simple, mechanical deduction, but intelligent connections, leaps of understanding, insightful shifts in explanatory focus, hold the whole together.

The most obvious import of this system of four viewpoints is its theoretical nature with implications for the meaning and function of the human sciences. Yet there are other implications inherent in this system.

Existential Implications

Each of the successively higher viewpoints depends on new and major presuppositions. And actually to work within those viewpoints requires acceptance of those presuppositions. For example, one does not work within the philosophic viewpoint just by noting that some people still hold a commitment to the pursuit of objective truth. To stand at such distance and to make such a detached observation is rather to work within the positivist viewpoint. To work within the philosophic viewpoint requires that one be committed to that pursuit oneself. So this system of four viewpoints is not only a theoretical matter but also a personal one. The viewpoints not only specify disciplines, they also determine the people engaged in them. The viewpoints have implications for human lives, existential implications.

Accepting any of the viewpoints entails some kind of personal conversion, some kind of faith (Fowler, 1981). This is so even for the positivist viewpoint, for it entails faith in the advance of human understanding. It depends on commitment to rigorous and disciplined research. In instructive contrast, peoples in some primitive cultures or some in affluent decadence or others in philosophical confusion shun even the kind of discipline, and lack even the kind of faith, characteristic of positivist science. They opt for the arational mentality. They choose to live by superstition or by personal whim or by social consensus. But commitment to pursuit of the true and the good within the philosophic viewpoint entails still further conversion, as discussed above. And even more obviously, because of the generally religious meaning of the word *conversion*, commitment to God or to deification in Christ entails still other conversions. Though once thought the more obvious, the exact nature of these latter conversions is now the more obscure. For any easily noted ethical meaning pertains to the philosophic viewpoint, and the difference between mere theism and the theotic concerns of Christianity now appears as radical as the difference between authentic humanism and theist belief. It is peculiar, however, that most theist believers are disturbed by the humanist who does not believe in God, yet most Christians are nonchalant about other theists who do not believe in the Trinity. Evidently, different groups put different emphases on the importance of different conversions.

Conversion in any form is always an ongoing process. No one could ever be fully positivist, philosophic, theist, or Christian. So this system of viewpoints is not to be used to categorize people. These categories validly apply to people always and only "insofar"—insofar as people do embody the presuppositions of the viewpoints. For example, despite the self-appellation, a close-minded, unthinking "Christian" might be operating only within the positivist viewpoint. Or a research team fudging its data would not really be operating within even the positivist viewpoint. Indeed, from the outside who can determine who is the real Christian, the true theist, the authentic human being, the committed positivist scientist?

Moreover, though this system of viewpoints has existential implications, its categories are theoretically defined. As with religion, so also with a person, all four categories could apply. An authentic Christian would be committed not only to the theotic viewpoint but perforce also to the theist, philosophic, and positivist viewpoints.

The obvious point here is that this system of viewpoints provides no easy way to categorize people as higher and lower, better or worse. Theoretical stances relate to one another as broader and narrower in purview, as higher or lower viewpoints. But people are not to be compared in that way.

The more subtle but more important point here is that theoretical pursuits entail existential commitments. It is all too easy to think that people can do science without taking a personal stance, without risking themselves. For the human subject is at the heart of every scientific enterprise, and science recedes or advances insofar as scientists are true to their commitments. Patently in the case of inner human issues, it makes no sense to believe that scientists could adequately understand in others phenomena totally absent in themselves. For they would be like blind people discoursing on the importance of color or like the deaf extolling the beauty of a symphony (Lonergan, 1967e, pp. xi–xii). Thus, developmentalists already recognize the difficulty in sketching the higher stages of human development when these transcend their own personal achievement (Loevinger, 1977, p. 26).

The present point has an even more challenging implication. According to the argument, human psychology can be adequate only within the philosophic viewpoint, and such psychology already is spirituality. If this is really so, development of an adequate psychology requires the development of authentic psychologists, requires personal formation.

In fact, such formation is already part of some professional programs in counseling psychology. Competent attention to clients and their problems requires an understanding of life, its meaning, and worthwhile values (Yalom, 1980), so senior faculty members carefully share their wisdom, while eager and grateful counseling students "sit at their feet." The process is similar to the seminary training of clergy. As one school phrases the matter, "The overall aim of the program is to facilitate the process of self-awareness for the benefit of others as well as oneself. It presupposes self-understanding as the basis for understanding and guiding others" (Department of Psychology, 1995). Deliberately or not, for better or worse, counseling programs engage in formation, imparting a vision of life and a set of values to match it (Browning, 1987).

But the present point applies also to academic psychology. The advancement of the academic field requires the spiritual advancement of its practitioners. On all fronts the training of competent psychologists presumes the work traditionally relegated to religion, namely, spiritual formation.

For science that would be "objective"—in the sense of detached, distant, personally uninvolved—this matter may be quite disconcerting. It brings theoretical issues too close to home. It exemplifies Lonergan's comment regarding knowledge, reality, and being: "Genuine objectivity is the fruit of authentic subjectivity" (Lonergan, 1972, pp. 292, 265). It calls would-be "objective" human scientists to attend also to their own souls. This system of four viewpoints has challenging existential implications.

Ontological Implications

The system of four viewpoints also entails ontological considerations. It turns on differences in reality itself. Two ontological differences are to be noted: first, differences in degree of humanness
in human subjects differently converted; and second, differences in
kind in the Christian version of the theotic viewpoint, compared
with the lower viewpoints.

As already noted, working within the different viewpoints
presupposes different personal conversions. But such conversions,
existential commitments, entail personal transformations.

Humans are self-constituting. What people are depends on
what they believe and value. For beliefs determine openness to
experience and constrain the possibilities of understanding. Narrow or erroneous beliefs restrict expansive self-development. Even
more importantly, values function in the same way. Not only do
values constrain beliefs. Values form the self. Choices about external things and events have the internal effect of forming the chooser.
What I give myself to in value choices determines what I am as a
valuer. I form my own self-forming self. As I choose, I more and
more become the kind of person who makes those kinds of choices
(Helminiak, 1996a, pp. 118–119, 201–217).

Now, according to the presuppositions of the present exposition, the human is intrinsically geared toward the true and the
good. It follows that deliberate commitment to the true and the
good enhances the very humanness of the one so committed. For
now concern for the true and the good is not merely the actual
condition of the human as she or he happens to be. Such concern
is also the condition that is deliberately known and affirmed and
chosen.

There is a compounding, a snowballing, effect here. For deliberate choice reaffirms what in natural spontaneity would already
be the case. Through such choice one becomes more surely what
one already is. But perforce one also becomes that in a more profound way. For what one is by nature, now one is also by choice,
and to be able to exercise such choice is precisely what one is by
nature. Therefore, to be this way knowingly and deliberately is to
enhance one's natural state. The difference is not one of kind, for
one was and still is a knowing and deliberating being. The difference is one of degree, for one now is more self-determinately the

self-determining being one is. Such a difference is a "higher degree of being" (Lonergan, 1958, pp. 98, 102–104, 127).

To be what one is, is a quality proper to any being. But to be knowing and choosing is proper only to humans. So in addition merely to being, humans may be knowingly and deliberately. Then, to be knowing and choosing knowingly and deliberately is to be human more humanly.

If this discussion seems circular or suggests a folding back on itself, that impression is certainly correct. For at stake in the discussion of human self-constitution is the spiritual nature of the human. To grasp the human possibility for self-determined increase in degree of being is to begin to understand what human spirit means. The essence of the matter is spirit's unmediated presence to itself. This peculiarity allows for the reflexivity, for the folding back on itself. This matter is not the easiest to understand; it was summarized in Chapter One and fully elaborated elsewhere (Helminiak, 1996a). Here, a more limited point is to be made. The succession of human conversions that correspond with the higher viewpoints entails successive increases in the degree of one's being human more humanly.

To work within the philosophic viewpoint is to be committed unrestrictedly to the true and the good. Since to be geared toward the true and the good is inherent in being human in any case, to embrace the philosophic viewpoint is to enhance one's own being. Then, as a knowing subject, ideally at least, one has an advantage over someone limited in personal commitment to science within the positivist viewpoint. For one's own self, one's questioning and knowing consciousness, is more deliberately itself, so, all things being equal, it is more likely to do what it is inclined to do, more likely to be attentive, to pursue understanding, to know correctly, and to choose responsibly. The difference is on the side of the subject who understands, not on the side of the data to be understood. No new data accrue to the person unreservedly committed to truth. Only a personal change occurs, and this change might allow more ready understanding of the commonly available data or allow openness to new data, which others might overlook or deem irrelevant.

So even when limited to a positivist investigation, the scientist personally committed also to the philosophic viewpoint would bring to positivist science a more finely honed knowing instrument and, at least in theory, would be at some advantage. For personal commitments entail ontological changes. Those changes are in the knowing subject. And the subject self-changed in the direction of human authenticity is more capable of being what he or she is, an understanding, knowing, and loving subject.

Likewise, in the shift from the philosophic to the theist viewpoint, the same argument pertains once again. This theist consideration brings up my reason for treating this matter at length. In *Spiritual Development* (Helminiak, 1987c), I was unclear about this ontological matter (Bain, 1987; Streeter, 1990). The question was whether belief in God entails any practical advantage. My answer was, No, but it turned on the ambiguous word, "practical."

To believe in God as understood here entails a commitment to the Fullness of Truth and Goodness. That Fullness is understood as the ideal terminus of the human pursuit of understanding. Then, to commit oneself to that Terminus would entail a commitment to that human pursuit in a way that goes beyond what is entailed in the philosophic viewpoint—though precisely what such a commitment might mean concretely seems to surpass the possibility of specification, just as to say what "God" is surpasses human capacity. The concomitant transformation of the human subject would represent another difference in degree of human being. That difference would again refine the human knower through a radical openness to absolute understanding and commitment to absolute goodness that transcend all human achievement. Such openness would confer on a knower an advantage in knowing whatever was to be known, for commitment to unlimited Transcendence confirms absolutely the absolute open-endedness of the human pursuit of understanding.

Such a transformation would be a true advantage, in the sense just explained. The advantage would be on the side of the subject, a refinement of human consciousness. But there would be no advantage on the side of the object to be known. That is to say, belief in God supplies no new data pertinent to questions about human life. Believer and non-believer alike must grapple with the same information to determine correct meaning and worthy purpose in life. Said in other terms, the data do not change because one shifts from one viewpoint to another. All four viewpoints regard one and the same reality, the human phenomenon as it in fact is. Higher viewpoints merely open broader questions on one and the same phenomenon. So believing in God provides no inside track on answering questions about life. This lack of advantage in supposed additional data was my main point in *Spiritual Development*. Emphasis on it obscured the possible advantage on the side of the subject, as emphasized here.

In addition, belief in God would entail an advantage also of an inspirational kind. This inspirational effect is to be expected. Psyche and spirit are both explanatory factors of a single reality, the human being, so increased integration of one's spiritual capacity would effect a restructuring of one's psyche. Said more popularly, human commitments entail emotional responses. Our loves move the heart. If commitments and loves are in line with the deepest inclination of the human being, they will express themselves in concomitant feelings of profound peace, harmony, enthusiasm, joy, hope, trust, and security. Such inspiration is the effect in psyche of the spiritual act of belief in God. Such inspiration leaves one free to live life more boldly. Thus, believers profess that their belief in God lets them live more fully and securely, especially in the face of hardship, suffering, and inexplicable human loss (Wicks, 1991, pp. 11–18).

Still, the critical mind might wonder whether the believer's strength and security are not evasion and blindness. Karl Marx commented that religion is the opium of the people. Unfortunately, his comment is too often apropos. For the "god" of false religion provides a hallowed reason for avoiding tough issues and for shrugging off responsibility for life. "Belief in God" is often the adult form of childish belief in Santa Claus. That was my point in *Spiritual Development*, and though religionists are reluctant to hear it, it remains valid, nonetheless. However, in that case theism is not really in question but some religious ideology, to be categorized within the positivist viewpoint, as explained above. When theism is true—ah, there's the rub!—it does legitimately convey the advantage of hope beyond hope. For it knows that there is Explanation of Everything about Everything and Absolute Goodness in the universe.

When consideration shifts to the Christian version of the theotic viewpoint, the same argument pertains still again. Christians believe that God poured the Holy Spirit into human hearts and that people—all people, I have argued—are accordingly transformed unto becoming one with God. If this is in fact the case and if one knowingly and willingly embraces it, then one not only is what one is in Christ but is that knowingly and willingly. Then one achieves a higher degree of being what all are in Christ. On the side of the subject one has an advantage over those who do not know and embrace the Christian mysteries. For one lives knowingly and willingly what all, indeed, live. This is the point clarified here. Still, on the side of the object, in the life that all live, there is no advantage, for whether people believe in Christ or not, the Holy Spirit is given to them, and their life is accordingly a sharing in the paschal mysteries of Christ. The substance of the life that all must live is one and the same. This is the point emphasized in *Spiritual Development.*

As is clear in theory, there are real ontological differences on the side of the subject that correspond to the system of four viewpoints. These differences entail subjective advantages, higher degrees of being human. Still, these advantages are not to be used to make comparisons between believers and others. The differences exist according to theory only insofar as people actually live the presuppositions of the various viewpoints. And who is to say who is truly authentic or who truly believes in God or who is truly a Christian? Indeed, the Creator-God and Christianity as understood in this exposition are foreign to the bulk of theist and Christian believers. Or again, some who deny the existence of God, disagreeing with the pious and naive, may well be more committed than "believers" to the unspeakable Mystery that defines the theist viewpoint.

This first ontological implication of the system of four viewpoints is subtle and at this point is really not to be pressed. This analysis is useful theoretically to explicate just what spiritual development might mean. But whether or not one is spiritually developed, whether or not one enjoys the advantage of a higher degree of human being, whether or not one is a better person—this is not to be determined by labels that people attribute. Rather, it should show in one's living and be evident in one's contribution. In the more direct words of Jesus, "By their fruits you will know them." Of course, if they are really known by their fruits, these fruits constitute discernable evidence that somewhere down the line, given some clever research design, could be used to test the theory.

The second ontological implication of the system of four viewpoints lies at the heart of the theotic viewpoint. Knowing no other truly theotic account, I must again rely on Christianity to supply the elaboration. However, I believe that the point to be made is pertinent to any theotic account. This is to say that the considerations that follow turn on the intrinsic rationale of the matter and do not depend merely on the religious authority of Christian tradition. This is not to imply that the assertions of traditional Christian orthodoxy must necessarily, therefore, actually be true, though the present discussion could provide a provocative apologetic argument to that effect. This is only to insist that the Christian treatment of the matter has hit upon unavoidable and irreducible issues. These are precisely the issues that constitute the theotic viewpoint, and any attempt to account for human deification must confront these issues.

According to Christian belief, through Christ and the gift of the Holy Spirit, humanity is introduced to a share in divine life. But humanity is not Divinity, so two different realities are in question. Human participation in Divinity entails reality beyond the human. Then the shift from the theist to the theotic viewpoint depends on an ontological difference. That difference is the distinction, within the one and the same human phenomenon, between what pertains to the human and what pertains to the divine.

It does pertain to the human to understand what happens to be the case, and it likewise pertains to the human to pursue human authenticity, and it also pertains to the human to acknowledge the mystery of created existence. So the positivist, the philosophic, and the theist viewpoints all derive from what is proportionate to humanity. But it does not pertain to humanity to understand everything about everything nor to love all that is lovable. It does not pertain to humanity to be like God. So the determinant of the theotic viewpoint, the possibility of human deification, is disproportionate to humanity.

This consideration of ontological differences highlights the theoretical nature of this system of viewpoints. The theotic viewpoint on the one hand, and the three lower viewpoints on the other, deal with different ontologies, one proportionate and one disproportionate to humanity. Yet both ontologies are givens-to-be-understood within one and the same human phenomenon. To explain the human intelligently requires the distinction between the proportionate and the disproportionate. To be able to distinguish and interrelate these is to explain that one phenomenon. The two are not separable, nor does to name and distinguish them separate them. The two are merely distinguishable aspects that intelligent insight can discern.

Similarly, the intelligible content contributed by, and thematized within, each of the four viewpoints is not a separable part or component to be added on. The viewpoints rather determine intelligent distinctions that are usefully made if coherent explanation of the human phenomenon is to be had. To speak of God within the theist viewpoint is not to add God to the human; it is merely to acknowledge another factor, createdness, which is essential to overall explanation and has been part of the picture all along. Or to prescind from God in the philosophic viewpoint is not to make things suddenly not-created. For whether God is acknowledged or not, if God is as understood here, God is there and God is operating as Creator all along. So to submit the human phenomenon to analysis within the four viewpoints is merely to sort out the factors that bear on complete explanation without losing any of them. There is no suggestion of adding or subtracting pieces. The analysis is theoretical. It pertains to an exercise of human understanding.

Why make an issue over theory and ontology? Because the difference between the theotic and the theist viewpoint, in contrast to the differences between any other two viewpoints, is not only theoretical but also ontological. And many confound these two. Acknowledging that there is a difference also in ontology does not disqualify the theoretical intent of this analysis. To speak of an ontological difference is not to introduce talk of components and pieces and parts. Distinctions are still what is at stake. The theotic viewpoint in its Christian version simply highlights another factor—this time a different reality, something additional in the realm of being—that needs to be intelligently distinguished if coherent explanation is to be had. In a word, this factor is "grace." But the term is not taken here in its popular usage wherein any experience of benevolence could be called *grace*. This term has a technical meaning, and it is what pertains here. In the first place *grace* is the divine Holy Spirit, who is God's gift to human beings (Romans 5:5), and in the second place grace is the concomitant transformation that makes the human able to receive the Holy Spirit (Helminiak, 1987c, pp. 193–194).

The disproportionate aspect of the human phenomenon, the participation in divinity which Christian belief highlights, is what traditionally has been named the "supernatural." But the supernatural has been taken to refer to some part or separable component that is given and taken away, enjoyed by some and withheld from or lost by others. The concept *supernatural* was reified and has fallen into disfavor (Gilkey, 1975, pp. 46–48; Gutierrez, 1973, pp. 69–72, 76 n. 44; Segundo, 1973, pp. 62–69)—and as reified, rightly so. "What is given to all and is everywhere pertinent to the human situation should not be considered additional or 'supernatural' but is simply natural," the argument goes. "What was always there must simply be natural, so talk of 'super'-natural is absurd." But the issue is not the addition and subtraction of parts nor chronology; the issue is, rather, explanation. Though grace may have always and everywhere been given in the human situation, it remains disproportionate to the human. It is a distinct factor in the human equation, and it requires specialized treatment.

If the truth be told, the system of four viewpoints is an expanded and refurbished version of the old natural-supernatural distinction. The supernatural pertains to the theotic viewpoint, and the natural has been subdistinguished and entails the theist, philosophic, and positivist viewpoints.

It occurred to me to differentiate the positivist and philosophic within the natural when I realized that empirical human reality can be of two kinds, the authentic and the inauthentic (or neutral). The two are significantly different, for only the authentic opens onto ideal human fulfillment, so only it is continuous with the possibility of union with God—or, as in the case of my personal problematic at the time, union in Christ (Helminiak, 1979). Further, I was forced to specify the theist viewpoint when, teaching a course in spirituality, I realized 1) that many spiritual or mystical accounts took for granted that participation in divinity is an inherent possibility for humans, and 2) that the confounding of humanity with divinity precludes any empirically-grounded treatment of spirituality. Thus, the study of empirical social science and a growing awareness of non-Christian religions prompted me to differentiate into a number of factors what in the medieval Christian world could be globally treated as "natural." The end result was the system of four viewpoints on the human. This conceptual system is nothing other than the best of medieval thinking recovered and expanded to meet the interdisciplinary needs of contemporary scholarship and science (Lonergan, 1957, 1958, 1967e, 1971, 1972, 1976).

For ontological reasons the theotic viewpoint emerges beyond the theist viewpoint. This is the important lesson that Christian doctrine contains. Any attempt to account for human union with

God or deification must somehow take into account the difference between humanity and divinity. This difference is already at stake in the emergence of the theist viewpoint, and it continues to demand its due in the theotic viewpoint.

The main thrust of this system of viewpoints is scientific account; the overall concern is coherent explanation. Yet beyond the theoretical, this system of viewpoints also has existential and ontological implications, and all entail one another. So all need to be noted and all be kept well in place.

Summary on the Four Viewpoints

Four different explanatory concerns determine four different approaches to the human phenomenon. Four different questions define four viewpoints on the human.

The positivist viewpoint limits concern to what actually happens to be the case in a broad range of physical, organic, and even human phenomena. Thus, the positivist viewpoint explains and sometimes even predicts the orderly functioning of the universe. Over and above that, the philosophic viewpoint asks also about human authenticity: Is what people really affirm actually true? Is what they actually hold really good? Are they true to what they affirm and to what they hold? Thus, the philosophic viewpoint explains a broader realm of human reality as it attends to the possibilities of human self-determination and the open-ended development implicit in authenticity. The theist viewpoint conceives a Fullness of Truth and Goodness, the Explanation of Everything about Everything, and affirms the Creator-God of the Universe as the ideal terminus of the human pursuit of the true and the good. Thus, the theist viewpoint explains existence itself, the givenness of phenomena to be otherwise explained. Finally, the theotic viewpoint envisages the human participation in the Fullness that is God. With Jesus Christ as paradigm and the Holy Spirit as divine gift, traditional Christian orthodoxy offers an example of a coherent theotic account. Explanation within the theotic viewpoint treats the attainment of human fulfillment in its ultimate and ideal form.

Those four different concerns differentiate different disciplines: positivist sciences of both the natural and human kind; adequate human science—like psychology, sociology, and anthropology—which is already really spirituality; theology, strictly taken, as the study of God; and theotics, critical treatment of the requirements of human deification.

Yet the questions that determine those four concerns are interrelated and linked to one another. The question, What happens to be case? prompts the further question in the case of humans, Is what happens to be the case right, is it true and good? Affirmation of the true and the good raises the further question, Is there a Fullness of Truth and Goodness, an Explanation of Everything about Everything? Acknowledgment of a Divine Fullness provokes the still further question, Can humans ever attain to participation in that Fullness?

Thus, a system of concepts results that unites distinct disciplines into a coherent, comprehensive, explanatory account. Since this system, explanatory in itself, envisages complete explanation, it is scientific in the core sense of the term. It is a contribution to the human pursuit of explanation, and it is a tool for furthering this enterprise. Like the periodic table of elements in the field of chemistry, this system of viewpoints is a heuristic structure that invites filling in the anticipated understandings. This system differentiates and relates scientific pursuit of the positivist, philosophic, theist, and theotic kind.

The philosophic viewpoint is at the heart of this comprehensive system. Because concern for human authenticity determines the philosophic viewpoint, study of the human within this viewpoint is already the study of human spirituality. So psychology within the philosophic viewpoint can be identical with spirituality. In contrast, psychology within the positivist viewpoint makes another contribution but can never in itself be adequate to the human. So two kinds of psychology emerge, psychology within the positivist, and psychology within the philosophic, viewpoints. In contrast on the other hand, spirituality is not the same thing as theology. And theology is not simply religious studies. Spirituality is a realm of human concern that may proceed apart from theism or theist religion. Although the religions and their discipline, globally called "theology," have much to contribute to the topic, spirituality theoretically differentiated within the present system is a distinct and autonomous discipline. Spirituality is a specialization within psychology. Those are some of the more relevant implications of this four-viewpoint analysis of interdisciplinary human studies.

This chapter has presented a comprehensive approach to interdisciplinary studies. The focal concern is the relationship of religion and the human sciences. A key suggestion has been that religion is too unwieldy a thing to be related effectively with science. There is need to sort out the various facets of religion. Once differentiated, aspects of religion can correlate rather easily with aspects of human science. Indeed, spirituality as distinct from religion is but another name for a particular kind of psychological analysis, one that takes human authenticity into specific account. This overall conception is summarized in a system of four higher viewpoints on the human. Application of this system represents an alternative approach to interdisciplinary studies.

The suggestion is that this approach is more adequate than the others available and in use. Broad comparisons in Chapter One made this suggestion plausible. Analysis of highly elaborated positions on interdisciplinary studies in the next two chapters will further support this suggestion and give it the weight of an argued claim.

Chapter 3

Revised Critical Correlation
à la Don Browning

"All roads lead to Rome." This was a maxim that expressed shrewd insight at the time of the Roman Empire. Literally, it meant that Rome was the hub of the world, so Rome was the place from which and to which all roads eventually led. Metaphorically, it meant that if anything was going to get resolved, it would eventually have to be dealt with in the capital. Today, the maxim might suggest that there are many ways of arriving at the same goal. Then this maxim must certainly be true if making a journey and other such practicalities are at stake. Even in questions of religion there are often different approaches. The proverb of Eastern religion insists that many different paths lead to the same mountain top.

However, things must be different when scientific explanation and not just religious practice is at stake. If by definition science, even human or social science, is eventually to give us *the* correct understanding of things, that understanding must be unique, so the many roads leading to Rome or the many paths up the mountain would not seem to apply. At some point—and that is the point

of this book: the attempt to deal scientifically with the spiritual—
knowledge and the means of achieving it codetermine one another.
The very object of study here, human spirit, is simultaneously the
instrument that must be used to do the study. Identical in themselves, the two could coincide in only one way. A successful scientific interrelationship of religion and the human sciences could follow
only one path.

Chapter Two presented a candidate for that sole approach.
Appealing to the nature of human spirit and its eros for ever more
comprehensive understanding, a system of four viewpoints sorts
out and interrelates different intellectual stances vis-à-vis the
human phenomenon. One stance is merely positivist concern, the
attempt objectively to specify and explain what are the facts of
some matter. Its disciplinary correlate is psychology as currently
conceived and, indeed, contemporary human or social science in
general. Another stance is philosophic and adds concern for human
authenticity. It questions and determines whether the facts are as
they ought to be. Its disciplinary correlate is a peculiar kind of
psychology that is, in fact, the discipline, spirituality. A third stance
is theist and seeks further to account for even the very existence
of the human. It affirms the createdness of the human and appeals
to the Creator-God of the Universe, to Divinity, to explain created
human existence. Its disciplinary correlate is theology. Finally, a
fourth stance is theotic, and its concern is human deification. Its
discipline, theotics, treats of ultimate human fulfillment, the possibility of human participation in qualities proper only to God.
Even as these four stances address one and the same phenomenon,
the human, they build on one another and interlock to provide one
coherent accounting. This system of four viewpoints allows a fully
secular treatment of things human, including things spiritual, while
also being fully open to questions of God and human participation
in Divinity. Thus, this system represents a peculiar approach to the
interrelationship of an array of specialized disciplines, secular and
confessional, that all treat the human phenomenon.

With this chapter, this book turns to other approaches to the
interrelationship of religion and psychology, other roads to Rome,
if you will. At the same time this book continues to argue for the
one approach that might not end in a cul-de-sac. Attention will be
on varied understandings of science, on the proposed competence of
different sciences, and on the resultant interrelationship of those

different sciences. Detailed comparison with other positions will serve a number of purposes. Not only will it summarize and criticize the other positions. The comparison will also help and elaborate the position of this book. This comparison will draw out implications in the present position, for one way of explicating a position is to contrast it with others. The suggestion is that, compared to the others, the present position is more adequate. It not only allows a coherent analysis of complex human and religious issues, as already shown. It also allows an incisive criticism of other interdisciplinary positions. It detects their flaws and ambiguities, explains the source of those shortcomings, offers the required correctives, and salvages the valid contributions. While it is able to account for the other positions, they do not seem able to account for it. Thus, this position recommends itself. It must be the one road to the intended destination. Or at least this book argues so.

The focus of the present chapter is the position of Don S. Browning's *Religious Thought and the Modern Psychologies: A Critical Conversation in the Theology of Culture.* His book is a major contribution to the dialogue between religion and psychology. Browning is an ethicist at the Divinity School of the University of Chicago. His focal concern is for social science adequate to human beings— which, I have argued, is nothing other than spirituality. Perforce he addresses in some detail the psychology-theology problematic, and his book is an extended application of the position he proposes. So a discussion of Browning's interdisciplinary position is relevant here— and especially so since he relies on the mainline position in Western thought. Thus, discussion of this single book by this single author will also be a discussion of the position more or less common to a list of important theorists, both social scientists and theologians.

Browning's True Contribution

Browning's original contribution is not his resolution of the interdisciplinary problematic. This he simply assumes from others. His real contribution is rather his "religio-ethical" (8)[1] analysis of five

---

1. Throughout Chapter Three numbers in parentheses refer to pages in Browning (1987).

different modern psychologies—Freudian theory, humanistic psychology, Skinnerian behaviorism, Jungian theory, and Eriksonian and Kohutian theory. This analysis is an exploration of three levels of thought buried in those psychological theories. In a former work Browning argued that any practical moral thinking implicitly contains these levels of thought. In applying this analysis to the psychological theories, Browning makes his main point, that these theories do, indeed, contain elements proper to "religion."

Uncovering Psychology's Metaphors of Ultimacy

Browning's deepest level of analysis concerns the universal human question, often silent and sometimes unconscious, "What kind of world do we live in and what is its most ultimate (in the sense of most determinative) context?" Browning continues, "In answering this question, we always resort to metaphorical language—deep metaphors which are themselves frequently embellished into myths, stories, or narratives" (9). So Browning's task is to uncover the "metaphors of ultimacy" (10) unwittingly at work in supposedly purely scientific theories of psychology.

For example, Freud initially supposed a metaphor of mechanics, a notion of the psyche as a hydraulic system of energy flowing in alternating buildup, tension, and release. Later, Freud relied on metaphors of life and death, eros and thanatos. These Freudian metaphors suggest that people should relate in "a modest and cautious reciprocity that would not overtax our limited libidinal investments or arouse our ready hostilities" (30). So Freudian theory envisages a culture of civilized detachment.

In contrast, the humanistic psychologies rely on "implicit metaphors of harmony which depict an image of the world where conflict can occur only if humans are somehow untrue to their own deepest selves" (30). These psychologies envisage a culture of joy— as does also Jungian theory. According to Jung, as interpreted by Browning, "tensions, imbalances, and one-sidedness can occur in the psychic equilibrium. But one's task in life is still to be faithful to one's own unique set of archetypal possibilities, that is, to practice a kind of sacred egoism. Such an egoism will lead to a deeper harmony because of the final complementarity between each person's archetypal possibilities and the structure of the world" (30).

Again, the behaviorist theory of Skinner suggests barnyard metaphors based on Darwinian principles of natural selection. The vision is a culture of control where conditioning and reinforcement lead everyone to live in justice, rather than seek self-actualization.

Finally, in their own way both Erik Erikson and Heinz Kohut propose metaphors of life as an interlocking system of care between one generation and another. Here, concern for self often coincides with concern for others. "The generative care of others is also an avenue for the actualization of each human's own deepest inclinations" (31). Erikson's and Kohut's theories and their metaphors of ultimacy allow for both self-regard and love of others, so Browning finds these theories the most acceptable of all.

The second level of Browning's analysis addresses the question, "What are we obliged to do?" (10). Browning maintains, for example, that Christianity's basic theory of obligation centers around the principle, Love your neighbor as yourself, the Golden Rule, and often includes some requirement of self-sacrificing love. But principles of obligation also underlie the various psychological theories, as already suggested in the summary analysis of those psychologies above.

Finally, the third level of analysis addresses the question, "What are the various fundamental needs and tendencies that should be morally and justly satisfied?" (11). To answer this question is really to propose an anthropology, in the etymological sense of the word: an understanding of what a human being is, what one ought to be, and what one needs to be that. To spell out these "psychobiological tendencies and needs" is to present an "image of the natural constitution of human beings" (11). One contribution of psychology is to do just that. That is, it is to help answer the question, What is a human being? (cf. Helminiak, 1996a, Chapter 1).

Browning speaks of these needs or tendencies as nonmoral or premoral goods (xi). He means to say that in themselves they are neither good nor evil. They are simply the possible objects of human choice, and it is human choice that is moral or immoral. To name these premoral goods is merely to list or order whatever would ideally be good for a person, the *ordo bonorum*. Said otherwise, Browning is pointing to what I discussed as the exigencies of organism and psyche, though his treatment unfortunately ignores the exigencies of spirit (Helminiak, 1996a, pp. 201–207). The ethical or moral task is to decide which of those goods one can justly seek and acquire in one's concrete situation. For one cannot always have what one wants or even what one ideally ought to have. The limitations of human life, broader concerns, or the rights of others—various ethical considerations prevent one from having all that might be ideally best.

Psychology as Religion

Browning's point is that the psychologies overstep their bounds. Although the psychologies claim to be science, they nonetheless propose answers to those three religio-ethical (and, supposedly, nonscientific) questions. Of course, this excess is not so true, or at least not so critical, in the case of experimental psychology. Closely associated originally only with physiological and animal research but later branching out into other areas of more specifically human concern, experimental psychology uses contrived experiments to test hypotheses and arrive at an understanding of basic psychological and social processes. This branch of psychology, "as does any rigorous science, narrows its task and tries to test propositions 'against the data'" (7).

But clinical psychology presents another picture. This is the branch of psychology that provides theories and techniques for psychotherapy and counseling, and it works to help people get their lives together. In Browning's words, the clinical psychologies are "concerned with the interpretation of basic patterns, modalities, themes, and narratives which give lives their underlying cohesion" (7). In my terminology, the clinical psychologies have hidden within their theories answers to the questions about the meaning and purpose of life. The clinical psychologies actually entail belief systems and norms for living. They treat matters of meaning and value. As Eric Fromm (1947, 1973) would say, they propose frames of orientation and devotion. So the clinical psychologies are unwittingly spiritualities. They propose particular ways of living as ideals to be striven for (Helminiak, 1996a, pp. 34–36). Whereas I speak of meanings and values, or beliefs and norms, or visions and virtues, or credos and commitments, and Fromm speaks of orientation and devotion, Browning speaks of "metaphysics and ethics" (124; see also 12, 14). The parallels are patent. Clinical psychologies covertly embody spirituality or, as Browning would say, religion.

Interdisciplinary Method

Doubtless, the psychologies do embody systems of meaning and value. As Viktor Frankl (1969/1988, p. 15) states, "There is no psychotherapy without a theory of man and a philosophy of life underlying it. Wittingly or unwittingly, psychotherapy is based on them." On my understanding no one should be surprised at it. All human endeavors entail meanings and values, for these spiritual realities are inherent in, and constitutive of, humanity as such. Also beyond doubt, Browning does a marvelous job of analyzing those matters. Astutely, he uncovers the beliefs and values hidden in the modern psychologies. This analysis is his original contribution.

But from this point on—as I impose my own organization on Browning's presentation—other, broader issues come into play. Browning's theory of interdisciplinary method now becomes the focus. (See Figure 3.1.) I will quickly sketch the many and far-reaching issues that come to bear in Browning's argument, and then I will present a detailed criticism of Browning's treatment of the matter.

Revised Critical Correlation

On Browning's analysis, if they are involved in metaphysical and ethical concerns, the modern psychologies are functioning as religions. For it is the task of religion to deal with such concerns. Adopting Dilthey's now classic delineation, Browning distinguishes the natural sciences or *Naturwissenschaften* and the human sciences or *Geisteswissenschaften*. The task of the natural sciences is to explain, predict, and control. The natural sciences are explanatory. But the human sciences are interpretative. Their task is to determine the significance of things—and the significance in question is the significance for human beings. Of course, psychology is a *Geisteswissenschaft*. But then, again, so is religion or theology. For both psychology and religion express the significance of things. Browning attempts to discern some difference between them by suggesting, "The clinical psychologies try to interpret *individual lives*; theology tries to interpret *life*—life as a whole, in its entirety" (7).

In any case, the point is that both clinical psychology and religion are dealing, to some extent or other, on the same level. Thus, there arises the possibility of a conversation between them.

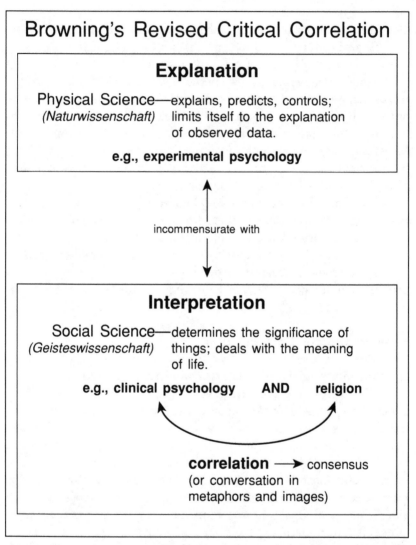

Browning's Revised Critical Correlation

Explanation

Physical Science—explains, predicts, controls;
(Naturwissenschaft)   limits itself to the explanation
of observed data.

e.g., experimental psychology

↑
incommensurate with
↓

Interpretation

Social Science—determines the significance of
(Geisteswissenschaft)   things; deals with the meaning
of life.

e.g., clinical psychology   AND   religion

correlation ⟶ consensus
(or conversation in
metaphors and images)

Figure 3.1 *Naturwissenschaften* and *Geisteswissenschaften* are fully incommensurate, for they depend on different ranges of data and different kinds of questions; that is, they serve different functions, to explain and to interpret. But both religion and clinical psychology fall within interpretative "science," for both propose answers about the significance of life. So when their answers differ, a conversation between the two, dealing in metaphors and involving rational assessment, is to arrive at an acceptable conclusion.

Browning conceives that conversation as an application of the *critical correlation* approach to religion and culture first proposed by Paul Tillich (1951, p. 61; 1952) and recently revised by David Tracy (1970, pp. 232–234). The end result is a *revised critical correlation*. It presumes that both psychology and religion have opinions about important human questions and that those opinions can be bounced off one another so that some kind of consensus, an acceptable answer, can arise. On this approach, psychology and religion are in conversation with one another and both profit by the dialogue. Such conversation is interdisciplinary cooperation. It results in a certain reconciling of diverse disciplines. Thus, the revised critical correlation is an interdisciplinary methodology. As such, it is an alternative to analysis within the system of four viewpoints presented in Chapter Two. Thus, Browning's presentation has become a topic of discussion in this book.

Browning states repeatedly that he is only performing an experiment; he is merely providing an example of what such a revised critical correlation might be like and how an answer might emerge from it. Here is his example.

The Conversation Between Religion and the Psychologies

An ethicist, Browning focuses on the moral issue of neighbor-love. He suggests that the Golden Rule expresses the rational core of all ethics. On some level it is important for Browning to specify clearly through human reasoning what the core of ethics is.

Yet he also looks to religion for the answer to this question. On the religious front, he discerns that the command to love one's neighbor is clearly part of the Judeo-Christian tradition. So this command is the religious voice in the critical conversation.

Yet, again, the religious voice is itself seriously ambivalent. For the Protestant tradition tends to lay heavy emphasis on self-sacrifice: one's ethical probity depends on how much one does for the sake of others. But the Roman Catholic tradition has stood by Saint Augustine's *ordo caritatis*, wherein Christian love requires a much more balanced emphasis on concern for self and concern for others. On this latter understanding, self-sacrifice is not the heart of Christian ethics but is only an extraordinary requirement that will inevitably come into play, but only now and again, to restore a favorable environment for a balance between love of self and love of others.

Moreover, there are still other voices in this conversation. As already noted, the clinical psychologies also imply norms about how one should relate to others. Freud's theory, for example, supports a cautious reciprocity with others. The humanists and Jung emphasize self-actualization, which appears to be more self-serving than other-regarding. Erikson's and Kohut's emphasis on interaction between the generations seems to suggest a more balanced concern for self and others.

So the conversation begins. The humanist call for self-actualization—certainly a villainous and covert selfishness!—challenges the Protestant ethical tradition to question its emphasis on self-sacrifice. Sure enough, consultation of recent biblical exegesis, especially in Roman Catholic circles, indicates that the biblical teaching does not call simply for self-sacrifice. Even Jesus' command was to love your neighbor *as you love yourself.* So the Catholic understanding of neighbor-love calls the Protestant emphasis into better balance. Browning now recognizes this refined understanding as simply "Judeo-Christian." It calls for correction of the humanist emphasis and also recognizes Freud's position of cautious reciprocity as more or less compatible with the religious norm. This same religious understanding also recognizes in Erikson's and Kohut's theories, compared with the other psychologies, a much more acceptable balance of concern for self and for others. Thus, the conversation comes to consensus and comes to a close. The example of the revised critical correlation of culture and religion is complete. The interdisciplinary methodology has been implemented.

Questions about the Conversation

However, serious questions remain about the unfolding of that conversation. These questions all relate to one, telling query: In that conversation among differing opinions, who or what was the final arbiter? For the conversation did come to a conclusion; some judgment was made. And supposedly, all the parties had an equal voice. What decided the question?

Indeed, it is not even clear who all the participant parties are. The "Religious Thought" in Browning's title and in the example conversation is as global a notion as one could want. On Browning's own understanding, even the modern psychologies qualify as religious thought. Narrowing the religion in question to Judeo-Christianity is only a slight improvement. For the call to neighbor-love, supposedly the contribution of Judeo-Christianity, is found in some form or other in all the great world religions. Besides, in practice "Judeo-Christianity" became the mainstream Protestant and the Catholic traditions, and both offered significantly different opinions on the question at hand. So which was the voice of "religion" in dialogue with psychology? Or was it that psychological religions and Judeo-Christian religions were dialoguing with each other?

I reconstructed Browning's conversation above in the best of faith, but, I confess, I am still not sure I have represented his position accurately. In the tangle of threads in the complexity of the tapestry he weaves, the individual strands tend to get lost. It is a tribute to Browning that he was even able to put an example of the revised critical correlation into written form. But that example, now in crystallized form, may ironically find its greatest value in evincing the difficulties with that methodology.

As best I can determine, religious opinion—that is, Roman Catholic biblical exegesis—carries the day in Browning's critical conversation. Then does religion hold ultimate authority and automatically outweigh that of "science"? But why accept the Catholic rendition of religion? Because it provides a coherent, reasonable, and critical account of the biblical data? Then does not a scientific opinion (reasoned argument, critical analysis, biblical exegesis)—albeit in a religious realm—and not religion as such settle the matter? Or was the Catholic rendition accepted because it better addresses the challenge of the self-actualizers? But what says their challenge is legitimate, in any case? Because their challenge does seem to make sense? Why so, when emphasis on self-sacrifice seemed rather to make sense for so long?

Then again, concern for reasonableness and good sense raises questions about the role of reasoning in this conversation. What happened to the concern to determine the rational core of ethics? If balanced emphasis on neighbor-love is that rational core, why did its determination depend on biblical exegesis? Or was it that, contrariwise, the rational core, already somehow known, sanctioned the conclusion of the biblical exegesis? Perhaps the point is precisely that the two worked together. Still, which had the telling authority, faith or reason? How did they work together? How was it determined that their working together did, indeed, confirm the accuracy of the conclusion? Could they not both be wrong?

To push the questioning further, what confirms the accepted answer as, indeed, the *rational* core? Perhaps the fact that it lies at the heart of a congenial consensus. But is the consensus congenial only to those raised in Judeo-Christian, Western civilization? Or, indeed, might the consensual conclusion be appealing because it is actually correct, because it actually expresses the core of ethics common to all humankind? (But see below.) Then anybody honest about it and in touch with his or her own humanity should agree on it, and the revised critical correlation method should be deemed a success—in this case. But was consensus in this case just a happy accident, a success in a relatively easy realm or in a realm already ripe for consensus? Then what of other realms and other more difficult questions? Recall, for example, questions about divorce, homosexuality, the subordination of women, and Jesus' subjection to the Father's will, which bedevil Evangelical Christianity's integration project, as noted in Chapter One, and which also bedevil the Christian Churches at large today. If the method of revised critical correlation is to be of further use, we still need to specify how exactly Browning's judgment was made. His example offers no criteria for making the judgment. Who or what is the arbiter in the critical conversation?

Criticism of the Revised Critical Correlation

All those questions raise doubts about the adequacy of Browning's interdisciplinary methodology. With the system of four viewpoints in mind, I will present seven considerations about the interdisciplinary conversation that Browning exemplified. While pinpointing the shortcomings in the revised critical correlation, these considerations will also suggest how the shortcomings can be corrected and how the legitimate contribution of the correlation method—namely, egalitarian engagement in sorely needed dialogue—can be preserved. The overall effect will be to suggest that the position introduced in Chapter Two provides a more appropriate environment and more incisive tools for an effective dialogue between psychology and religion.

Who Is Arbiter?

First, who or what was the arbiter in Browning's conversation? Though Browning himself gives no explicit indication, there is no doubt about the arbiter's identity. It was Browning himself. Reviewing the evidence, assessing the arguments, aware of broader considerations, concerned about ultimate implications, Browning the seasoned ethicist made the final judgment. The conclusion in his book is his own.

Well, so what? Of course the conclusion is Browning's own. He wrote that book.

Granted all that, we must not overlook the obvious. In this case its methodological implications are far-reaching.

The point is not to deprecate a decision because it is made by some one person. In fact, Browning provides an extraordinarily fine treatment of a very complex problem. The point is to emphasize that judgments result from human beings. This is the same point that Chapter One made by highlighting Crabb's requirements for the faithful Evangelical Christian who wishes to engage in interdisciplinary dialogue. Not religion or science, not theology or psychology, not faith or reason, but the human subject is the source of judgments, and to human subjects alone may judgments be correctly attributed.

Authenticity as Fundamental

Second, it follows that the adequacy of the judgment will depend on the adequacy of the human subject making the judgment. That is, granted the requisite scholarship, human authenticity is the fundamental factor. If Browning came to what seems an adequate solution, it was because he is a person of competence and good will—not only learned in his field but also attentive, intelligent, reasonable, and responsible in his judgments and decisions. Giving Browning the deserved benefit of the doubt, let us grant that he is an authentic person. The point is that in these and all human matters, authenticity is the bottom line.

The Role of Faith

Third, however, Browning is a believer, an adherent to Christianity, and in his book he appeals to the Judeo-Christian tradition. Is it perhaps not, then, his faith, rather than his reasoning, that legitimates his judgments? Is his response perhaps a religious answer, rather than a scientific one?

That form of the question precludes intelligent answer, for that construal of the matter is simply misguided. Faith—in contrast to beliefs (Lonergan, 1972, p. 123)—is not a set of answers, a list of formulas expressing opinions about the way things are and about how one should behave. Rather, faith is a determining characteristic of a human subject. Faith entails a horizon of concern and commitment within which a human subject operates.

Undoubtedly, then, because he is a believer, Browning's faith played a part in his grappling with his ethical question. His theist faith set a horizon of concern, open to ultimate transcendence, which requires that his eventual answer be valid without reservation. Certainly this concern for ultimacy colored Browning's treatment of the question, just as his faith, a quality of the agent subject, must influence everything he does.

Then faith and reason are not two separate sources of answers to two different kinds of questions. Misunderstanding on precisely this point is the flaw in the question that asks about faith *or* reason (Lonergan, 1972, p. 343). Misunderstanding on this point is also the basic flaw in any position that construes the interdisciplinary problematic in terms of religion *or* science or again, religion *versus* science.

No human being operates without some kind of faith (Fowler, 1981; Hiatt, 1986, p. 738; Van Leevwen, 1996, p. 152). Even positivist scientists work within a horizon of faith. They believe in, and commit themselves to, the possibility of correct understanding about certain limited questions. And they dedicate their lives to the pursuit of answers within those limits. So the question is not whether faith or reason is functioning in a given discussion. The question is, Within which horizon of faith is it appropriate for a particular discussion to proceed? As argued in Chapter Two, horizons of concern may vary, and with them, presuppositional commitments, that is, faiths. Discussion may go on within horizons of concern that are positivist, philosophic, theist, or theotic. So the question is not whether Browning's conclusion resulted from faith or reasoning. The question is, Within which horizon of faith, within which viewpoint, does Browning's ethical question legitimately move?

Within the Philosophic Viewpoint

Fourth, then, Browning's experiment was conducted within the philosophic viewpoint. For neighbor-love is an ethical question. It asks about how people ought to behave. The concern is for what is right and good. The task is to specify the implication of authenticity in a specific context. The ethical question finds a correct answer through the judgment of sufficiently informed and authentic human subjects (who, as authentic, it must be noted, are not solipsistic and do not work in isolation).

That the discussion be called "religious" is only an accident of history, an accident of definition of terminology. In relatively recent Western history, and especially given the clumsy separation of "church and state" in the United States, ethics was determined to be the concern of the religions. So any ethical concern was deemed a religious concern. But "religion" in Western society almost invariably also means theism. So in common practice, ethics and theism have tended to be married, if not identified (Taylor, 1989). Yet ethics is a human concern, it pertains in every society whatsoever, and intrinsically it has nothing to do with belief in God. Granted, one's belief in God may lead one to be more radically open to embracing ethical conclusions that do indeed have ultimate validity—or a misguided or imbalanced belief in "God" may prevent one from doing any reasonable ethical thinking whatsoever. But belief in God does not change, rather it confirms, the spiritual exigencies determinative of human authenticity, and the topic of God is not an intrinsic part of ethical consideration. Accordingly, although ethics may be called a religious concern and though it is a *part* of religion: more precisely said, ethics is proper to the philosophic viewpoint.

On the other hand, that the ethical discussion *not* be called "scientific" is also an accident of history and an accident of definition of terminology. For narrow empiricism has taken the term "science" to apply only to treatment of sensible and measurable data. But even physical scientists *as such* have limited concern about right and wrong—about the rightness of pursuing this experimental design rather than that, about the rightness of following this line of research or another, or about the implicit rightness of scientific commitment at all. Science also entails value questions that are themselves ethical, so even taking the term in its current, narrow usage, these ethical questions could be called "scientific." More to the point, a rigorous treatment of broader ethical questions, like Browning's, marshals all the relevant data and methodically applies the appropriate axioms, so it could itself also be called somehow "scientific." This line of argument was elaborated in Chapter Two.

Thus, in the present context, whether Browning's experiment in revised critical correlation is scientific or religious hardly seems to be a profitable question. More on this below. With far more precision, it can at least be said that this experiment unfolded not within the positivist, nor within the theist, but within the philosophic viewpoint.

A Religious Discussion?

Fifth, Browning called his discussion "religious" and specified that religion as Judeo-Christian. Yet the hallmarks of Judaism and Christianity, God and Christ, figure only incidentally in Browning's presentation. So, analyzed differentially against the technical definitions inherent in Chapter Two's system of four viewpoints, Browning's presentation appears to be neither Christian nor Jewish (that is, theist).

Not a Christian Discussion

As for its being Christian, consider the three distinctive core Christian doctrines. First, Trinity plays no part in Browning's analysis. Second, Grace does get a mention in a popular form that suggests forgiveness and empowerment, but the indwelling of the Holy Spirit or its deifying implication goes completely unnamed, so the concept is merely theist (59, 88). Finally, Jesus Christ is mentioned because of his teaching about love of neighbor (e.g., 148, 155). He is also mentioned as redeemer, that is, "a source of renewal and revitalization in the midst of human brokenness" (137). And Jesus' example of "impartial and self-sacrificial love" is mentioned and suggests, according to Reinhold Niebuhr, what agape means (145).

In none of those instances is there anything specifically Christian at stake, namely, the possibility of human deification, as explained in Chapter Two. Rather, Christian sources and images—metaphors, as Browning prefers to phrase it—are invoked because of the implications they carry for human affairs. That is to say, the focus throughout is on philosophic-viewpoint concerns couched in this instance in terms of the Jesus story and of God. So the Christian tradition serves here simply as a source and a vehicle of ideas that bear on the ethical question, just as the humanist psychologies are another contrasting source.

From Browning's treatment of the notion of agape, it is clear that the Christian metaphors really are not the telling factor in the argument. Browning rejects Niebuhr's emphasis on self-sacrifice, though it has colored much of Christian history, because that particular understanding has been proved untrue to the biblical sources. Evidently, such metaphorical usage of Christianity differs from an approach, like mine, that would specify the determinative essence of Christianity, which cannot be changed. That Browning's ethical analysis supposedly corrects the Christian tradition, suggests that he is not working within the Christian viewpoint. Rather, he is working within the philosophic viewpoint, where Christianity has no unique competence or authority. So humanist insistence on self-actualization can legitimately provoke rethinking. The discussion is not between Christianity as such and psychology. The discussion is among ethical considerations derived from a wide range of human sources, including Judeo-Christian religion and humanistic psychology. Then the adequacy of the ethical judgment Browning eventually made depends on its reasonableness and responsibleness. That is, it in no way depends on the authority of Christian revelation, though it may be explicating in reasonable argument what the Christian tradition claims as revealed.

Despite the name *Christian* and the appeal to metaphors found in the Christian tradition, Browning's analysis is simply not Christian, if this term be given distinctive content.

Not a Theist Discussion

A similar conclusion applies to Browning's appeal to God and its possible categorization within the theist viewpoint, though in this case the argument will be harder to make. For "metaphors of ultimacy" are at the heart of Browning's analysis; and for Judeo-Christianity, the "religious" partner in Browning's conversation, metaphors of ultimacy mean metaphors of God. So it might appear, as Browning surely intends, that the discussion is really theological, that is, that it deals with the question of God and moves within the theist viewpoint. But the evidence suggests otherwise. The consideration that will sort out the matter is this: How much are Browning's ethical concerns and arguments really tied up with belief in God?

One argument that belief in God is linked with universal love is particularly strong. That argument occurs in discussion of Janssens's (1977) exegesis of biblical texts on neighbor-love. Browning writes, "Janssens resorts to the basic metaphors of Christian faith—every person is a child of God and redeemed by Christ—to ground the basic valuation of the other, and indeed all others, as of 'irreducible worth and dignity'" (150).

Surely, belief that all are children of God and sisters and brothers of one another is consistent with an ethic of love for all others. Again, preaching God as parent of us all surely fosters neighbor-love. But the telling question here is whether that belief is the source of the ethic. Which came first, the awareness of the correctness of respect for every person or the belief in God as parent of us all? Did ethics determine theology, or did theology determine ethics?

I do not pretend to answer that question. I suspect the issues are inextricably entangled in the Hebrews' and early Christians' human subjectivity, which always entails both meanings and values, belief and ethics, simultaneously and initially undifferentiatedly. But one would be hard pressed to show that ethic depends on that theist belief, for non-theist Buddhists respect every sentient, let alone every human, being.

Besides, the meaning of those metaphors, children of God and redemption by Christ, is not what resolved Browning's own discussion of neighbor-love. The metaphors may point to neighbor-love, but it was Janssens's exegesis that determined precisely what that neighbor-love means—and this, after centuries of misunderstanding and debate among Christians who never doubted the parenthood of God or their redemption in Christ. The connection between Judeo-Christian theism and neighbor-love is really not as clear as it might first appear.

A second argument of Browning also attempts to make the connection between the God of Judeo-Christian belief and a particular ethical outlook. Talk is of vitality and form. Vitality means energy, impulse, urge, drive, power, dynamism. Form refers to order, rules, exigencies, inherent requirements. So Browning writes,

> In the Christian vision, Niebuhr tell us—and I believe correctly—God is seen as a perfect union of vitality and form, and humans, at the levels of both ["lower"] nature and spirit, are finite unions of vitality and form. The practical upshot of these affirmations is that both Judaism and Christianity have very positive views of nature and instinctuality. Our instinctuality has form. . . . Being a civilized person is not a matter of spirit, reason, and conscience beating instinctuality to the ground and forcing it into submission. . . . And all of this at the anthropological level reflects the fundamental unity of vitality and form in the life of God. (45)

The point of this elaborate argument is that the human, including the body, is good and inherently ordered. Created in the image of God, humans could not but be good even in their biological nature.

That anthropological vision does square with the theological one. Yet the correlation is much more obviously crafted, or even contrived, than in the previous example. And that the two visions require one another is hardly a sustainable claim. For one thing, cultures do have elaborate anthropologies without any notion of God. Non-theist Buddhism can again provide the appropriate example. For another thing, even Christian history shows wide fluctuation in reverence for human instinctuality. Protestant emphasis on fallen humanity and Catholic Jansenist tendencies deprecate the human condition even while still worshipping the Creator God of Judeo-Christianity. If belief in a good God can affirm human instinctuality, belief in the same God as governor, judge, and unrelenting chastiser can also sustain hostility toward one's body. While Browning would argue that the nature of God determines a particular ethical understanding of humankind, the pundit would suggest rather that people create God in their own image and likeness.

Theology Does not Determine Ethics

An important difficulty in Browning's argument is its basic ambiguity. It is not clear if talk is of God or of how various religious movements might conceive God. It is not clear whether at stake is the nature or a notion of God. The difference between the two was discussed in Chapter Two.

If at stake is a notion of God, then the pundit's comment carries the day, and a correlation between an understanding of God and of human ethics is not surprising at all. Such correlation hardly attests that theology determines ethics. Such correlation is no evidence that the ethical position is grounded in God.

And if at stake is the nature of God, another more sure argument can be mounted. Granted the classical understanding of God, as recounted in Chapter Two, it follows that the nature of God does not necessitate the nature of humankind. This is to say that God could have chosen to make "humanity" other than what it actually is. Or, said more precisely, humanity as it is, is a contingent vis-à-vis God. Humanity is but one among an infinity of possible creations, all of which would be compatible with God and all of which could well exist. Since the link between divinity and humanity is not necessity but contingency, one cannot deduce the nature of humanity from the nature of God. That is, no one anthropology with its inherent ethical requirements follows simply because God is what God is. Rather, humanity is as it happens to be, it is as God freely chose to create it. To understand it and its inherent requirements, one must attend to it. The ethical requirements inherent in humanity, the rational core of morality, must be known from human nature itself and not from consideration of God. This argument appears definitive: a concrete ethics cannot be derived from the nature of God.

Moreover, at least on the classical understanding, we do not know what God is. What we do know of God is what we extrapolate from our experience in a contingent world, which only happens to exist as God happened to create it. So our understanding about what this world is, about how it functions and how we should function in it, though couched in terms of the Divine Creator and in metaphors of divine governance and providence, is nothing more than our understanding of this world as it happens to be and as we have thus far come to understand it.

That argument cannot be faulted in that it, too, relies, not on the nature, but on some notion of God. For it does not claim to say what God is. It gives no categorical content to its talk of God. For it "God" is a purely heuristic notion (Helminiak, 1987c, Chapter 5). That argument merely insists that there must be ultimate explanation and names whatever that is, "God." The account of God in classical theology still seems to represent the best available opinion of the day.

Ethics Determines Theology

Other evidence in Browning's text—namely, his own methodology in other places—confirms that theology does not determine ethics but, for Browning, just the reverse. Browning invokes an understanding of ethics, the rational core of morality, to criticize metaphors of ultimacy, including metaphors of God. Browning's discussion of mysticism provides an example.

Again following Niebuhr, Browning argues that "monistically oriented forms of mysticism" are inadequate. Their flaw is their "turning the inner self into a sacred reality and then identifying and merging this self with the divine itself." The criticism "is primarily a moral critique: monism minimizes the sense of individuality prerequisite to the possibility of moral action. . . . In addition, monistic mysticisms tend to minimize the reality of evil and thereby lower one's sense that there are any really serious problems in the world that need to be addressed." To be preferred is a mysticism that leaves room for "a transcendent God and an individuated person in a finite and differentiated world" (88).

Note that the brunt of the criticism comes from an understanding of the requirements of ethics. Adequacy to ethics is the criterion of metaphors of ultimacy, including metaphors of the divine, incorporated in notions of mysticism. To wit, a mysticism that loses the self in the divine and so minimizes individual responsibility is unacceptable.

My point is not to fault Niebuhr's and Browning's conclusion. Their conclusion is sound. Nor do I fault their way of reaching that conclusion. I argue similarly in criticizing Ken Wilber's position in Chapter Four—if not from an ethical concern there but from an epistemological one, still, however, on the basis of rationality, that is, consistency of argument. The point is that Browning's discussion is within the philosophic, not the theist, viewpoint. For Browning, as for myself, the priority of the philosophic viewpoint constrains even theist belief. But Browning is not always clear about this matter.

When Browning turns specifically to criticizing metaphors of ultimacy, his criterion is again ethical. The criterion is whether or not the metaphors are open to human freedom and responsibility, the requisites of ethical behavior. The metaphors of Freud and Skinner and, supposedly, even those in the self-actualizing theories of humanistic psychology, fall short on this score. "In contrast to these psychologies, the metaphors of ultimacy of the Christian tradition explicitly allow for and promote understandings of human freedom and agency." "Within the Christian tradition the major models for the representation of God as the ultimate context of experience tend to portray God as compatible with the possibility of freedom on the part of human beings" (134). Evidently, the requisites of the rational core of morality validate or disqualify even the metaphors of God in the Judeo-Christian tradition. For Browning, ethics determines theology.

The Appeal of the "Process God"

So much is that the case that, without clearly expressing his opinion, Browning seems to prefer the God of process theology. He seems to agree with Reinhold Niebuhr and William James in their support of Charles Hartshorne's "neo-classical understanding of God." The concern is to save human freedom at any cost, even at the cost of qualifying divine omnipotence, perfection, and infinity. So there is a movement against "the classical metaphysical tradition," caricatured in this way: "so concerned to protect God's aseity (God's self-caused nature) that it envisioned God as beyond all influence from the finite world, as eternal in all respects, as omnipotent in all respects, and as beyond both enjoying and suffering"

(134). To be preferred is a God that can be "*affected* by the events of the world, open to the subjectivity and initiatives of humans." Such a God is "consistent with the popular piety of the Judeo-Christian tradition" (135).

Such an understanding of God is, indeed, compatible with popular piety. The Bible itself presents images of God as angry or sad, repenting of decisions or anguished over human infidelity. If one would take these images literally, one must conclude that God does change. Yet taken equally uncritically, other texts seem to make the opposite, metaphysical point. Malachi 3:6 reads, "I the Lord do not change." And James 1:17 speaks of "the Father of lights, with whom there is no variation or shadow due to change."

How does one reconcile those differences in biblical statement? Distinguish between a popular, pious, rhetorical, metaphorical, inspirational, or descriptive statement, on the one hand, and a systematic, scientific, metaphysical, or explanatory statement, on the other (Helminiak, 1986d, pp. 47–64, 87–90). If the concern is to accord with popular piety and to speak so as to foster devotion, one should realize that one is about the task of preaching, a valuable, important, and noble task. Nonetheless, if one's task is to answer critical questions and to present a consistent account of theist belief, one must resign oneself to pursuing more and more technical, systematic, conceptualization and formulation. One must begin doing theology.

Doing theology, one runs the risk that one's technically formulated statements will be ripped from their systematic context and preached as "the latest thing" to a baffled and bored congregation. Or else, as is more likely in our day, when awareness of the difference between rhetoric and science is lost and even proscribed from religion, the systematic formulas of theology will be rejected outright as misleading nonsense. Such, it seems, has been the fate of the classical understanding of God, discredited because it does not square with the metaphors of the Bible and of preachers. Yet those technical formulations were not meant to be popular fare. Taken for what they are, they provide a perfectly coherent account of traditional Judeo-Christian belief about God, including the inviolability of human freedom in the face of an omnipotent, unchanging, and concerned God (Lonergan, 1971).

In contrast, the God of process theology, I believe, entails an inherent self-contradiction. When even God is changing in response to human initiative, nowhere is there an absolute against which the movement of change can be judged. On these terms, it is impossible to effect a coherent and comprehensive account, for the criterion of adequacy is a moving target. If process, change, is the ultimate constant, any change can be deemed good. Then "goodness" really means nothing. Then is the goodness, the value, of a coherent account also unimportant? Is it merely the preoccupation of a particular phase or era? If so, process theology as a performed enterprise is in conflict with process theology as an intellectual enterprise. Process theology's enacted attempt to construct a coherent and comprehensive system conflicts with its theoretical presuppositions that discredit and, indeed, logically preclude such a thing. Praxis contradicts theory. And if coherent explanation is not merely the preoccupation of a particular phase or era, some perduring criterion of ultimate truth and good must somehow still be at work. Then an unchanging absolute, something like the classical God, must still be in the picture.

Thus, the project of process theology seems inherently doomed. It depends on human thinkers subject to the requirements of rational discourse—intelligence, reasonableness, logical coherence. Built into the structure of the human mind, these are real absolutes with universal implication and validity. Yet process theology seeks to create a coherent system of thought free from the constraints of an absolute.

Of course, that absolute could be the very structures that guide the process and assure its continued unfolding—much like the normative, four-level structure of open-ended, dynamic consciousness in Lonergan's (1957, 1967a, 1972) analysis. But if that is the case, if the normative is already built into the human process, why even bring God into the discussion? Evidently, just to satisfy the requirements of religious belief. But in this case, if the intended theoretical understanding of that God is to be in ultimate harmony with religious belief, the theoretical understanding must make sense; it must withstand criticism; it must respect the requirements of rational discourse. Then we are right back to extrapolating the *classical* understanding of God on the analogy of normative, dynamic, human spirit (Helminiak, 1987c, Chapter 5).

Alternatively, that supposed, built-in normativity might be conceived as constraining both the universe and God. Then, from within the process, as it were, it would supposedly guide the process of both a changing God and a changing universe. But in this case, the ultimacy that is usually attributed to God has merely been shifted to another function, which itself impinges on God. That is to say, this supposed, built-in normativity now functions as the classical conception of God, and the suggestion that God changes is really a sleight of hand. In addition, this construal of the matter is already starting down the path of infinite regress.

Moreover, that construal of the matter suffers from picture thinking. It imagines God as *outside* the universe or imagines a normative structure as *inside* the process. Use of imagination rather than understanding, use of images rather than insight and concept—reliance on psychic rather than spiritual functions (Helminiak, 1996a)—precludes any possible intellectual solution to the matter. (More on this general issue again and again below.)

Finally, howsoever the supposed guiding principle of the process is conceived, the question about its very existence and the existence of the process—the question that defines the theist viewpoint—still remains to be answered.

One does not teach physics in grade school as one does in college. In grade school, examples, stories, and metaphors elicit interest, foster enthusiasm, and suggest explanation: electricity is like water running through a pipe. In college, one presumes interest, commitment, and requisite learning; and Maxwell's equations precisely express hard-won and pure understanding about electricity. No one faults theoretical physicists because they are not engineers or mechanics nor because most of the population really hasn't a clue what they're talking about. Yet religionists reject theoretical formulations because they do not meet the immediate needs of the people in the pew. If metaphor is to be the coinage of theology and ability to portray life's significance in popular terms, its criterion, then theology is but sophisticated preaching (Smart, 1997), and there will be no coherent ultimate explanation of things, no science in the realm of the humanities. How could there be? The option has been for rhetoric, not science. Then matters must be settled in a loosely defined conversation wherein the identity of the differing voices remains unclear, the criterion of judgment is unknown, and the arbiter goes unnamed.

All that represents, of course, the inadequacy inherent in Browning's methodology, and his emphasis on metaphors is at the heart of the matter. All that also bespeaks, I believe, a major shortcoming of process theology, but this matter of process theology is too big to pursue further here.

Human Requirements Determine the Nature of God

The point here is that, for Browning and for the theologians he follows, concern about human requirements for ethics determines even the supposed nature of God. According to Browning's *modus operandi*, human realities evaluate the supposed divine. The rational core of ethics judges the adequacy of metaphors—and whole theories—about God.

Browning is explicit about the matter. He writes, "The first and most obvious question to raise about any metaphor of ultimacy is this: Does it provide for the possibility of the freedom and self-transcendence which are the presuppositions for the possibility of mutuality?" (132). A reasoned understanding of ethics is the criterion. "Mutuality is the core of morality, and this is true without reference to the justifications of religio-cultural paradigms or deep metaphors" (138).

Evidently, Browning's adjudication of metaphors of human ultimacy moves within what I call the philosophic viewpoint. Although Browning may speak in terms of "religion" and call his project "theological," determination of the ethics that must govern human life prescribes an understanding of God, and not vice versa. This matter is not a matter of God—according to Browning's own practice and statement. This matter does not move within the theist viewpoint. For as Browning seems here to agree, ethics is essentially a matter of human authenticity and its task is to spell out the implications of authenticity in particular cases. And human authenticity does not depend on belief in or metaphors of God. Here is a major point of consensus.

A Fluid Presentation

In fact, Browning's presentation shifts back and forth. Now it appeals to God and theology; now, to the rational core of morality. This back and forth flow may well be part of the intended conversation. But on my analysis, the shifting of positions occurs because of a confusion about the relationship of theology and ethics. Browning seems to want to identify the two, giving ethical requirements the authority of God or, alternatively, seeing moral responsibility as the call of God and the meaning of belief in God.

I wonder if his Protestant roots do not partially explain this state of affairs. For classical Protestantism emphasizes that God's revealed word imposes itself on a fallen, wholly corrupt, and helpless humanity, supposedly incapable of discerning the good. I wonder if the Reformation debates on human justification are not coming back to haunt us in the postmodern crisis of interdisciplinary studies. For unless one can allow the validity of a merely human understanding of human nature, the human sciences can have no legitimacy in dealing normatively with meanings and values.

When one identifies theology and ethics, ethical claims are called "religious." Then the modern psychologies are exposed for being religion in the guise of science. And since religion is construed in terms of God, the religions that treat of God can assume some special authority in the ethical discussion. So an exegesis of the Bible provides the argument that settles the debate. Yet the whole time an understanding of the rational core of morality is also supposedly controlling the discussion. The whole affair is confusing. Despite itself, it still appears to be the standard fare of religion versus science and secularity.

On my understanding and in my terminology, what Browning does is not theology at all. Browning's problematic has nothing explicitly to do with God; it does not move within the theist viewpoint. Rather, the whole discussion is among possible equals, all operating within the philosophic viewpoint. In this case, what is telling is one's commitment to authenticity, the depth of one's analysis, and the cogency of one's arguments. This alternative approach respects the process of conversation or dialogue that Browning so meticulously exemplified, but this approach also clarifies any ambiguity as to what is going on. This approach also seems to give all considerations their due, including eventually even theism. So this approach via spirituality, this analysis of higher viewpoints, recommends itself as methodologically more adequate.

The Rational Core of Morality

A sixth consideration is the rational core of morality. I have been arguing that Browning's presentation is a matter of the philosophic viewpoint. Not theist belief in God nor Christian belief in Trinity, Christ, and Grace, but human concern for the true and the good is the telling thing. This construal of the matter suggests another solution to Browning's ethical concern. For the philosophic viewpoint is already defined by what Browning calls the rational core of morality. And it is not mutuality but authenticity.

Browning's appeal to mutuality as the rational core of morality seems to derive from the Judeo-Christian teaching about neighbor-love. Within some strains of this tradition, altruism as opposed to selfishness is the touchstone of all moral decisions. Important arguments can demonstrate the necessity of mutuality for the possibility of society. That there be honor even among thieves is necessary so that the band hold together.

But that position does not appear to be fully adequate. Emphasis on mutuality seems to focus on maintenance of a structured and functioning society. But this emphasis does not readily allow for transformation of society and is weak in highlighting the human thrust toward self-transcendence. Moreover, an ethics built on mutuality highlights concern about you and me, about them and us. The dichotomy of selfishness and altruism is inherent in this conceptualization. I submit that this dichotomy is false. As Aristotle argued in his *Ethics* (VIII, 5, 1157a 16ff, IX, 4, 1166b 2ff, IX, 8, 1169a 12ff), not whether a thing benefits you or me but whether it is right—this is the ultimate criterion of ethical decision making (Lonergan, 1967c, p. 24).

Besides, issues of right and wrong often transcend the category of mutuality. Even Mahatma Gandhi admitted that his policy of non-violence in India was successful only because the British are a civilized people. Liberation movements in South Africa learned Gandhi's wisdom by bloody experience and then adopted violent and destructive means to advance their just cause. Marcus Aurelius pursued discussion with the barbarian invaders of the Roman Empire until it became apparent they were impervious to reason. Then he, the paragon of Stoic virtue of his day, reluctantly but ruthlessly slaughtered the barbarians for the sake of civilization. Christian just-war theories and theories of self-defense attempt to formulate principles that apply in such cases.

Sometimes doing right and furthering the good requires offense to, or even destruction of, the other. The good sometimes requires doing what, except in the most idealistic and unrealistic of scenarios, you would never want the other to do unto you.

Besides, many moral issues do not turn primarily on relationship with others but on anguished questions about choice among an array of seemingly legitimate and equally urgent options—environmental concerns versus business concerns, the universal availability of medical attention versus the soaring costs of medical technology, the frightening risks attendant to a nuclear energy industry already in place versus the increasing world-wide demand for readily available energy. The more concern turns from individual to social ethics, the more surely does the supposed conflict between selfishness and altruism become irrelevant.

So alongside the Golden Rule are other formulations of the rational core of morality. Thomas Aquinas held that the ultimate moral principle is, Do good and avoid evil. Bernard Lonergan, explicating Aquinas, summarizes the rational core of morality in one word: authenticity. Four transcendental precepts specify authenticity: Be attentive, Be intelligent, Be reasonable, Be responsible.

Virtue versus Moral Principles

No doubt, talk of authenticity appears very abstract. The notion is merely heuristic. It does not specify what is to be done but how one is to do whatever one does. As a result, this notion applies to, and is valid in, every possible human situation. Authenticity certainly qualifies as a "rational" core of morality, especially when formulated in terms of the four transcendental precepts, for the notion results from an analysis of human consciousness or spirit and does not, in contrast, appeal to God or religion. Indeed, this notion seems to distill the core of ethical teaching fostered by a wide range of religious traditions. Authenticity has neither a selfish nor an altruistic emphasis; it is not a solipsistic nor an externalistic notion (Helminiak, 1996a, pp. 106–110; 1996b; 1996c). Authenticity implies commitment to the pursuit of objective truth and goodness, so it entails ethical concern that necessarily includes but also transcends both self and other. The power of this notion is that it speaks of the human subject him- or herself. It specifies what a human being is to be and only derivatively specifies what behavior is required. This notion determines an aretaic ethics, that is, an ethics built on the centrality of human virtue.

The contrast is Browning's focus on mutuality. It entails certain prescriptions of required behavior. It is the core of a proposed deontic ethics, that is, an ethics built on fundamental rules or principles of behavior.

Browning is well aware of the debate over an aretaic versus a deontic ethics. He rightly notes that the two approaches are not necessarily opposed to one another. Indeed, in practice an aretaic ethics needs formulated ethical principles to help nurture virtuous people of good conscience throughout their formative years. Reciprocally, a deontic ethics depends on virtuous people to formulate its ethical principles in the first place. Browning is also aware of Alasdair MacIntyre's (1984) work, a seemingly conclusive argument that the attempt to formulate ethics deontically is futile. And Browning knows full well "that no principle can ever exhaust what is meant by virtue, character, or the good person" (11). Still, he would analyze the modern psychologies, which carry implicit understandings of the good person, on the basis of an ethics of moral principles. The point is to note the consequences of this option.

Spirituality and Ethics

My emphasis on authenticity and Browning's on mutuality, usefully highlight the difference between what I call spirituality and what is generally known as ethics. Spirituality is concerned about the person and his or her openness to self-transcendence. In contrast, ethics would specify the behaviors that a good person should perform. The deontic approach to ethics fits this conception of ethics well, but when the aretaic approach enters the picture, spirituality can start looking like ethics (Helminiak, 1996a, pp. 235–236). It becomes harder to specify precisely where the one ends and the other begins, for, indeed, ethics flows naturally from spirituality.

On my understanding, spirituality presents a general picture. It specifies what a human being is and how one ought ideally to function. To this extent spirituality is really a philosophical anthropology, an understanding of the human being. Anthropology in this case is called "spirituality" simply because it insists on self-transcending authenticity as essential to all human concerns and so involves itself with what religious traditions of various kinds have implied by the term "spirituality." In contrast, ethics becomes more specific and focuses on behaviors. It attempts to spell out the implication of authenticity for action in concrete cases. Thus, ethics helps people to make authentic decisions, to further their authenticity, as they determine their lives in a particular personal, historical, social, and environmental context.

Said in Browning's terminology, spirituality is concerned with the *ordo bonorum*, the explication of all that constitutes humanity and would ideally allow human life to unfold at its best (157–159, 229). And ethics is concerned with the *ordo caritatis* or with some other way of determining which of the ideally desired goods might be responsibly pursued in a specific, concrete case (153, 156–157, 229). Since Browning allows that psychology does have a role in spelling out the *ordo bonorum*, his understanding seems also to allow that at some point the disciplines of psychology and spirituality may coincide.

However, on my understanding, authenticity remains always at center stage. Responsibility of choice is always the focal issue. So an aretaic, not a deontic ethics, is at stake. Then, the rational core of ethics coincides with the determinative of spirituality: authenticity. Ethics and spirituality—or psychology within the philosophic viewpoint—both have the same core because both, as academic human disciplines, intend contributions to personal integration and growth. Accordingly, both must respect the human essential, the call to authenticity. But ethics differs from spirituality in going further, indicating the lived concrete implications of authenticity, which spirituality only thematizes within a broad explanatory account of the human being.

In any case, Browning opts for a deontic ethics and posits mutuality as its first principle. In light of what has been said thus far, this option must certainly be mistaken. Just as the conscious subject is the logical presupposition of any thought, so the authentic subject is the logical presupposition of a moral act. So a logical priority falls to the aretaic approach.

A Reevaluation of the Modern Psychologies

Emphasis on authenticity, rather than on mutuality, results in different judgments about the psychologies that Browning analyzed.

Browning is rather mild in his criticism of Freud's ethical position. Although "its cautious character strips it of the kind of fully reversible thinking that would lead one to take initiatives" (139), Browning writes, "Freud's cautious mutuality in the sense of reciprocal respect begins to approach the fully reversible thinking that exhibits the rational core of morality" (131). But concern for dynamic human spirit and authenticity suggests a harsher judgment. Freud's conception seems to apply to some static system of social interaction. His version of conscience, superego, is but the internalized expectations of the status quo. Freud's understanding of the human being is fully limited to the positivist viewpoint (Helminiak, 1996a, pp. 223–232). Still, on the criterion of mutuality, his position scores at least a passing grade. Evidently, Browning's analysis has missed something important.

A similar assessment must be made of Browning's treatment of Erikson and Kohut. Because their positions explicitly advocate a reciprocity between generations and, as a result, advocate some form of selflessness, Browning rates these psychologies as the most adequate. Yet Browning's criterion is still confounded with the false dichotomy between altruism and selfishness. And this criterion undervalues the ethical importance of the human thrust toward self-transcendence. This thrust discredits any mere maintenance of the status quo. The human thrust toward self-transcendence implies transformation of social relationships and envisages the emergence of new social orders. These key ethical concerns are weak in these psychological theorists, but they easily slip by Browning's criticism.

My own research on adulthood (Helminiak, 1994a) can highlight that weakness in Erikson's psychosocial theory of human development. Erikson provides only one stage to cover the long expanse of adult life. That stage is defined by the "crisis," generativity versus stagnation. While Erikson is clear that generativity need not involve biological parenthood, almost universally he defines generativity in terms of concern for the upcoming generation. Thus, this stage can begin in late adolescence or early adulthood, the usual childbearing age, and supposedly characterizes the remainder of adulthood, until old age. Commentators vary in opinion about what chronological age this "crisis" characterizes. Regardless of which chronological age is suggested, this characterization seems to overlook important experiences of middle adulthood. At that point in life the raised, schooled, experienced, and established adult is on the leading edge of society's move through history. At that point in life adults often seem plagued by bigger questions like these: What is life all about? What makes life worth the effort? Then concern focuses not primarily on the upcoming generation but on oneself and one's own generation. Then concern is to transform these and thereby, perhaps, to influence one's world and so the upcoming generation. Then this concern, transformation, subsumes and reworks the concern of early adulthood, generativity. Erikson's stages miss the self-and-society-transcending moment open to the experienced adult. Only in his analysis of Dr. Isak Borg, from Ingmar Bergman's film, *Wild Strawberries*, have I found focused mention in Erikson's writings of this critical human issue (Erikson, 1978). So perhaps the ongoing project of adulthood involves at least two "crises": the concern of early adulthood, generativity versus self-absorption, and the concern of midlife, transformation versus stagnation.[2]

Emphasis simply on mutuality, operative in Browning and also, evidently, in Erikson, can overlook the transforming dynamism essential to human living, the need for authenticity.

By the same token, Browning's harsh assessment of the humanists' emphasis on self-actualization needs to be reconsidered. Browning's criticism stems from concern about selfishness and altruism—that same bugaboo, again. If the self in question is understood as the human being, endowed with dynamic spirit, inherently geared toward the fullness of truth and goodness, then, self-actualization must seem the most adequate emphasis among the modern psychologies (Helminiak, 1996a, 108–109). It alone takes into explicit account the intrinsic human inclination ever to pursue what is beyond on a path of cumulative unfolding. Reading Carl Rogers, Abraham Maslow, Gordon Allport, Viktor Frankl, and Eric Fromm, I myself have no difficulty whatsoever finding this same emphasis on page after page. Granted, the formulations are not always as clear and precise as one would find in scholars trained in ethics or religious studies. There is certainly room for correction and for explicit emphasis on this pivotal issue. But on

---

2. I am grateful to Nancy Schweers of San Antonio for this conceptualization of the matter.

my reading Browning himself did not squarely hit the pivotal issue, whereas, again on my reading, the humanists are deliberating calling for authenticity—not only in the existential, but also in Lonergan's, sense. The humanists are already engaged in the academic discipline that I call spirituality.

By way of example, consider Joseph Campbell's famous dictum, "Follow your bliss." Though Campbell, a student of Carl Jung, is not a humanistic psychologist, his humanism could be equally criticized for advancing the supposed egocentric or individualistic culture of our day. But what does Campbell's dictum really mean? A disciple of his interprets the matter as follows:

> This means to pursue that which inspires one with a sense of wonder and connectedness, full of the rapture of life. It doesn't mean pursuing simply materialistic happiness or middle-class (even academic-class) fulfillment, though it may incidentally result in those. Bliss is a technical term in Buddhism, *ananda*, for being enraptured in enlightened wonder and living in harmony with truth and being. This doesn't mean being narcissistic in the sense of being concerned only with one's own happiness and satisfaction, though it does mean following one's own path and not looking to "what other people think" for the measure of one's success. It means paying attention to what life is telling one one ought to be doing, paying attention to the promptings of one's soul, to the urgings of compassion, and to one's sense of being part of the grand process of life. (Johnson, 1992, pp. xii–xiii)

While some might hear in "Follow your bliss" only an invitation to selfishness, obviously it is nothing other than an invitation to authenticity.

Inspired by a religious tradition, Browning proposed mutuality as the rational core of morality. Relying on an analysis of human consciousness, the present account suggests, rather, authenticity. This difference has important implications for the delineation and interrelationship of the disciplines, ethics and spirituality. This difference also results in very different assessments of the adequacy of some modern psychologies.

Religion and Science: Interpretation and Explanation

A seventh and final consideration addresses head-on the relationship of religion and science. Browning presupposes a position more or less common to a number of important theorists. He lists Ian Barbour, Ludwig Wittgenstein (6), Paul Tillich, Reinhold Niebuhr, Malcolm Jeeves, David Myers, and David Tracy (12–15). This position is Wilhelm Dilthey's distinction between the *Naturwissenschaften* (natural sciences) and the *Geisteswissenschaften* (human sciences), built on Max Weber's distinction between *Erklärung* (explanation) and *Verstehen* (interpretation) (Palmer, 1969). The suggestion is that religion deals with the meaning or significance of life, while science limits itself to the explanation of observed data. Religion is interpretative, and science is explanatory.

However, as Browning argues so well, the modern psychologies also propose interpretations of the significance of life, so they are implicitly acting like religions. In this state of affairs, if the psychologies be taken seriously, they must be allowed to speak their piece. So an interdisciplinary critical conversation is to settle the differences. I have already summarized that conversation as Browning presents it and have also provided significant criticism of it. That approach appears to be wanting. For we were never sure how the final judgment was made; the involvement of issues about God, Christ, and "religious" authority significantly muddied the discussion; and the nomination of mutuality as the supposed rational core of ethics did not seem to hold.

Here, discussion of the interdisciplinary methodology that Browning represents goes one step further. Here, further analysis intends to expose the flaw in Browning's presentation at a deeper level. If Browning's attempt at a critical conversation proved inadequate, a major reason is that its presupposition seems mistaken. That presupposition is precisely the above-noted, longstanding, and widely held distinction between science and religion as explanatory and interpretative.

Criticism of Browning continues to be criticism of a commonly accepted position. The criticism is focused on Browning merely because he so effectively formulated an application of this position. Summarizing those other theorists and specifying that distinction between interpretation and explanation, Browning suggests that religion or theology differs from science on two scores: religion deals, first, with "different kinds of questions" and, second, with "different ranges of human experience" (13). The different kinds of questions are precisely questions for explanation and for interpretation.

Not a Matter of Further Data

Let attention first turn to that second difference. It relates to the first, for supposedly the different ranges of experience provoke the different kinds of questions. These different ranges of experience mean different sets of data. Supposedly, the sciences handle "discrete and controlled empirical data" while religion handles "larger networks of human experience which make up the ongoing flow of human life" (13). It is not necessary here to attempt and clarify what these "larger networks" might be—or even what the supposedly contrasting "discrete and controlled empirical data" might be—for the matter comes back once again to the same, one contrast: interpretations about life versus explanation. The point here is to note and quickly treat an initial difference in my construal of the matter.

In Chapter Two I argued at length that, if human studies are at stake throughout, there is no increase in available data as one moves from positivist to philosophic to theist and to theotic considerations. One and the same reality, one and the same set of data to be understood, is available throughout. Only the breadth of understanding that one is willing to bring to these data changes as one moves up the system of explanatory viewpoints.

For example, a traditional Freudian analyst will be concerned about the meanings and values that poignantly structure the client's life. Such concern is necessary if the analyst would help the client alter those meanings and values and "adjust." Though treating spiritual realities, meanings and values, or visions and virtues, or beliefs and ethics—but inadequately!—such treatment moves within the positivist viewpoint. But a humanist psychologist might ask whether the meanings and values required by adjustment to the current society are really something good. No new meanings and values in the client and in society, but only a broader consideration about them, shifts the focus of understanding from adjustment to authenticity. No new poignant struggle in the client, but only a different understanding of it, suggests the struggle might be about authenticity, not adjustment. Now treatment moves within the philosophic viewpoint. Still, a psychotherapist who happens to be theist might marvel at the very fact of the human experience unfolding before her or his eyes, or the client might anguish over the metaphysical question about his or her very existence. Again, no new data have entered the picture, just a broader understanding. So the believer or the client now shift toward the theist viewpoint. Finally, a person might wonder about the furthest possible implications of the client's holding authentic rather than inauthentic meanings and values. Thus, the very same data, now implicated in the process of deification, receive treatment within the theotic viewpoint.

I maintain that study of the human within the philosophic viewpoint, taking authenticity into explicit account, allows for an adequate treatment of the human phenomenon (Helminiak, 1996b). But not study within the positivist viewpoint. Nonetheless, the concern for authenticity, proper to the philosophic viewpoint, is still a vital factor in the lives of human beings studied within only the narrower positivist viewpoint—just as are the createdness that is proper to the theist viewpoint and the deification that is proper to the theotic viewpoint. The data remain one and the same. Only the explanatory viewpoint from which they are considered changes. This identity of data is one important source of possible unity among all scientific study of the human.

Interpretation versus Explanation

If that understanding of the matter is correct, Browning's talk about broader ranges of human experience does not accurately imply different data sets. Rather, this talk must be but another way to attempt and specify the different kinds of questions at stake. This talk is just a way of insisting yet again that religious questions deal with interpretation and scientific questions with explanation. The suggestion is that interpretation is a realm of human understanding different from, or beyond, explanation. And that supposed realm entails the supposed broader range of human experience. Thus, attention to ranges of human experience directs attention back to talk of the contrast between interpretation and explanation. Evidently, the real issue is about interpretation versus explanation. So our discussion reverts back to it.

Then, this discussion needs a better fix on what constitutes "interpretation" in Browning's account. Relying on Tillich, Browning explains that the specific task of theology is to deal with "the question of the significance and meaning" of life (13). To interpret is to determine the significance of things. So this appears to be the argument: while science explains things, religion tells the significance of things for us.

As a clue in this matter, note that talk of *meaning* as constitutive of human experience can be ambiguous. Most talk about the meaning of life or about finding meaning in life refers to the *significance* or import that life may hold. In contrast, my frequent reference to "meanings and values" as determinative of human experience takes meaning in a restrictively cognitive sense. Thus, in the cognitive sense, meanings parallel credo, vision, beliefs, understandings. But when in general usage meaning means significance, it actually includes both meanings and values in my sense of the term. In addition to meanings, significance also includes commitment, virtue, ethics, evaluations, the second elements in that list of pairs that I use in parallel to "meanings and values." Meaning as significance includes both cognitions and volitions. This particular ambiguity supports the impression that religion cannot be dealt with scientifically, cannot be dealt with consistently and coherently. For in this case meaning means meaning for me or for you or for an innumerable number of different referents.

Common Sense versus Theory, Description versus Explanation

Since Weber and Dilthey, it has commonly been accepted that there are two ways of approaching things: interpretation and explanation. These two ways appear to parallel what Lonergan (1972, pp. 81–99) also distinguishes—not as interpretation and explanation, but rather as description and explanation.

According to Lonergan's usage, "description" depends on a commonsense mentality, and "explanation" depends on a systematic or theoretic mentality. Elsewhere I have spoken of these as the functional and the ontological mentalities (Helminiak, 1986d, pp. 45–55, 87–90, 284 n. 21). Common sense understands things insofar as they relate to us. Common sense is a *quoad nos* affair. It

expresses itself in description. That is, it expresses itself—in metaphors! And in images, contrasts, stories, repetition, emotional appeal. It is wrought with paradoxes—like "Look before you leap" but
"Those who hesitate are lost"—which confound simplistic thinking
and provoke deeper consideration. Precisely such paradox is the
cornerstone of Ken Wilber's integral paradigm, discussed in Chapter Four. Common sense uses all the tricks in the rhetorician's bag
to try in any way to get its message across. In contrast, the systematic or scientific or theoretic mentality understands things by relating them to one another. Systematics is a *quoad se* affair. It deals
in explanation. Some examples will help.

When I say, "It's hot in this room," what I really mean is, "I
feel hot." I am really relating the heat of the room to my own
feelings. In general, such announcement of feelings carries some
validity. Unless I have a fever or suffer some other extenuating
circumstance, my feeling hot does say something about the heat in
the room. This is to say, to contrast common sense with theory,
description with explanation, is not to deny a qualified validity to
common sense and its descriptions. However, I could also check the
thermometer and say, "It's eighty-eight degrees in this room." This
formulation might be expressing the very same reality, but the
manner of understanding and conceiving it are different. This time,
the matter depends, not on how the room's heat relates to me, but
on how a column of mercury in a small, graduated cylinder responds to the thermal energy in the room. Here, reality is expressed by relating aspects of it to one another. Here, a new measure
of precision and constancy is introduced. Here, a measure of heat
is expressed apart from my wishes, feelings, regrets, or delights.
Here is an expression of reality significantly independent of me.

Feeling hot is a matter of common sense and descriptive
understanding; it relates things to myself. Citing a temperature is
a matter of systematic or theoretic or explanatory understanding;
it relates things to one another.

Again, my car is a vehicle I use to get from place to place. My
car plays an important role in the overall scheme of my life's purposes. The convenience of a car requires that I have money to fuel,
repair, and insure the car, that I have the key to get it started, that
I know how to use it, and that I have a licence that allows me to
drive. All these considerations express the *meaning* of the car *for
me*. They express the car's significance. They emerge from a

commonsense mentality. Now, my mechanics view my car in a very different way. Apart from my car's importance to the maintenance of their income and their own standard of living, they also understand my car in a more explanatory way. Not just a means of transportation, my car is an ingenious combination of parts and intricate mechanisms that relate in precise ways to effect the intended functioning. While I approach my car in a descriptive mode, my mechanics approach it in an explanatory mode.

Here is another example from the realm of biology: "If a biologist takes his young son to the zoo and both pause to look at a giraffe, the boy will wonder whether it bites or kicks, but the father will see another manner in which skeletal, locomotive, digestive, vascular, and nervous systems combine and interlock" (Lonergan, 1972, pp. 82–83).

One can take this matter even further. For example, consider a circle, and attempt to specify what makes it a circle. I have presented this exercise in detail elsewhere (Helminiak, 1996a, Chapter 5). You could express how the circle appears to you, how it affects your senses. That is, you can *describe* the circle as something flat and equally round on all sides. Or else you could take another tack. You could invoke the formula, $C = 2\pi r$, to express with universally valid precision the inherent intelligibility of any circle everywhere and always in the Euclidean world. Rather than describing, you could cite a formula and *explain* circularness.

In the first case you have description; in the second, explanation. The key to explanation in its purest achievement is what David Hilbert called "implicit definition" (Lonergan, 1957, pp. 12–13). It depends on having grasped the essence of some matter and having expressed that essence with a set of terms nested in a particular interrelationship. The terms define the relations and the relations define the terms, and both terms and relations are grounded in insight into the matter. So, for example, in the equation for a circle, C and r are defined by a relationship of 2π. The relationship specifies the terms; given this relationship, they can be nothing other than circumference (C) and radius (r). Conversely, this precise relationship (2π) only applies when a circumference (C) and a radius (r) are in question. So the terms also specify the relationship. Terms and relations codetermine one another, and understanding this fact makes the formula lucid. To achieve such precise accounting of things is the epitome of science; this is explanation.

Religion as Common Sense

Now to get to the point. Browning's understanding of religion as expressing the significance of things for us seems definitively to relegate religion to the realm of common sense—in Lonergan's technical sense of the term. On this understanding only natural science could be scientific, systematic, explanatory, and function in the theoretic mode. Religion or theology would always function descriptively, suggestively, metaphorically, in the mode of common sense. This is precisely also the position that Ken Wilber takes, as discussed in Chapter Four. Then, no wonder there would be an unbridgeable divide between science and religion. It is not that science and religion are really dealing with different kinds of questions and different ranges of human experience. They are, rather, merely approaching experience with different modes of understanding—commonsense versus theoretic, or functional versus ontological.

Throughout, Browning and Wilber understand religion/theology as a commonsense affair—a matter of metaphors, images, symbols, stories, myths, and inspirational accounts, a mode of thinking that understands things by relating them to ourselves. Indeed, Browning and Wilber almost seem unaware of any other possibility. Browning portrays even science in terms of metaphors and models. He writes, for example, "Disciplines that are designed to account for highly discrete ranges of observed data, such as chemistry or physics, may be able to make progress with a limited number of fairly specific metaphorical models. But disciplines such as theology that are attempting to account for experience in general must resort to a wide range of metaphors and models" (121). Wilber makes similar statements.

But metaphor and model are simply not the characteristic coinage of science. In this matter, Browning seems to rely too heavily on theorists who have not appreciated the advance from metaphor to model to systematic statement (Barbour, 1974) and who do not understand implicit definition as the precise expression of the intelligibility inherent in some reality or other. The periodic table of chemical elements is hardly a metaphor or model. Nor are Newton's or Maxwell's' or Einstein's or Heisenberg's equations. Rather, these scientific formulations represent the insightful breakthroughs that moved physics and chemistry precisely from metaphors and models into systematic, theoretic, formulation: science in the strictest sense of the term. Insofar as metaphors and models do function in the scientific enterprise, they express for lay people a popularized version, or else they represent attempts at understanding that have not yet reached explanation, that are not yet truly scientific.

In contrast to science, theology still does commonly rely on metaphors. Yet ultimately the task of theology is also that of science, to express the intelligibility of reality, "the meaning of life." Theology is just dealing with more difficult questions. Contrary to popular parlance, theology is the "hard science." It still looks for the breakthrough that will result in systematic formulation, implicit definition. But the goal of theology, just like that of natural science, is to propose a precise, coherent, and accurate understanding of things. If theology were to achieve its goal, it would, like natural science, propose an explanatory account.

Contrariwise, the natural sciences, just like theology, also deal in "the significance of things." For science is both theoretical and applied. Isolation of HIV, the virus responsible for AIDS, led medical personnel, *scientists*, to speak out about its mode of transmission and its implications for personal behavior. Was it wrong for medical researchers to speak about the *significance* of HIV for the populace? Not at all, since they were legitimately sharing the fruits of their specialized research. God help us if only the religionists have the right to "interpret" such things! The horror of the AIDS pandemic would be far worse than it already is. Evidently, then, within its own realm of competence, science must also portray the significance of things.

The differentiation of religion/theology and science as interpretation and explanation, respectively, simply does not hold. This dualism rather bespeaks two different kinds of understanding, common sense and theory. Both are instances of the same thing, human understanding. Both entail operations proper to the second level of consciousness, in Lonergan's analysis. Their difference is that one understands things by relating them to us and the other understands things by relating them to one another. But on the popular level, the word "explanation" implies the achievement of greater success at understanding, and this popular usage too easily obscures the fact that common sense also represents an understanding of things.

Sort those issues out, and the supposed incommensurability between religion and science disappears. For both can be presented in a popular, commonsense, mode; and both can achieve the systematic, theoretic understanding that determines science as such. Or at least this is my claim (Helminiak, 1979, 1984b, 1986d, 1987c, 1988a, 1994a, 1996a, 1996c). If the traditionally "religious" questions can indeed be addressed systematically, then treatment of things human and divine—in addition to treatment of the physical universe—can also be science in the strictest sense of the term.

Granted that eventuality, what is then the difference between the physical sciences and the human sciences, including theology? And how do they relate? The difference is not the one between common sense and theory, between interpretation and explanation, for in the present case all the disciplines stand on equal intellectual footing as strict sciences, systematic understandings of reality. The difference is that they work within different realms of competence, determined by different presuppositional commitments. These realms can be defined within a system of higher viewpoints, as explained in Chapter Two: positivist, philosophic, theist, and theotic. And this very system of higher viewpoints accounts for their interrelationship. This system itself is an implicitly defined account (Helminiak, 1996a, pp. 78–79). It is science in the strictest sense of the term.

Theology as Systematic

However, can religion/theology really be scientific, systematic? That it can, has been the bold presupposition of this book. Contributions toward that achievement have been a system of four viewpoints that systematically interrelate questions pertinent to human studies and religion; a tripartite understanding of the human being that makes room for spirituality within strictly human studies; and an understanding of human spirit or consciousness explicated in terms of two modes and four interrelated levels. These contributions rest on what appear to be significant theoretical breakthroughs—the determination of the pivotal concepts that define the four viewpoints: correct understanding, authenticity, creation, and deification; the determination of spirit and psyche as distinct factors in human mind; and the determination of consciousness as simultaneously, concomitantly, and intrinsically both reflecting and non-reflecting and as empirical, intelligent, reasonable, and responsible. The present differentiation between common sense and theory, between description and explanation, also belongs on this list of contributions. The suggestion is that now it is possible to treat even "religious" questions scientifically, that is, within an explanatory or theoretic or systematic mode of understanding. Hopefully, the fruits of such an approach are already evident in this presentation.

Granted those contributions, many of the ambiguities that befuddle the position that Browning's presentation exemplifies can be readily clarified. The revised critical correlation is fuzzy because it is an exercise in commonsense thinking. It attempts to relate various opinions without a clear conceptual framework within which to work. When metaphors are the coinage of discussion and one wants clear and precise understanding, one must first clearly determine what the metaphors mean—and in the process, one moves into systematics. Again, sorting out the theist and theotic viewpoints from the philosophic, makes clear that Browning's ethical concern is not strictly a theological matter. Or again, Browning's interchangeable use of the terms "religion" and "theology" is now simply intolerable. His "religion" is now known to include positivist, philosophic, theist, and Christian theotic elements, and the validity that pertains to one is not the same as what pertains to the others. And the term "theology"—in contrast to preaching or "religious discourse" (cf. Smart, 1997)—now has specific meaning: the *theoretic* or *systematic* treatment of questions only about God. If "science" is to relate to "religion" (read: theism), it must be to the theoretical treatment of religion, to theology, that science relates. Then the relationship is not one of competing authorities over some one and the same subject matter. Rather, the relationship is one of differing breadths of understanding—theist versus philosophic and/ or positivist—about one and the same human phenomenon. Finally, the differentiation of spirit from psyche in one human mind allows that matters formerly assimilated to theism, like ethics and spirituality, are indeed a legitimate—nay, necessary—concern of psychologists (Helminiak, 1996a, 1996c). For psychology conceived as truly adequate to human beings entails not merely "psychobiological tendencies and needs" (12) but also spiritual ones. Moreover, the delineation of spirit as non-reflecting and reflecting and as unfolding on four levels, introduces the possibility for a highly refined treatment of the human issues that have concerned both psychology and religion.

More needs to be said about the possibility of attaining objectivity (that is, correctness) in the human sciences or *Geisteswissenschaften*. For their concern is meaning or significance, and of that, people do create their own. Apart from such objectivity, how could one really speak of science? how could one speak of a unique and valid account of things? This topic, which pervades this whole book, surfaces again in the criticism of Ken Wilber's position in the next chapter. There, the context will allow for a more convenient treatment. There, more will also be said about the possibility of a systematic spirituality and the liabilities of a merely metaphorical expression of meaning.

Review and Preview

Those seven considerations highlight ambiguities and flaws in Browning's interdisciplinary methodology:

1. Browning himself is the unnamed arbiter in his revised critical correlation;
2. authenticity is a key condition for the validity of Browning's or any person's judgments;
3. not faith in contrast to reason, nor reason in contrast to faith, but a human subject who reasons within some horizon of faith—this is what determines judgments;
4. the horizon within which Browning's analyses legitimately move is the philosophic viewpoint;
5. Browning's analyses, though called "religious," are neither Christian nor theist, if these terms are given distinctive meaning;
6. the fundamental rational core of morality is not mutuality, as the Bible-inspired "Golden Rule" might suggest, but rather authenticity, for it includes neighbor-love and much more;
7. religion/theology and science, construed as interpretation and explanation respectively, are, indeed, incommensurate disciplines—not because they deal with different questions and different ranges of data, for both are instances of the human quest for understanding about the human situation, but because so construed they confound common sense and theory, two different modes of human understanding.

Those considerations also suggest an alternative approach that might better achieve Browning's goal of relating the human sciences and (Judeo-Christian) religion. In general, there is need for a more systematically conceived discussion that is more precisely situated within its interdisciplinary context.

Two Further Issues

The call for a more systematically conceived discussion applies to two other issues: the legitimate role of metaphors and the two forms of psychology. Brief treatment of them will conclude this criticism of Browning's work.

The Importance of Metaphor

Though emphasis here has been on systematic formulation, Browning's emphasis on metaphors does have its validity. Let this acknowledgment be clearly noted. Though repeatedly I call for a systematic or scientific treatment of religion, in no way do I deny the validity of metaphors or call for a cessation of their use across the board. And of course, when I say "metaphor," I mean to infer a whole range of phenomena: symbol, myth, ritual song, poetry, proverb, paradoxical statement. Within the practice of religion these all have a legitimate and absolutely valid role. Indeed, spare me the cleric whose heart knows no poetry but who tries nonetheless to facilitate a religious service! But the topic of this book is not effective religion, at least not in the short run, so here I do not elaborate the valid use of metaphor. Rather, my argument is that there can also be a scientific treatment of religion and in this case metaphor is not appropriate.

Of course, many will deny that a precise science of religion or of the spiritual is possible; they suppose that only metaphorical speech can address these matters. While fully appreciating metaphorical speech in its commonsense usage, I challenge that supposition. The real question here is not about the validity of metaphor in religious discourse; hopefully, no one would deny it. The real question is rather about the possible validity of systematic formulation in the study of religion.

Browning's concern is the structuring and transformation of cultures. By nature culture is a commonsense affair. Culture implies the embodied and lived beliefs and values of a people. And the carriers of beliefs and values on a popular level are myths, stories, proverbs, metaphors, images, ritual—the very focus of Browning's analysis and the coinage of common sense.

Indeed, the differentiation of psyche and spirit makes clear why myth and metaphor are the structures of culture. Whereas systematic formulation achieves pure, precise, and clear expression of meaning, systematic formulation remains jejune and sterile. It has explanatory power, but it lacks motivating power. In contrast, metaphorical or mythic expression of meaning includes values and motivational components. It bespeaks global significance rather than cognitions and evaluations in differentiation and interrelationship. For metaphor is an undifferentiated medium. It inspires, motivates, delights, and entertains even as it informs, educates, and "explains." While addressing the spiritual issues, meanings and values, it also engages the more primitive and more gripping facets of humanity, the psychic and the visceral. It addresses the whole human being. It meets people where they live. So when concern is the shape of cultures, emphasis on metaphor is well placed.

But the use of myth and metaphor always entails a danger. They are inherently ambiguous. They carry a surplus of meaning (Ricoeur, 1967), so they can be easily misunderstood. That God is governor may imply gracious care, but it may also imply punitive dictatorship. That people treat others as they themselves would like to be treated may imply benign passivity that never opposes evil for fear of offending someone. So metaphorical expression of meaning and value cannot be sufficient in itself. When conflicts of understanding and commitment emerge, as they do when different cultures meet or when religious concerns encounter secular ones, someone somewhere needs to determine what the metaphors must and must not mean. To do this would be precisely the task of systematic human disciplines like psychology, spirituality, and theology, as envisaged in this book.

From one point of view, Browning is certainly correct (137). A world conceived only in scientific terms would be narrow, dull, and uninspiring—a world without poetry and song. So the multidimensionality of religion's metaphors is a real asset. This positive assessment also applies to Ken Wilber's reliance on metaphor, symbol, and yes, even paradoxical statement. But Browning and Wilber seem not to appreciate the eventually unavoidable need for a systematic, a scientific treatment even of religious issues. Indeed, they and most of the world seem to believe that such scientific treatment is just not possible.

Granted, talk of authenticity is abstract, distant, and technical. But such talk does make a contribution—on the systematic side of the issue. Of course, there remains the task of transposing onto the popular level the understanding achieved through systematic analysis. There remains the task of using the scientific understanding in a way that can transform cultures. This other task does need to be done. It is the specialization that Lonergan (1972) called Communications. Still, this task is not proper to the systematician, to the scientist. This applied task belongs to the popularizers, to the preacher, the teacher, and the politician. The task of the systematician is to help the popularizers through their professional training to really understand what their own task is about.

In contrast, the systematic understanding proposed here, *as such*, does not need to be presented popularly. This scientific project is not intended to spawn a new religion—like the French Revolution's religion of rationality or some supposed religion of authenticity. Rather, this project merely proposes an explanatory account that is useful for analyzing already existing religions. Indeed, the powerful archetypal metaphors that could foster authenticity or authentic theism or positive spiritual growth are undoubtedly already in use among the religions. So the need is not to popularize—and inevitably distort—this scientific analysis in metaphorical form. The need is simply to help religion make clear the intended meanings of its already current metaphors. Then, when taught, preached, and ritually enacted, they will more surely have only the desired positive effect. To elucidate for the practitioners these intended meanings is the sufficient purpose of this systematic account.

Browning's analysis of stories, myths, images, and metaphors is surely a valid and necessary enterprise. Similar to Lonergan's (1972) theological specialization, Dialectic, Browning's critical conversation about the adequacy of particular metaphors is also a necessary enterprise. However, the purpose of this critical conversation would be more surely achieved if the conversation could be grounded in a prior systematic understanding.

Two Kinds of Psychology

Browning's call for two kinds of psychology (xi, 124, 242–245) seems to parallel my call for a similar thing. Indeed, my understanding of the matter seems to bring clarity and firmness to Browning's suggestions.

Browning and I share an important, common, starting point, the awareness that adequate treatment of human beings cannot avoid questions of normative meaning and value—or, as Browning phrases it, metaphysics and ethics. The Frankfurt Institute of Social Research, known most commonly today through the work of Jürgen Habermas (1970/1991), offers important support for this awareness (Bernstein, 1976; Geuss, 1981). The Marxist analysis of the *Frankfurterschule* led to the realization that the social sciences are hardly value-free. Rather, they unwittingly embody the values of the societies that support them. So, to be truly objective as sciences, the social sciences must somehow critically address the questions about what is a good person and a good society.

I address that issue by distinguishing a higher viewpoint, so I propose a psychology within the positivist, as well as a psychology within the philosophic, viewpoint. I insist forcefully that only the latter can be humanly adequate, but I allow also the former—not only because it is a powerful academic reality with which we remain saddled but also because a merely positivist study can indeed make valuable, if limited, contributions to an understanding of the human.

However, my conception of the matter is systematic, scientific, throughout. So psychology within the philosophic viewpoint is also a fully scientific enterprise even though attention to human authenticity, a spiritual matter, is its determinative factor. Indeed, the argument is that, without such attention to authenticity, psychology omits an essential explanatory aspect of the human, so only with such attention can psychology be truly scientific. My concern is to present a coherent, comprehensive, and explanatory account of the human. The goal is always correct understanding. So in addition to psychology, a science within the positivist viewpoint, I propose another science, psychology within the philosophic viewpoint or, said otherwise, spirituality. On my view, both forms of psychology are strictly scientific.

In contrast, Browning's two forms of psychology are scientific, on the one hand, and practical, on the other. These more or less parallel the distinction between experimental and clinical psychology, noted above. "One model envisages psychology as a relatively objective and scientific discipline dedicated to the development of a body of knowledge about the patterns in human symbolic and behavioral activity" (xi). For Browning, this form of psychology deals with "strictly descriptive statements" in a "relatively value-free form" (244). Obviously, despite a terminology that differs from my own (for Browning descriptive means scientific), this first form of psychology squares with my first form, psychology within the positivist viewpoint. But Browning continues, "This form of psychology will be distinguished from another view which conceives psychology as a practical discipline based on a critical ethic and a critical theory of society" (xi).

Of course, that second kind of psychology in Browning's mind is foremost among the psychologies he criticizes throughout his book. This form of psychology is, indeed, practical. It is nothing other than psychotherapeutic. Even as Browning demonstrates, these clinical psychologies do include presuppositions about normative meanings and values, so Browning sees in them covert forms of religion. As a result, they are to be lumped together with religion in the category of *practical* human enterprises.

Notice a pernicious presupposition there: the deeper questions about life, the significance of human life, the "religious" issues, supposedly cannot be treated in a scientific, systematic, explanatory way. So religion, and, indeed, even theology, and the clinical psychologies are all relegated to the category of practical disciplines.

Even Browning is not completely satisfied with that construal of the matter, but he seems to see no way around it. In addition to the psychotherapies, he correctly realizes, other forms of psychology must also entail spiritual matters: "personality theory, developmental theory, and all aspects of social psychology" (244). But these forms of psychology are hardly practical disciplines. Rather, they are strictly methodical pursuits of understanding about the human being—science. Thus, at this point Browning intimates a scientific psychology much like what I have called psychology within the philosophic viewpoint. Indeed, Browning even attempts to qualify this kind of psychology somehow as science: "Both forms of psychology could rightly claim to be scientific since both would attempt to be public and follow arguments that could be publicly examined, reviewed, and tested. But they would indeed be sciences in different senses of the word" (244).

At stake is the question of what constitutes science. Chapter Two conceived science as resting on a generalized empirical method, such that investigation need not be limited to the observable, though it must appeal to some kind of evidence or data. Moreover, the essence of science was conceived as the ongoing advancement of explanatory account. This understanding of science can apply across the board. So developmental, social, and personality psychology— within the philosophic viewpoint—can qualify as science in the strict sense of the term. This understanding seems to provide what Browning knows is somehow needed and what he struggles to propose. But he identifies the psychologies as a covert form of religion, and he confounds religion/theology with the solely practical. These ambiguities preclude resolution of the matter.

As for the psychologies as psychotherapies: they are indeed practical disciplines. They are applications of the hoped-for fully scientific psychology, or spirituality, just as engineering is the applied form of the physical sciences.

Browning would like to leave a role for religion or theology in that proposed critical, scientific, study of psychology (245). But again, the confounding of common sense and theory, religion and theology, befuddles the attempt.

Clearly, religion does have something to contribute to the broader issue of scientific study of the human. But the term "religion" applies to a very mixed bag. When "religion," globally taken and vaguely defined, so often means self-declared authority on all matters, human and divine, no wonder Habermas and other social scientists allow it no role.

On my understanding, only one small part of religion is theology, and it treats solely of God. This treatment is technical and, hopefully, also systematic. So understood, theology has no place in the human sciences and should be removed from the discussion. No one should be disappointed by this eventuality. The human is not the divine, so the two require different treatment. I suspect that the central figure in this matter, God, far from being disappointed, would rejoice at long last being withdrawn from the fray.

But another part of religion is its understanding of the human being, spiritual wisdom built into traditions over long centuries.

This part of religion is, indeed, relevant to social-science concerns. But neither does this part of religion enter the discussion as "religious" per se. Rather, this contribution of religion enters as *human* understanding about a topic that also concerns other parties and about which those parties also legitimately have opinions. Discussion at this point is simply discussion of the human—revised critical correlation—within the explicitly noted philosophic viewpoint. Such discussion is open to anyone committed to authenticity and learned in the matter.

So authenticity, not belief in God, not revelation, not religion, becomes the critical factor. And if "religion" does have a contribution to make to the social sciences, religion is not to make that contribution as religion but simply as another human attempt to explicate authenticity.

Conclusion Regarding Browning

Explanatory analysis of the human problematic differentiates the positivist, the philosophic, the theist, and the theotic. Religion, like life in general, can include all of them. These distinctions determine parameters within which diverse issues can be intelligently engaged and all parties be given their due. This approach seems to lose nothing of Browning's concerns or contributions. Rather, it places them in a broader and more focused context. It corrects the flaws, redresses the misemphases, and preserves the valid intent. Here is an interdisciplinary methodology that directly addresses Browning's theme: religious thought and the modern psychologies.

Chapter 4

The Perennial Philosophy of Ken Wilber

"Oh, East is East, and West is West, and never the twain shall meet." So goes Rudyard Kipling's oft-quoted line from *The Ballad of East and West*. But the times have changed. Not only have East and West met; they begin to interpenetrate. As they do, it becomes clear that, as another adage goes, "People are people." In many respects, the concerns of the East have also been the concerns of the West. So Westerners concerned about spiritual things have found a treasure of resources in Eastern thought. And attempts to relate religion and the human sciences have borrowed from that treasure, for in many ways this interdisciplinary task presupposes an understanding of spirituality.

This book is spelling out its own understanding of how religion and the human sciences relate, and at center stage, of course, stands spirituality. Contrast with other approaches helps explicate this understanding. The previous chapter considered the reigning approach in Western thought as exemplified in the work of Don Browning. This chapter turns to another approach, still in Western thought, but significantly colored by the Eastern. This state of

213

affairs belies the adage, for evidently East and West have met and mixed. Nonetheless, in the end the analysis here will validate the adage. For the Eastern approach differs from the Western in fundamental ways, so the attempt to integrate them must eventually prove incoherent.

The case in point is the position of Ken Wilber (1996), his *Eye to Eye: The Quest for the New Paradigm*. This book is an elaborate 315-page statement. It easily stands alone as a complete exposition of Wilber's interdisciplinary position apart from his many other and voluminous works (Wilber, 1977, 1980a, 1981, 1995). Published now in its third edition, this book may safely be taken as Wilber's well-considered opinion. The similarities between Wilber's project and the present one are striking—and especially since I had not read Wilber before I completed the full formulation of my own position, which remains essentially unchanged. Yet differences with Wilber are also striking, and they lie at the critical junctures.

Wilber is sometimes characterized as the arch-guru of the transpersonal psychology movement(Rothberg, 1996b; Walsh, 1996; Walsh & Vaughan, 1994; Wilber, 1982). He was schooled in modern biology and chemistry, he studied Eastern psychological and philosophical systems, and he is widely read in Western thought. He is a long-time practitioner of Zen. On a lifelong pursuit of the meaning of life, he has struggled to integrate the insights of genius wherever he found them and to reconcile the thinking of East and West. He speaks for a very widely held position, which in the end is a version of Hinduism.

Knowingly or unknowingly, that position colors much, if not most, of current discussion about spirituality or "metaphysics," at least in popular circles, transpersonal and otherwise. That position is now also prominent in academic psychology (Assagioli, 1965/ 1976; Chandler, Holden, & Kolander, 1992; Deikman, 1982). For this reason, among others, Wilber's work deserves and will receive extensive and detailed criticism here. Those familiar with "spiritual" writings, especially writings influenced from the East, will easily recognize common themes, apart from any familiarity with Wilber's own works.

This criticism will begin with a summary of the concerns common to this book and to Wilber's. Above all, Wilber is explicit about developing a science of the spiritual and about proposing a comprehensive interdisciplinary paradigm. There will follow a brief summary of Wilber's position and then a detailed analysis of our points of difference. The hope is to show that the position that I developed in this book can meet the need for a comprehensive paradigm, as envisaged by Wilber, while avoiding what appear to me as ambiguities, inconsistencies, and flaws in Wilber's presentation.

The hope of the present criticism is to salvage as much of Wilber's vision as possible. For the breadth of explicit treatment in Wilber's book far exceeds that presented here. *Eye to Eye* includes valuable analyses of the rise of "scientism" in Western civilization, discussion of the excessive claims all religions have tended to make, and balanced criticism of the use that New Age religion and other contemporary spiritualities make of quantum mechanics and holographic theory. His other works, especially his latest and monumental *Sex, Ecology, Spirituality* (Wilber, 1995), reach into still broader and more diverse fields. If that expansive treatment can be incorporated into the present position—for much of that treatment remains valid despite the criticism on other matters presented below—the actual achievement of a truly comprehensive paradigm may, indeed, be near at hand.

Common Concerns

As his subtitle suggests, Wilber intends to present a "comprehensive-integral paradigm" (123)[1] that can unite the sciences, the humanities, and spiritual disciplines. It is significant that in that project Wilber insists on a list of issues similar to the ones discussed in the preceding chapters.

His account of three "eyes"—the eye of flesh, the eye of the mind, and the eye of the spirit—shows some parallel to the three factors in the tripartite model of the human: organism, psyche, and spirit. He conceives the unification of science as a hierarchical system—like the Four Viewpoints in Chapter Two—in which the higher unities include the lower unities, yet each has its own proper and autonomous domain. On this understanding, Wilber speaks of violations of that autonomy as category errors (7ff), even as Chapter Two

---

1. Throughout Chapter Four, numbers in parentheses refer to pages in Wilber (1996).

objected to such violations as instances of reductionism and fideism. While the notion of dynamic human spirit undergirds the whole of the present interdisciplinary position, Wilber also grounds the unity of science, of consciousness, and, indeed, of the cosmos, in a dynamism that is spirit—or "Spirit." As also in the present position, Wilber insists that a comprehensive paradigm must provide a common account of knowledge or science, applicable across the board, in all sciences and disciplines, including the treatment of the spiritual, though individual disciplines will have their specialized methodologies. And he proposes such an account. Clearly, then, as is obvious in his treatment and in mine, epistemology is a key to the present enterprise. Moreover, Wilber is well aware that theorizing is an attempt to use symbols and concepts to articulate data from varying domains of experience. Accordingly, he argues that there can be valid knowledge of the spiritual insofar as such knowledge is grounded in real evidence. This evidence is the experience of the spiritual adept. Of course, this evidence will not be sensate or empirical (in the narrow sense). Thus, Wilber also acknowledges the distinction between the data of sense and the data of consciousness; in the face of narrow scientism, insists on the validity of both; and so would allow what Lonergan (1957, pp. 72, 243) would call "generalized empirical method." Finally, Wilber is aware of a possible experience of consciousness wherein all distinctions are transcended: formlessness, no-thing-ness; and he attributes an ultimacy to this experience. The parallel is in the treatment of consciousness as conscious (Lonergan, 1972, pp. 6–13) or as nonreflecting (Helminiak, 1984a, 1996a).

The parallels between Wilber's position and the present one are numerous. The importance of this fact should not be overlooked, though I can but state the fact and then must pass on to other lengthy considerations. It is obvious that Wilber's and my project are the same and that a similar understanding of the issues supports our respective proposals. This convergence of understandings, coming from very different starting points, is significant and encouraging. The bases for a true science of spirituality do seem to be emerging. In an effort to secure those bases, the detailed analysis that follows will attempt from my point of view to clarify ambiguities in Wilber's presentation and also to indicate some differences that are pivotal.

The Core of Wilber's Position

The theoretical core of Wilber's position is two sets of concepts: first, the notion of three eyes, which relate to different kinds of human awareness and thus to different sciences; and second, the notion of three strands of knowledge, which constitute science as such. (See Figure 4.1.)

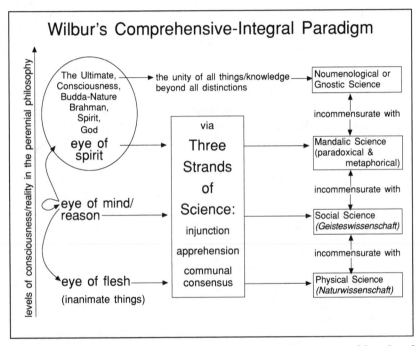

Figure 4.1 Three eyes (actually part of a wider range of levels of reality/consciousness, as in the perennial philosophy) result in three kinds of theoretical knowledge or science as the eye of reason reflects on itself and the other two eyes. All are science because all in their own way entail the same three strands. But resulting from three different eyes, the sciences are incommensurate. So mandalic science, unlike physical or social science, is inevitably paradoxical. Moreover, mandalic science is also incommensurate with another form of spiritual science, noumenological or gnostic science. In it, in the experience of The Ultimate, all paradox and, indeed, all distinction and formulation are transcended, and all is known to be one.

The Three Eyes

Wilber borrows the metaphor of three eyes from St. Bonaventure, the medieval Christian mystic. Supposedly, people

> have at least three modes of attaining knowledge—"three eyes" . . . : the *eye of flesh*, by which we perceive the external world of space, time, and objects; the *eye of reason*, by which we attain a knowledge of philosophy, logic, and the mind itself; and the *eye of contemplation*, by which we rise to a knowledge of transcendent realities. (3)

Emphasis on these three eyes recurs throughout Wilber's presentation, expressed in different terminology and in broadly differing parallels. Thus, the three eyes parallel the "hard ware" of the physical science, the "soft ware" of philosophy and psychology, and the "transcendental ware" of mystical-spiritual religion (1). They relate to facts, principles, and God (9). They parallel flesh, mind, and spirit (9) or, again, body, mind, and spirit (67, 173), or else the biological, the mental, and consciousness (125–129). They correspond with sensation, reason, and contemplation (10) or with Aristotle's *techne*, praxis (*phronesis*), and *theoria* (173) or with knowing that is sensory, symbolic, and spiritual (38) or else sensory, mental, and spiritual (67) or else sensory, symbolic, and intuitive (171). What exactly these groupings and parallels may be intending is the topic of criticism below. Clearly, however, the overall brunt of Wilber's argument is that three different kinds of human experience allow for three different general realms of knowledge.

Wilber is "saying (and will try to demonstrate) that there are legitimate data—*direct apprehensions*—to be found in the realms of flesh, mind, and spirit; that is, real data in these *real* object domains, object domains that we can call *sensibilia, intelligibilia,* and *transcendelia*" (38), namely, things sensible, intelligible (67 suggests "mental"), and transcendental.

Those Latin words best summarize Wilber's conception. They serve as technical terms and recur throughout his presentation. (Note that the Latin form for "things that transcend or go beyond" is *transcendentia*. "Transcendelia" appears to be a combination of the Latin stem, *transcendere*, to climb over or step beyond, and the Greek stem, *delein*, to make manifest, familiar in the word "psyche*delic*." "Transcendelia" may be deliberately coined to suggest indicators of the transcendent rather than transcendent things themselves. But Wilber never makes this point, and his usage and overall argument do not support such an interpretation.)

By insisting on the validity of a third eye, the eye of contemplation or the eye of spirit, Wilber argues forcefully for the reality of the spiritual realm and for our capacity to know it. This insistence is a major contribution and a rallying point for Wilber's disciples and, indeed, for many people committed to spiritual pursuits. By championing the third eye, in addition to the eyes of flesh and of mind, Wilber's hopes to achieve a comprehensive paradigm. This paradigm would embrace religious, spiritual, contemplative, mystical knowledge as well as knowledge within the physical sciences and within philosophy, the human sciences, and the humanities.

Although the three eyes have their individual realms of competence, the eye of reason (or the eye of mind) can be turned onto the knowledge derived from any of the three eyes. The result is the formalized presentation of knowledge, for it is precisely the work of the mind or reason to symbolize, conceptualize, and form propositions. "Neither the sensorimotor [fleshy] realms per se, nor the spiritual realms per se, form theories. They can be the *object* of theories, but do not themselves produce theories" (68). Thus, the logic of the mind plus a fleshy starting point results in "indubitable facts" or "irreducible and stubborn facts" or simply the empiric-analytic facts of hard science. Logic plus a mental starting point results in "indubitable principles of reference" or "intuitively self-evident truths" or "direct phenomenological apprehensions" of philosophy or psychology. Logic plus a contemplative starting point results in revelation or mandalic reasoning. "At any rate, let us note the three starting points for reasoning: irreducible facts (flesh), self-evident or axiomatic truths (mind), and revelatory insights (spirit)" (9).

Said otherwise, the eye of reason may be used to "map" or "mirror" (52) input from itself or from the other two eyes.

Whereas the *data* in *any* realm is itself immediate and direct (by definition), the *pointing* by *mental* data to *other* data (sensory, mental, or transcendental) is a mediate or intermediate process—it is a *mapping, modeling,* or *matching* procedure. And this mapping procedure—the use of mental data (symbols and concepts) to explain or map *other* data (sensory, mental, or transcendental)—simply results in what is known as *theoretical knowledge*. (68)

The accumulation of such theoretical knowledge constitutes science (63), and this accumulation can occur in any of the three fields of human experience.

However, Wilber insists repeatedly and forcefully that the theoretical knowledge possible in the field of transcendelia is of a different kind compared to that possible in the other fields. Treatment of transcendelia results in "mandalic science"—which is to say, deliberately paradoxical formulations. Application of the mind's or reason's conceptualizing ability to contemplative experience can result only in "theory in a looser sense . . . paradoxical reason . . . mandalic science" (179). "When the mind attempts to reason about the absolute, it will necessarily generate paradoxes" (173; also 174, 175). Supposedly, Immanuel Kant "demonstrated that any time we attempt to *reason* about this transempirical reality, we find that *we can create arguments for either of two completely contradictory views with equal plausibility*—and that plainly shows that such reasoning is futile (or, at any rate, does not carry near the weight it had so generously given itself under the title of 'metaphysics')" (18). Likewise, the Buddhist genius Nagarjuna supposedly showed that "Reason cannot grasp the essence of absolute reality, and when it tries, it generates only dualistic incompatibilities" (19).

The Three Strands of Knowledge or Science

If knowledge of transcendelia can only be expressed in paradoxes, how can one claim science in this realm? The answer to this question depends on what "science" means. So here enters the second of the two sets of concepts at the core of Wilber's position. The answer is this: the paradoxically expressed knowledge of transcendelia is like the knowledge of the other sciences because all valid knowledge or science shares a common form.

All valid knowledge is essentially similar in structure, and thus can be similarly verified (or rejected). That is, all valid knowledge—in whatever realm—consists of three basic components. . . .

1. *An instrumental or injunctive strand.* This is a set of instructions, simple or complex, internal or external. All have the form: "If you want to know this, do this."

2. *An illuminative or apprehensive strand.* This is an illuminative *seeing* by the particular eye of knowledge evoked by the injunctive strand. Besides being self-illuminative, it leads to the possibility of:

3. *A communal strand.* This is the actual sharing of the illuminative seeing with others who are using the same eye. If the shared-vision is agreed upon by others, this constitutes a communal or consensual proof of *true seeing.* (31–32)

An example will help clarify the notion of the three strands of knowledge. Let the issue be whether or not it is raining. This issue pertains to the eye of flesh, for the knowledge in question depends on using sense perception. The injunctive strand runs something like this: "If you want to know if it is raining, go to the window and look." The injunction tells what needs to be done to attain the knowledge in question. Next, the illuminative or apprehensive strand is the actual looking of the person willing to follow the injunction. According to Wilber's account of the matter, the person goes to the window, looks, and knows that it is raining. Finally, whether or not this knowing is correct depends on corroboration from others who follow the same injunction and have their own illuminative or apprehensive experience. So if a number of people also went to the window and agreed that it was raining, it would be true that it was indeed raining. Valid knowledge would be the result (32).

Granted, that is a simple example, and Wilber does elaborate the notion of three strands in great detail. That detail will be examined below. Wilber's main point is simply that all valid knowledge is of that kind. Then, if that same three-strand structure of knowledge occurs in other areas of experience, the knowledge in those areas is just as valid as is the knowledge in the physical sciences. And the accumulation of such knowledge constitutes real science.

Of course, one must be willing to train the appropriate eye if one wants to claim validity for one's opinion in some realm. The trained eye is the public eye. Training and consensual validation move knowledge from the realm of the merely personal into the public realm. Someone unwilling to learn mathematics cannot demand an explanation from physicists. Someone unable to read cannot argue the meaning of a text. And "someone who refuses to learn contemplation cannot be allowed to vote on the truth of Buddha Nature or Spirit" (32–33).

On that basis Wilber argues for the validity of spiritual knowledge as science:

> If by "science" one means the three strands of knowledge accumulation in any realm, then indeed the purer schools of Zen, Yoga, and so on can be called scientific. They are injunctive, instrumental, experimental, experiential, and consensual. That being so, then we could legitimately speak of "spiritual sciences" just as we now speak of social sciences, hermeneutical sciences, psychological sciences, and physical sciences. (63–64)

Knowledge of God

Indeed, Wilber goes so far as to insist that there is proof for the existence of God. "The knowledge of God is as public to the contemplative eye as is geometry to the mental eye and rainfall to the physical eye. And a trained/contemplative eye can *prove* the existence of God with exactly the same certainty and the same public nature as the eye of flesh can prove the existence of rocks" (34–35). What is that proof? The experience of those who come to know the existence of God. Wilber explains, "There *is* an instrumental proof for the existence of God, but the instrument is contemplation, not reason, and the proof is direct, not mediate" (63). It is "an experimental, verifiable, repeatable proof for the existence of Godhead, *as a fact*, as a penultimate Datum, but that proof is not—indeed, could not be—merely rational or logical (let alone empirical [in the narrow sense])" (62). The experience of adepts in contemplative techniques, corroborated by others also so trained, constitutes proof for the existence of God, proof based on replicable experiments, so to speak, among those willing to perform the experiment.

The conjunction of two basic notions—the three eyes and the three strands of knowledge—constitutes Wilber's comprehensive paradigm. The supposed scope of this paradigm is broad indeed. It even envisages treatment of God.

The Perennial Philosophy

But when did the question of God enter this discussion of an inter-disciplinary paradigm? In fact, God was in the discussion from the start, included in the notion of the eye of spirit. So further explanation is in order.

Wilber speaks of three eyes, but such talk is only a shorthand form of a much more elaborate system. The real basis of Wilber's position is what he, following Leibnitz and Aldous Huxley (1945), calls the perennial philosophy, the *philosophia perennis* (124–131). Here is a conception of reality as the Great Chain of Being, "a hierarchy of dimensional levels, moving from the lowest, densest, and most fragmentary realms to the highest, subtlest, and most unitary ones" (124). In question are "realms" both of consciousness and of reality. For all reality is conceived as expressions of con-sciousness. All is consciousness. The highest state of consciousness would correspond to the ultimate reality, and the lowest state would correspond to physical, inanimate objects. Physical reality is but consciousness in a gross, dense form.

Between the lowest and the highest is a series of ever more subtle forms—forms both of conscious experience and of reality. On this understanding, stages of possible human development corre-spond with levels of reality. As one dedicates oneself to meditative practice, one's consciousness is successively transformed and one is more and more able to experience and appreciate the single reality of all things, consciousness, that has been such all along.

That understanding presumes a notion of *"involution,"* namely, the emergence of reality in declining stages from the one absolute, ultimate consciousness. Such an understanding is central to much New Age thinking and characterizes the long-standing Hindu, Neo-Platonic, and gnostic traditions. Adepts in those traditions differen-tiate numerous stages. Generally six or seven are presented, and the higher ones, corresponding to ever-further states of meditative experience, often have substages. Wilber points out that these stages of emergence of reality can also be considered in reverse order, the order in which, in fact, they come to be known. Then the movement would go from inanimate objects to living beings to perceiving and thinking beings and finally, via stages of ever-refined awareness, to ultimate consciousness. Thus, one could also discern here a process of *evolution.* Likewise, one could understand how three realms—

flesh, mind, and spirit, ignoring now the lowest realm, the inanimate—could conveniently be used to approximate the six or seven realms in the complete theory. So talk of the three eyes is an abbreviated form of a much more elaborate theory.

Wilber's intention is sweeping indeed. With that conception he intends to unite Eastern thought about consciousness and Western physical and evolutionary theory. He also suggests parallels between the states of consciousness in the perennial philosophy and the stages of human development detailed by Western psychologists like Jean Piaget, Lawrence Kohlberg, and Jane Loevinger. So Wilber's attempt at a comprehensive paradigm identifies the process of evolution with the process of human development and again identifies all that with the states of consciousness noted in the perennial philosophy. Full discussion of this theory—which is all too easy—is beyond the scope of this presentation, though significant criticism will be given below. Elsewhere I have already provided a detailed study of human development as it relates to consciousness (spirit) and to God (Helminiak, 1987c, 1989c).

Here, note only one point, relevant to interdisciplinary method. The ultimate ground of, and hope for, the unification of all knowledge in Wilber's position is the unity of all things/knowledge in the absolute, beyond all form and all formlessness, beyond all knowing and all not knowing. Wilber's position at this point seems to be this: all knowledge can be unified because in God/consciousness all is one.

Actually, Wilber describes that unifying transcendent reality in widely differing terms. It is God, a Transcendent Ultimate, the noumenon [evidently in Kant's sense] (18) or else reality (169) or else reality as a whole (175) or else the absolutely real (165) or else Being (61) or else consciousness (289ff) or else Hegel's Spirit (60–61) or else Brahman (290–292) or else "God or Buddha Nature or Tao" (34) or else "Godhead or the absolute" (162) or else the "deity-form" or "*dhyani*-buddha" or "Deity" or "one's own Self or highest Archetype" or "(choose whatever term one prefers) God" (93).

So God (or something of the sort) has been at the heart of Wilber's position from the beginning. Attention to the full sweep of the perennial philosophy behind his notion of the three eyes highlights this fact.

It should be noted that Wilber's understanding of "the perennial philosophy" is more precise than that of Huxley. From the outset and consistently thereafter, Huxley (1945, p. vii) understands the perennial philosophy as "the metaphysics that recognizes a divine Reality substantial to the world of things and lives and minds; the psychology that finds in the soul something *similar to, or even identical with*, divine Reality" (*emphasis added*). In this formulation it is not clear whether God is distinct from other reality or is to be identified with it. The vague and repeated phrase, "divine Reality substantial to the world," does not clarify the matter. Though Huxley does tend toward identifying the self and the Divine, it appears that Huxley was deliberate in his ambiguity, and thus he was able to propose a "philosophy" that does, indeed, emerge universally in theist religion of all kinds. In contrast, Wilber posits an explicit and deliberate identification of God and other things. Wilber (1980b, pp. 75–76) lucidly phrases the matter elsewhere as follows: "The core insight of the *psychologia perennis* is that man's 'innermost' consciousness is identical to the absolute and ultimate reality of the universe, known variously as Brahman, Tao, Dharmakaya, Allah, the Godhead."

That discrepancy in usage regarding the term *perennial philosophy* is typical of Wilber's reliance on his sources. However, the more important point is this. Wilber's identification of God, the Ultimate, with human consciousness sets him squarely in alliance with the Eastern thought of Hinduism and some forms of Buddhism and sets him squarely in conflict with the Western theism of Judaism, Christianity, and Islam. It is on this very point that in Wilber East and West do meet; it is also on this point that in fact they retain a fundamental incompatibility. More on this pivotal issue below.

Two Conflicting Bases of Unity for Science

Note the implication for interdisciplinary method in Wilber's rendition of the perennial philosophy. His emphasis on the ultimate seems to imply a second basis of unity among the sciences—physical, mental, and spiritual. To the question, How can all sciences be united under a comprehensive paradigm? Wilber seems to answer, In two ways.

First, the sciences, including knowledge of the spiritual, are similar because they all depend on the three strands of knowledge. This first answer refers to explicated knowledge, articulated insights, formulated experiences, elaborated theories, shared and tested understandings. This is "science" in the usual sense of the term. This is the science that results when the eye of reason/mind turns onto knowledge that comes from the eyes of flesh or of mind or of spirit.

Yet the result of such science in the case of transcendelia can only be paradoxical. There can be no consistent formulations in this case. Such mandalic science is nonetheless valid because it finds confirmation in the experience of adept meditators. Still, one must wonder how they are sure they are meaning the same thing since they can only express themselves paradoxically. There certainly is ambiguity in the matter.

The second and conflicting basis of unity comes to the rescue at this point. What the adept meditators know is that consciousness/God is everything. All is one, so distinctions, concepts, formulations, theories, differences among things, are illusory. Ultimately, they have no validity. The absolutely real is the one that is everything, beyond form and beyond no-form, beyond knowing and beyond not knowing, beyond knowledge and beyond ignorance. Knowledge of reality in this sense is "science" of a very peculiar kind—immediate apprehension that all is one.

That second basis of unity ultimately disqualifies the first. And the first basis of unity cannot adequately deal with the second. Two competing approaches to science seem to compensate for the shortcomings of one another, but the upshot is that no coherent, comprehensive paradigm is provided. This lack of coherence is another pivotal issue that will be treated in detail below.

From Summary to Criticism

Those considerations have already turned discussion from an objective summary of Wilber's position to a critical analysis of it. To this latter task attention now turns in earnest. This critical analysis unfolds under five main headings. Each focuses on a key facet of Wilber's theory, and each raises major methodological questions.

The Three Eyes:
Different Sciences, Data, and Knowing

The metaphor of the three eyes is central to Wilber's presentation. In many ways this metaphor summarizes his proposed comprehensive interdisciplinary paradigm. On closer inspection, however, the metaphor of three eyes represents a very fuzzy vision indeed. In fact, the notion of eyes serves three different functions in Wilber's theory, and these three functions are not sorted out. First, the list of eyes serves to differentiate different kinds of sciences. Second, the eyes provide people with access to different kinds of data. And third, the eyes are themselves different modes of human knowing.

The Eyes Determine an Array of Sciences

That first function is relatively unproblematic. In this usage the metaphor of three eyes serves merely as a shorthand way of listing an array of possible scientific concerns. That array ranges from concern for inanimate objects (no corresponding eye), as in physics and chemistry; to concern for living things (the eye of flesh), as in biology, botany, and zoology; to concern for perceiving and thinking beings (the eye of mind or reason), as in philosophy, mathematics, psychology, sociology, anthropology, and to some extent even spirituality; and finally to explicit concern for consciousness, spirit, and God (the eye of spirit), as in, once again, spirituality and also (using my terminology) theology and theotics.

However, the array of sciences is not clear-cut once the eye of mind enters the picture. From my perspective, the problem here is precisely the confounding of psyche and spirit within "mind" and the identification of spirit with God. More on this to follow.

Another glitch is this: in Wilber's array of sciences, physics and chemistry have no corresponding eye, for the eye of flesh corresponds with biology. Yet for the other two functions of the eyes (source of data and modes of knowing), the eye of flesh does correspond with the "hard sciences," including physics, chemistry, and biology. More on this to follow, as well. Despite these ambiguities, in a more or less satisfactory way the three eyes legitimately function to sort out an array of sciences.

Comparison with the Four Viewpoints

The obvious parallel in my position is the system of four viewpoints. It also sorts out disciplines or sciences in a hierarchical array. However, there are significant differences. Physics, chemistry, and biology certainly fall within the positivist viewpoint (though only the human sciences are my explicit concern), so the system of four viewpoints does represent a comprehensive interdisciplinary position. Yet, in this book focus has been on the human being and, in the positivist viewpoint, on the *human* sciences. This restriction makes obvious that the higher viewpoints beyond the positivist, which apply only to human studies, do not result because of the availability of new data but because of the emergence of further questions about the selfsame, already fully given data on the human. Such an approach promises complete unification of knowledge for a number of reasons: because of the ontological unity of the object of study, because of the focus of human questioning on that one object of study, and because of the unity of human intellectual capacity applied to the successive questions.

In contrast, on Wilber's understanding, the engagement of further eyes does add further data, for a second function of the eyes is to be the source of data. Indeed, the eye of spirit supposedly even adds data about God. Moreover, with the opening of the further eyes, as is especially obvious in the case of the eye of spirit, the knowledge from the lower eyes is relativized and even disqualified. Fully opened, the eye of spirit recognizes that consciousness is everything and everything is consciousness. This knowledge transcends the knowledge of the eyes of flesh and of mind and renders it meaningless. Not a unification, but a replacement, of knowledge is the result. Furthermore, because of an identification of the spiritual and the divine, Wilber's position leaves no room for the theist and the theotic viewpoints. Their determinitive questions cannot even arise. Besides, even the pivotal concern for authenticity in the philosophic viewpoint receives little attention in Wilber's presentation. In every case, the crucial issues at stake in each of the viewpoints are obscured, and the four viewpoints are collapsed into one.

Accordingly, the system of four viewpoints may be the most obvious parallel to the first function of the three eyes, namely, to sort out an array of sciences, but in fact the system of four viewpoints represents a theoretical elaboration that is simply lacking in Wilber's position.

The Eyes as Sources of Data

The three eyes serve a second function. Respectively they are the source of separate data: "each eye has its own object of knowledge (sensory, mental, and transcendental)" (6). Or again, by way of example, behaviorism and psychoanalysis "are two sets of data gathered through two different eyes, both of which are valid, one of which is empirical, and one of which is mental-phenomenological" (16).

Undoubtedly, there are different realms of data, and humans do have access to those different realms. Because of the physiological organism and its capacity for sense perception, humans can and do have access to sensory data: sights, sounds, tastes, smells, and sensate feelings. Because they are partially constituted by psyche, humans can and do have access to psychic data: emotions, images, and memories. And because of nonreflecting consciousness, identical with spirit, humans can and do have access to spiritual data: consciousness, and meanings and values. Human access to differing realms of data does depend on the polymorphous structure of the human being: organism, psyche, and spirit.

If that is all that Wilber means at this point, our positions square well enough. He does suggest that that is at least part of what he means. He states, for example, that science is "*grounded* by the eye of flesh" (12); and he notes that scientific formulations result when the eye of reason operates on the eye of flesh. So on this formulation, science is not simply the product of the eye of flesh, but "eye of flesh" is but a way of speaking of science limited to empirical, sensory, data.

Yet Wilber's treatment of the matter also suggests something else. It suggests that each of the eyes *alone* acts as a source of, or is a specialized receptivity to, different data. In stark contrast, following Lonergan, I have argued that availability of data occurs on the first level of *consciousness*. For example, hearing a voice on the beach, clearly a sensate, empirical act, can be the starting point for the analysis of the four levels of consciousness or spirit (Helminiak, 1996a, pp. 82–85). For the hearing provokes questioning: What is it?

And the ensuing idea provokes a judgment of fact: Is it so? Have I understood correctly? And the ensuing judgment of fact provokes deliberation and a judgment of value: What am I going to do about it? In this and in every case, data are presented for cognitive processing via conscious, spiritual, actuation. In every case we are aware of data, we are aware that there is something to be understood, because we are conscious. Forcing Wilber's terminology into this foreign system, one must say that the eye of spirit is essential to every experience of data whether sensory, mental, or spiritual.

There are not three separate sources or receptivities of data in the human being. Rather, there is only one, human consciousness itself, by which humans are aware and self-aware and thus are confronted with data. The human being is not equipped with three separate knowing systems, each valid in its own right, with the one, reason, sometimes interacting with the other two (unless, of course, one speaks analogously of "knowing" in the sense of classical or operant conditioning that results in purely physiological or psychic [meaning related to psyche in my sense of the term] responses, but such "knowing" is not human conceptual affirmation, which characterizes science, the topic here). Rather, the human being him- or herself is the knower, a single though polymorphous agent, capable of experiencing various data, of understanding, and of knowing. In every case human knowing results from the coalescence of acts on three levels of consciousness as the judgment of fact confirms the validity of an idea in light of the data. Precisely this singularity of cognitive process allows for the possible unity of all human knowledge. Consideration of the third function of the three eyes makes this pivotal difference between Wilber's and my position even clearer.

The Eyes as Modes of Knowing

In the third place, in Wilber's theory the three eyes also function as three modes of knowing. The eyes appear to be three separate knowing capacities. Thus, Wilber insists that the eye of contemplation "embodies a valid mode of knowledge" (35). This knowing, "a direct apprehension of spirit, by spirit, as spirit ... is quite beyond the capacities of objective-empirical [eye of flesh] or subjective-phenomenal [eye of mind] cognition" (60–61). So it is mistaken to believe that "Godhead can never be directly known or absolutely intuited," to think that God is "hidden to direct awareness" (19). Although "trying to prove with the eye of reason that which can only be seen with the eye of contemplation" (18) is futile, "a trained contemplative eye can *prove* the existence of God with exactly the same certainty and the same public nature as the eye of flesh can prove the existence of rocks" (34–35).

So one eye knows this, another knows that; one eye can prove this, another can prove that. Apparently, the eyes are separate cognitive capacities, separate knowing faculties. Indeed, the second strand of knowledge, the illuminative or apprehensive strand, is precisely "the illuminative *seeing* by the particular eye of knowledge evoked by the injunctive strand" (32). Different seeings, different kinds of knowledge, pertain to the three different eyes.

That supposed state of affairs is even used to explain why consensus is reached more easily in the physical sciences than in philosophy, psychology, and the humanities—"because everybody is given the same eye of flesh but different mental outlooks" (34). So the eye of flesh produces knowledge much more clear cut than that produced by the eye of mind or the eye of spirit. But this argument is glaringly specious.

Does not human variation in organism far exceed that in psyche or spirit? The structure of spirit, articulated by Lonergan, holds universally among humans; there is also a common structure in human psyche, characterized by archetypes, though it is yet to be precisely determined (Helminiak, 1996a). In contrast, however, the structure of the human eye or ear varies widely from person to person. That all humans have the same "eye of flesh" is fantasy. The blind and the deaf certainly do not perceive in the same way as the rest of the population. Nonetheless, they can come to understand the physical world as do any others. In their own way all can come to understand $C = 2\pi r$. Evidently, then, consensus of understanding, even regarding physical things like circles, is not primarily a function of sensory perception nor of imagination and feelings but rather of insights that occur on the second and third levels of consciousness. In Wilber's terminology: such consensus is neither a function of the eye of flesh nor of the eye of mind but in every case a function of the eye of spirit.

Wilber himself is aware that science is not an affair simply of the eye of flesh. It was already noted above how different kinds of knowledge supposedly result when the eye of reason adds "logic" to fleshly or mental or contemplative premises. Indeed, the genius of Bacon, Galileo, and Kepler was "to yoke the eye of reason to the eye of flesh" (15). But more than that, Wilber writes, "I believe it [empiric-analytic science] even uses the eye of contemplation for creative insight" (21). Indeed! Isn't creative insight at the very heart of all scientific discovery and explanation? Then which eye is really the eye of physical science?

The presentation of physical science as the domain of the lowly eye of the flesh, sensory perception, is misguided. Such a presentation attributes modern physics, surely among the most abstract of human achievements, to a low-level "knowing" capacity, "the eye we share with animals" (12). Surely, that attribution is not Wilber's intention, but the ambiguity in his talk of "three eyes" supports such an interpretation.

Similar problems result when Wilber tries to argue for the unique functioning of the eye of the mind. He writes, "there is no *empirical*-scientific proof for the meaning of *Hamlet*. It is a mental-symbolic production and can thus be understood or apprehended only by a mental act—sensory evidence is almost entirely worthless" (48). Wilber's insistence on a valid realm of reality available only to understanding minds is certainly welcome. It is indeed foolish to conclude that there is nothing there to be understood because a team of physicists could not, with all their sophisticated gadgetry for observation and measurement, thus determine the meaning of a Shakespeare production. But it is equally foolish to suggest that seeing and hearing the production is incidental to anyone's being able to determine that meaning. In this case, even as in the case of the physical sciences, sensory evidence is far from worthless. On the contrary, it is one condition for the possibility of human understanding.

When the three eyes are taken to imply separate modes of human knowing, foolishness or equivocation must be the result. There can be no validity in this use of the metaphor.

Finally, it was suggested above that the three eyes seem to parallel the factors in the tripartite model of the human: organism, psyche, and spirit. In fact, beyond consideration of the physiological organism, the parallel breaks down. For Wilber, the eye of mind/ reason has to do with reasoning, logic, and conceptual formulation. Wilber seems to have bought the modern notion of reason as rationality or "logic-ing," what has been called instrumental reason (Taylor, 1989). But the modern notion of reason is distorted and impoverished, so there is need to make room somewhere for insight, intuition, creativity—and Wilber makes room in the eye of spirit.

For me, following Lonergan, spirit or consciousness entails both the creative and the propositional dimensions of human understanding and knowing. Insight and logic are two sides of the same coin. So for me, mind is not reason and contemplation, as for Wilber, but psyche and spirit; and spirit explains both reasoning and contemplation. One of Lonergan's (1957) main tasks was to understand understanding. His conclusions show that the modern notion of reason overlooks the determinative characteristic of human cognition, namely, insight. Accepting Lonergan's understanding of cognition, I need speak only of consciousness/spirit (in Lonergan's sense of the terms), whereas Wilber needs to posit an eye of reason as well as an eye of spirit.

Another drawback results in Wilber's model. It includes no specific accounting for the purely psychic processes—emotion, imagery, memory, and personality structures, which constitute psyche in my model. For Wilber these things are somehow packaged up in the eye of mind/reason. So this eye deals with things as disparate as mathematics and philosophy, on the one hand, and psychology, sociology, anthropology, art, and literature, on the other.

Moreover, in his understanding of the eye of spirit, Wilber includes the divine. But this I differentiate from the human spirit by understanding God as Creator and the human spirit as created.

The parallel between Wilber's three eyes and my tripartite model of the human is only apparent. Wilber began by unfortunately building into his account the modern and distorted notion of reason, so he had to supplement it with a broadly conceived eye of spirit, and in the process he gave short shrift to matters of psyche and their role in human cognition and becoming. In contrast, I took a whole other starting point. I began with Lonergan's radically different and richer understanding of cognition, epistemology, and metaphysics, so I could see not only that human spirit, as it functions in the process of knowing, entails both logical reasoning and insightful creativity but also that human spirit is different from psyche on the one hand and from divinity on the other.

Summary on the Three Eyes

Wilber's conception of three eyes is a real chameleon. It holds some validity when the intent is merely to indicate an array of possible sciences and when the intent is to indicate an availability of different kinds of data, which determine that array of sciences. However, the conception has no validity when it is taken to suggest actual, separate, human capacities or faculties whether for gathering data or for producing knowledge.

Taking the three eyes to refer to separate modes of knowing or separate cognitive capacities not only results in inconsistencies, as noted. It also fractures human knowing by projecting separate realms of knowledge, dependent on disparate knowing capacities. So Wilber's conception appears to be but an expansion of Dilthey's distinction (80–81) between the physical sciences (*Naturwissenschaften*) and the human sciences (*Geisteswissenschaften*). In some way or other this unfortunate distinction underlies every counterposition considered in this book. The distinction's core error is oversight of the difference between common sense and theory as two different ways of expressing understandings, as explained in Chapter Three. This error is related to the anemic modern notion of reason, which does not understand what understanding is. Buying into this error, Wilber's contribution is to add yet a third separate level of *Wissenschaften*: mandalic or spiritual science. This contribution is precisely an addition. It posits a separate realm of human experience and insists that it, too, is a realm of valid knowledge, though of yet another kind. Wilber's unwavering insistence on a spiritual realm is certainly welcome, and to a large extent his defense of the spiritual explains his near hero status in the transpersonal psychology movement. But as presented by Wilber, knowledge in this realm is incommensurate with that in the other two, just as in Dilthey's position the physical and the human sciences are incommensurate with one another. On this understanding there is juxtaposition but there is no unification of the sciences. There is no comprehensive paradigm.

A Theory of Knowledge

The need is for a theory of knowledge that can apply equally to different realms of data and sustain the claim of validity for the knowledge in each of those realms. Wilber's account of the three strands of knowledge is to supply just such a theory. Criticism must now turn to that account.

According to Wilber, all valid knowledge is similar because it entails 1) a prescription for attaining the knowledge in question, 2) the actual attainment of the knowledge, and 3) social consensus as to the validity of the knowledge attained. These are the "three strands" that constitute all knowledge and science.

Knowledge as Immediate Apprehension

Strand #2 represents the key issue. It explains the actual knowing. In what does such "knowing" consist? Well, strand #2 is the "illuminative or apprehensive strand" (31). It entails "intuitive apprehension" (43). Its knowledge is such that, "To know if it's raining, go and look" (32); or, as regards spiritual knowledge, proper contemplative training allows "direct seeing into one's spiritual nature," "a direct apprehension" (60). Evidently, Wilber holds a theory of immediacy of knowledge. One knows simply by attending. Like light striking the retina, knowledge is immediately given to the opened eye. Look and you see. Attend to the matter and you know. On this basis, attending with different eyes results in different kinds of knowledge. The key to the matter is simply to be willing to train the proper eye. Open the eye, and the rest happens automatically.

But that account of knowing is too simple. Consider what actually goes into the training and what one actually does in some supposed "apprehensive" moment. In the physical sciences, for example, the young, budding scientist must certainly learn more than attentive looking, for even observation is guided by theory. Scientific training includes questioning, theorizing, planning and carrying out experiments, measuring and running statistical analyses, interpreting results, drawing conclusions, checking the conclusions against replicated experiments, and so on over and over. Obviously, attaining scientific knowledge requires more than looking. Scientific knowledge is hardly an immediate given, ready to impinge on anyone who wants it. The theory of knowing as direct apprehension is an illusion. Strand #2 projects a fantasy, alluring but overwhelmingly deceptive.

Knowledge as Achievement

The obvious contrast is Lonergan's theory of knowledge. There, knowing is the result of the coalescence of numerous acts on three distinct levels of consciousness. Through an act of conscious awareness, one experiences data. Then question arises as to what one is experiencing. Pondering the data provokes an insight, which expresses itself in an idea, concept, theory, or hypothesis. Further question arises as to the accuracy of the hypothesis. Consideration of the data in light of the hypothesis results in another insight about the adequacy of the hypothesis to the data. With this final insight one knows, one grasps whether one's understanding—the idea or the hypothesis—does account for the data or not.

Notice how this account of knowing parallels the textbook account of the scientific method. Accumulation of data leads to the formation of hypothesis. The formation of hypothesis calls for experimental testing. Verification of the hypothesis depends on its demonstrated adequacy to the data.

On Lonergan's (1957, 1967a) understanding, there is a major difference between data and knowledge (Helminiak, 1996a, pp. 62–65). *Data* are immediately given in the awareness that constitutes the first level of consciousness. The immediacy of this givenness is the immediacy of the nonreflecting presence of consciousness "to" itself. Experiencing him- or herself as the experiencer in the immediacy of nonreflecting self-awareness, a person can then come in reflecting consciousness to wonder what it was that she or he was experiencing. The experience constitutes the data, which one can then question. In contrast, *knowledge* only results from questioning the data and after two different kinds of insights are added to the experience, one for understanding and one for judgment of fact, and insight itself is oftentimes only arduously achieved. Knowledge is a composite of experience, understanding, and judgment.

Wilber does not make such a detailed analysis of the actual process of knowing. As a result, he presents a global account of knowing as a moment of "direct apprehension." Of course, this oversimplification allows him to deal easily with spiritual experiences by treating them as moments of knowing, but such treatment is misguided. The confusion of data, given in immediate experience, and knowledge, achieved through correct insight into data, has far-reaching consequences—especially when one attempts to relate different sciences or to deal with consciousness itself and claim knowledge of the spiritual.

Data, Not Knowledge

Some of Wilber's presentation does seem to make a distinction between data and knowledge (but in the end, it seems, only because of an ambiguity of terminology). Wilber does seem to be arguing for the validity of different realms of data, which can become the basis for valid knowledge. So what Lonergan articulates explicitly may well be part of what Wilber is trying to say. For example, opposing the "empirical verification principle" of narrow scientism, Wilber insists, *"this does not mean verifiable by direct experience in general; it means verifiable by sense experience"* (23). Wilber clearly wants to insist that there are different kinds of direct experience, different kinds of valid data. He writes at length,

> The core of the problem is that there is a great ambiguity in the meaning of the word "experience." It can be used to mean only sensory experience (as empiricists do), but it can also be used to cover virtually all modes of awareness and consciousness. For instance, there is a sense in which I *experience* not only my own sensations and perceptions (sensibilia) but also my own ideas, thoughts, and concepts (intelligibilia)—I see them with the mind's eye, I *experience* my thoughts, my personal ideals, my imaginative displays. . . . Likewise, there is a sense in which I *experience* spirit—with the eye of contemplation or *gnosis*, I directly and immediately apprehend and experience spirit *as* spirit, the realm of transcendelia.
>
> In all these broader senses, "experience" is simply synonymous with direct apprehension, immediate givenness, intuition—sensory, mental, and spiritual.
>
> Stated thus, there is indeed a sense in which all knowledge is grounded in experience (as empiricists claim)—but not in *sensory* experience (which they also claim). Thus, various *a priori* or rational truths are those I *experience* in the mental realm but not in the sensory realm (e.g., mathematics). And transcendental truths are those I *experience* in the spiritual realm but not in the mental or sensory realms (e.g., satori).

And in that sense, there are all sorts of knowledge outside of sensory experience, but none that is finally outside of *experience* in general. Sensibilia, intelligibilia, and transcendelia can all be open to direct and immediate experiential apprehension or intuition, and those apprehensions constitute the data of the knowledge quest in each of those domains. (42)

There, verbally at least, Wilber seems to come close to sorting out three realms of possible experience, one sensible and two mental. Insisting that the data of experience can be more than sensory input, he seems to be affirming with Lonergan a "generalized empirical method" (Lonergan, 1957, pp. 72, 243). Stating that "all knowledge is *grounded in* experience," he seems to be making the distinction between data and knowledge. But serious ambiguity soon enters the picture.

What Wilber has clearly and correctly discovered, is the immediacy of experience—the presence of consciousness "to" itself, the nonreflecting aspect of human consciousness. That this is so is not surprising, since Wilber finds his most illuminating instruction in the Eastern traditions of meditation. His insistence on that immediacy is a valuable contribution. So he says, the datum is "the immediate display of experience"; and again, "the point is immediateness or givenness in direct experience" (39).

Data as Knowledge

But Wilber has not appreciated the difference between what is immediately given, the data or experience, and human knowledge as "processed" data. So Wilber quotes William James to support his understanding of datum: " 'If our own private vision of the paper be considered in abstraction [or bracketed off] from every other event, then the paper seen and the seeing of it are only two names for one indivisible fact which, properly named, is *the datum, the phenomenon, or the experience'* " (38). This quote does support Wilber's insistence on the immediacy of experience, for it does posit some (never-explained and ultimately erroneous) identity between the seen and the seeing. But Wilber overlooks the fact that James has already smuggled in understanding and judgment in what he calls the datum. For the term "paper" implies more than mere sense perceptions. "Paper" 1) *correctly* 2) *interprets* and 3) *names* the perceived. One does not immediately perceive paper; one immediately perceives visual data which one correctly understands as "paper." The example is not the best because at stake is simple recognition (Helminiak, 1996a, p. 85), which even brute animals can do in their own way. Still, the point is valid.

But again, in the last long quote above, Wilber suggests that we *experience* truths, rational truths in the mental realm and transcendental truths in the spiritual realm. But if "experience" is to refer to the apprehension of the immediately given, to the apprehension of data—and that is how Wilber uses the term—it is simply untrue that we *experience* truths. What we do experience is data. But only after we have correctly understood these data do we know and can we speak the truth pertaining to them. Truth is not something lying out there to be stumbled upon or seen or intuited, something that is gained through perception or some other kind of immediate apprehension. Truth or knowledge is the product of correct human understanding. When Wilber suggests that we experience truths, he confounds data and knowledge.

Or again, the task of the second strand of valid knowing is "immediate *data*-apprehension" (43). Though Wilber italicizes "data," he means something else. For strand #3 is "checking the results (apprehensions or data) with others" (43). But the "results" one checks with others are formulated understandings or conclusions or supposed knowledge—and not immediate apprehensions: one cannot share one's immediate apprehensions as such with another. Wilber confounds data and knowledge. Indeed, while on page 43 Wilber says, "valid data accumulation in any realm has three basic strands," on page 31 he says, "all valid knowledge . . . consists of three basic components," the three strands. And later on page 31, Wilber italicizes "valid knowledge"—just as he italicized "data." Evidently, data and knowledge are meant to mean the same thing.

Verification as Communal Confirmation

Consideration of the third strand of valid knowledge will again highlight Wilber's confusion of data and knowledge and will expose a latent relativism in his theory. By "relativism" I mean the general philosophical position that objective human knowledge is impossible.

I refer to the skeptical insistence that no knowledge can apply equally across cultures, across times, and among different individuals.

Wilber's third strand of valid knowledge is "communal confirmation" (44). The suggestion is that verification is constituted by social consensus and that the agreement among a community of "experts" is what assures the validity of some knowledge. On this basis, the explicit criterion of truth is social consensus. Whatever people tend to hold is what will be deemed true. Here, again, it is evident that not data, not immediate apprehensions, but some kind of processed cognitive product, knowledge, is submitted to communal scrutiny. Although Wilber speaks of the overall knowing process as "data-gathering and verification procedures" (43), it is clear that he is talking about knowledge and not about mere data. Likewise, because the position ultimately appeals to social consensus, the relativity in this position is already evident, for this position suggests that truth is whatever a group of people can agree on.

However, what Wilber really means by "communal confirmation" is far from clear. The one thing he maintains throughout is the possibility of the "rebuff" of theories. This possible rebuff guarantees their correctness.

Wilber gets this notion of rebuff from Karl Popper (1985). In Popper's theory the rebuff arises from critical thinking. If a theory cannot stand up to questioning and new data and the criticism of others, it is rebuffed.

Note that on Popper's understanding an inherent flaw in an argument or theory is the basis of rebuff. Though the rebuff comes from others concerned about the matter, not the sheer opinion of the others but the inability of the theory to meet the issue is the basis of rebuff.

Wilber confounds those two matters. In Wilber's words, "a 'bad' fact . . . will be rebuffed, not only by other facts but by the community of investigators" (46). For Wilber there appear to be two possible bases for rebuff: adequacy of the theory to the facts (read: to the data) and acceptance by others. Wilber never sorts these two out. As a result, on his theory, someone's "immediate apprehension," that is, vision, insight, intuition, supposition, or whatever, may find its ultimate validation in the fact that others happen to agree with it. Again, Wilber certainly does not intend such a simplistic stance, but his words allow and support it, and he does not seem to know how to avoid it.

In fact, it is only in treating spiritual knowledge that Wilber insists almost solely on social acceptance as the criterion of truth. The consensus community in his example is the Zen Master and the other meditators. They judge whether a student's meditative experience is valid or not: "*all* apprehensions are struck against the community of those whose cognitive eyes are adequate to the transcendent, and such apprehensions are soundly nonverified if they do not match the facts of transcendence as disclosed by the community of like-spirited" (61–62). Taken as it stands, this statement could apply to a Fundamentalist church, a racist fraternity, a Nazi military base, or a Jonestown or Waco or Heaven's Gate community just as well as to a Zen monastery. For the express criterion is social consensus. If the determination of "eyes adequate to the transcendent" has no other criterion except "those whose cognitive eyes are adequate to the transcendent," there is no criterion given. The argument is circular. It will fit any group where people agree or can be made to agree.

This analysis is not meant to disparage the Zen tradition. It is to criticize Wilber's rendition of that tradition. That tradition does work, and it does maintain its purity. But more than social consensus is at work in it. The consensus is about *something*, and that something imposes itself on the meditators. (Surely this is also the point Wilber wishes to make.) That something also imposes its own criterion on the consensus—and not vice versa. Moreover, the meditators must *express* their experience in some way before others can test it against their own. So at work in that tradition is an experience that many have not only been able to achieve but that they have also been able somehow to express. In that expression, halting as it must be, others who have had the same experience recognize their own experience. They then agree that they are speaking of the same experience.

Wilber's account ignores the role that reflection on the experience and articulation of the experience play in that tradition. His jump from "immediate apprehension" to "communal confirmation" is all too easy. Mutual confirmation of findings certainly plays an important part in the growth of any body of knowledge. But that confirmation is not itself the criterion of validity for the knowledge. Adequacy to the data is the criterion. The contribution of the community is precisely to ensure that this intrinsic criterion is met. This is the meaning of Popper's insistence on critical thinking. This is also the meaning of Lonergan's determination that knowledge results from a correct judgment of fact.

Verification as Adequacy to Data

Wilber probably also agrees with that assessment, for he is aware of the criterion of adequacy to data. Talking about the same three strands of valid knowledge, he insists on this criterion quite clearly as regards empirical science and even to some extent as regards the "mental" sciences. For example, opposing the mere imposition of an opinion through social pressure, he says, "what distinguishes a theory or hypothesis from a merely dogmatic formulation is its call to experiential or data-based verification" (69).

But more elaborate statements suppose a difference between dealing with sensibilia and with intelligibilia. Wilber writes,

> [I]f you are working with the empirical-analytic mode, then you are basically working with the "mirror" model of truth. . . . Propositions are true if they reflect the facts correctly—that type of thing. An empiric proposition is true if it more or less accurately mirrors or pictures or represents the sensory world. That is all as it should be. That model is just right for empirical truth. But when it comes to the purely mental or phenomenological world, the simple mirror or only reflective model no longer works. In a sense you are still doing reflective work— you know, you are still proposing theoretic maps and models, as we earlier discussed; but you are no longer using symbols to represent nonsymbolic occasions. You are using symbols to look at other symbols, a process which *creates* new worlds with new possibilities and new truths. . . . [I]n the mental world where symbols look at symbols, it's like using one mirror to reflect another mirror which reflects the reflection, and so on in a circle of meaning that you and I cocreate whenever we talk. That is the hermeneutic circle. (193)

That theories reflect the facts correctly is the criterion of truth in the empirical sciences. But supposedly, this same criterion does not hold in the human sciences. Why? Because the circular function of human exchange of meaning creates new worlds, new truths. Then in this case, it seems, truth and reality are not something objectively determined; rather, they depend on the circle of communicators who create them. Under these circumstances, social consensus must be the criterion of truth. Agreement determines "reality" and "truth."

That Wilber would entertain such a conclusion, if he does, is really very peculiar. It is peculiar, in the first place, because it is based on a false supposition. Wilber suggests that in the empirical sciences truth mirrors or maps or models or pictures reality. But how much does $C=2\pi r$ actually look like a circle? Physicists entertain no illusion that they are describing something visible. They use complex mathematical formulae to express an *understanding* of physical reality. What they articulate mathematically is the intelligibility of the universe. They do indeed maintain a criterion of responsibility to the data, but they make no attempt to mirror or picture reality. So the "mirror model of truth" is no more appropriate for the physical sciences than it is for the human sciences. And meaning or intelligibility is as much the concern of the physical sciences as it is of the human sciences. Granted, treatment of meaning in the human sciences is more difficult because, as Wilber rightly states, humans do create their own meaning. But to conclude that the physical and human sciences are therefore basically different, is really to misunderstand what science is in any case.

That conclusion, that social consensus would be the criterion of truth in the human sciences, is peculiar for a second reason—namely, that elsewhere Wilber argues perfectly well that correctness in these sciences depends on adequacy to their data. For example, correct translation of hieroglyphics requires an interpretation that squares with other known translations. "The point is simply that, though we are working with a largely subjective production—a language—nonetheless that doesn't mean I can pop out any ole interpretation that suits me, because intelligibilia possess intersymbolic and intersubjective *structures* that will themselves *rebuff* erroneous claims" (50). Again, to say fully what Goya's painting, *May 3, 1808*, objectively means may be impossible. "But any ole meaning or interpretation will not do—this painting is *not* about the joys of war" (57). Or again, the field of psychology, though far from coherent, is showing significant convergences among different researchers and areas of study. "The point, however, is that in a very impressive number of areas, there is a decent intersubjective consensus on fact, theory, and practice; a general and ongoing intersubjective movement of *intelligibilia* that not only produces repeatable data but rebuffs incongruent apprehensions and dislodges them from the ongoing sweep of the knowledge quest" (59–60).

Flip-flopping between an Objective and a Subjective Criterion

Perhaps it is easier to conceive objective interpretation in those examples than in other areas within the humanities. To determine the meaning of hieroglyphics is easier than assessing the validity of a culture or judging the acceptability of a religion or a *Zeitgeist*. Wilber would like to maintain objectivity throughout, and he struggles to do so, but with varying success. For example, in answer to the question, "But using phenomenology and hermeneutics as an example, wouldn't mere interpretation make truth a wildly subjective affair?" Wilber responds:

It depends upon the caliber of the community of interpreters. Real philosophy, psychology, and phenomenology . . . depend in large measure upon the quality of the community of interpreters. Good interpreters, good thinkers, ground good phenomenology. They discover those truths that apply to the subjective realm, and in that sense the truths are subjective truths. But that doesn't mean mere individual whim. First of all, a bad interpretation will simply not mesh with general subjective consensus. It is rebuffed by a reality that is subjective but very real and very lawful, just as a bad empiric fact is rebuffed by other facts. Second, a phenomenological truth, in order to be recognized as truth, must be *tested* in a community of like-minded interpreters, just as an empiric fact, to be so, must be tested against the community of other facts. It's no mere wishful thinking and subjective license. The hermeneutic test is just as stringent and demanding as the empiric test, but of course the empiric test is easier because it is performed by a subject on an object, whereas phenomenology is performed by a subject on or with other subjects. Much more difficult. (185)

Three observations about that response can conclude this discussion of the third strand of knowledge, communal confirmation. First, note that while Wilber listed two safeguards against mere individual whim, the two are actually the same. The first is "general subjective consensus," and the second is "a community of likeminded interpreters." Here, the criterion on consensus seems to hold full sway.

However, second, Wilber's appeal to "a reality that is subjective but very real and very lawful" is provocative. In the quote three paragraphs above, Wilber emphatically refers to "intersubjective *structures*." Repeatedly Wilber makes this appeal to "phenomenological facts, as *embedded and disclosed in intersubjective consensus*" and "the domain of intelligibilia and its *intersubjective structures*" (49–50) and rebuff "by the very *structures* of the intersubjective realm of intelligibilia (the other mental facts themselves and the community of interpreters)" (51). For the life of me, I cannot figure out what Wilber is trying to say. The insistence is surely an appeal to some source of objectivity as real as that found in empirical science's reliance on sensory data. But what that source of objectivity is supposed to be remains a mystery.

My most likely interpretation is this: just as in the realm of physical science there are objective constraints on acceptable conclusions, namely, the sensible data that must be accounted for with reasonable argument; so in the realm of interpersonal belief and sharing there are some kinds of objective structures that constrain acceptable conclusions. These structures emerge in some intersubjective realm that is created when people interact.

I believe that Wilber is actually imagining some kind of other realm, another world of human experience, a parallel universe, for he also proposes that the transcendental realm is yet a third world into which people, properly trained, might enter, and there have a whole other kind of experience and a whole other kind of knowledge, all incommensurate with experience and knowledge in our present shared world. And I believe Wilber means all this quite literally. I imagine scenes from the movie version of *The Hobbit*. When a character in the movie put on the magic ring, the screen went fuzzy and, as if a scrim were raised, there slowly emerged a whole other dimension of reality, another world, which supposedly had been there all along, but one could not perceive or enter into it without the magic ring. This would be Wilber's intersubjective world, which exists as a parallel to the physical world, with its own structures and its own laws.

According to the supposition, the structures of this inter-subjective world constrain life there just as the structures of the physical world constrain our living. Is this or something like it what Wilber is suggesting? To my mind the suggestion is sheer fantasy, an exercise in imagination, like *The Hobbit*. Yet my interpretation does square with Wilber's conception of three incommensurate kinds of knowledge which, supposedly, correspond to three eyes, which give information on three separate realms.

That this notion of parallel worlds is mistaken is patent. It misunderstands what understanding is. The physical sciences entail an exercise in meaning as much as does literary interpretation. The physical sciences are not dealing in the physical but in the mental. Their task is to *discern* the inherent *intelligibility* of the physical universe, to propose a coherent *interpretation* of the sensible data. The "world" of physical science is not a world different from the "world" of intersubjectivity. Shared *meanings* constitute them both. As Lonergan puts it, unlike the other animals who live in a habitat, we humans live in a world mediated by meaning and motivated by value. This value-laden meaningful world coincides with the physical world as much as with the intersubjective world. It is the one world in which we live, although this world has many dimensions for possible exploration, including the physical, the psychic (in my sense of the term), and the spiritual, and the charting of these dimensions is always an intersubjective, a shared, enterprise.

More optimistically, maybe Wilber means something else. By intersubjective structures, maybe he is alluding to human mental structures, like Jung's archetypes of the psyche or Lonergan's levels of consciousness (Helminiak, 1996a), which all people share in common. In this case, the argument would be that even regarding "subjective" experiences, as also regarding physical experiences, the cognitive enterprise ever engages the same process of human knowing, namely, operations on the first three levels of consciousness. Within this process the exigencies of proper functioning on each level of operation—attentiveness, intelligence, and reasonableness—constrain the process, rebuff nonsense, and thus eventually arrive at truth. However, this optimistic interpretation presupposes Lonergan's cognitive theory and epistemology, which Wilber does not share. Still, this interpretation does suggest that Lonergan's understanding of things can make reasonable sense of the "intersubjective" matters with which Wilber is struggling.

In contrast, as initially suggested, Wilber's phraseology puts the emphasis on social consensus, and his insistence on the *inter*subjective diverts consideration from the structures of the individual human mind. Indeed, the intersubjective structure in question might well be the imposing reality of an opinion deeply felt and widely held. Where objectivity and a guarantee of correctness come in here is hard to say. But what about "other mental facts themselves"? Who knows?

Third, the above long quote contains hints as to what that elusive source of objectivity might validly be. Wilber talks of "the caliber" and "the quality" of the community of interpreters. His reference to "good interpreters, good thinkers" is quite different from the reference to "like-minded interpreters." Certainly, if really good people, interpreters of the highest all-around caliber, were to do the interpretative work, that work would, as best as humanly possible, approach objective validity. Here, Wilber is onto something that would, indeed, meet the issue.

Yet what is the measure of caliber or quality? What is meant by "good"? To these questions, Wilber has no explicit answer. The closest he comes to an answer shifts the criterion back again to consensus. Precisely this shortcoming is the flaw in his third strand of knowledge.

Objectivity in "Subjective" Domains

But there is an answer to the question, What is the criterion of "good"? Lonergan has provided that answer: human authenticity. Objectivity is possible even in the realms of supposedly "subjective" humanities studies. How so? Let Lonergan (1972, p. 265; see also p. 292) speak for himself.

> There are areas in which investigators commonly agree, such as mathematics and science; in such fields objective knowledge is obtainable. There are other areas, such as philosophy, ethics, religion, in which agreement commonly is lacking; such disagreement is explained by the subjectivity of philosophers,

moralists, religious people. But whether subjectivity is always mistaken, wrong, evil, is a further question. Positivists, behaviorists, naturalists would tend to say that it is. Others, however, would insist on distinguishing between an authentic and an unauthentic subjectivity. What results from the former is neither mistaken nor wrong nor evil. It is just something quite different from the objective knowledge attainable in mathematics and in science. . . .

. . . it is now apparent that in the world mediated by meaning and motivated by value [that is, the world of human inquiry and thought, including the realms which Wilber calls intelligibilia and transcendelia], objectivity is simply the consequence of authentic subjectivity, of genuine attention, genuine intelligence, genuine reasonableness, genuine responsibility. Mathematics, science, philosophy, ethics, theology differ in many manners; but they have the common feature that their objectivity is the fruit of attentiveness, intelligence, reasonableness, and responsibility.

So Wilber's "new worlds with new possibilities and new truths . . . in a circle of meaning that you and I cocreate" (193) may indeed be anything we can succeed in creating. But whether those "new worlds" will really be good and those "new truths" true, depends on the measure of authenticity of the ones creating them. The human creation of meaning is one thing. The objective validity of that meaning, a function of authenticity, is something else.

Once again Lonergan's position meets the needs and suggests corrections to the flaws in Wilber's presentation. The three strands of knowledge are mere extrinsic considerations. They do not touch the intrinsic nature of human knowing and so cannot account for the validity of knowledge or science.

Wilber's Treatment of Authenticity

But Wilber does treat the issue of authenticity. He devotes a whole chapter to it (244–263). Still, for Wilber, "authenticity" is a measure of validity for a social or religious movement or a belief system. That is, authenticity pertains to a social organization, not to an individual. Wilber defines authenticity in relation to his stages

of human development. Organizations that foster such development are deemed authentic. This criterion of human development
is, indeed, more or less valid. I argued that emergence of the *higher*
stages of human development, the post-conventional stages, depends on some degree of authenticity, in Lonergan's sense
(Helminiak, 1987c, pp. 79–82). So somewhere authenticity in
Wilber's sense does coincide with authenticity in Lonergan's sense,
and this is a happy realization.

In fact, Wilber never clearly resolves the question about the
inherent nature of truth, reality, objectivity, and goodness, despite
the chapter on authenticity and despite long discussions about
scientific knowledge. Wilber's adherence to the "perennial philosophy" probably explains this fact. In the "Ultimate State of Consciousness" none of these things really matters anyway. Ignorance
is supposedly enlightenment (300), and the difference between good
and evil is supposedly transcended (241). Wilber's philosophical
commitment allows him to take these things seriously at one point
and then at another point to suggest that they are ultimately
meaningless. The suggestions that samsara is nirvana and that
maya is Brahman (318)—that is, that the present realm is the
ultimate realm—do not explain the inconsistency; rather, they highlight it. Indeed, on Wilber's position these suggestions, part of the
world of samsara and maya, can themselves be taken seriously or
can be treated as ultimately meaningless.

Paradox in Wilber's Position

Authenticity, a notion pivotal in my position as prerequisite to any
valid human discourse, ultimately plays no explicit part in Wilber's
presentation. For him, the Ultimate State of Consciousness is the
final guarantor of all validity. Nonetheless, he would want his
position in the realm of samsara to be taken seriously. Obviously,
consideration must now turn to the scientific legitimacy of what
Wilber calls "paradox."

Wilber's insistence on paradox has already been noted. Supposedly, logical inconsistencies or paradoxes are inevitable whenever one attempts to reason about transcendelia. Wilber is adamant
on this point. His insistence on the legitimacy of paradox in the
realm of transcendelia is a cornerstone of his integral paradigm.

But this cornerstone does not hold, and the intellectual edifice it supports begins to crumble. For there is further evidence on the matter. The paradoxes depend on ambiguities and oversights. Sorting these out eliminates the supposedly inevitable paradoxes. The discussion that follows substantiates this claim.

But first, let me state again my appreciation for metaphor, for myth, symbol, ritual, and yes, even paradoxical statement—but all in their proper place, and I do not believe that scientific account is the place for paradoxical statement. I treated this matter in detail in Chapter Three under the section, "Religion and Science," and under the later subsection, "The Importance of Metaphors."

The Supposed Paradox in Self-Actualizing People

A relatively easy example, which Wilber cites, is Abraham Maslow's characterization of self-actualizing people. Those who touch the heart of self-transcending experience "can only be described as 'simultaneously selfish and unselfish, Dionysian and Apollonian, individual and social, rational and irrational, fused with others and detached from others, and so on'" (75). These descriptions may seem like inconsistencies, oppositions, or flat contradictions, as Maslow suggests, but a little thought shows that they are not.

Take "individual and social," "fused with others and detached from others." If spirit partially constitutes humanity, as I have argued, it is of the very nature of the human to embrace the universal. So the more any person actualizes him- or herself, all the more will she or he live with what transcends individuality. Add authenticity to the equation, and the matter is explained. Increased authentic individuality entails increased sociality, increased universality (Helminiak 1979, 1987c, pp. 69–70, 91; 1988a; 1996a, pp. 210–212, 252–254, 258).

The same point can be made much more simply. All the truly great—artists, statespersons, humanitarians, athletes—are both highly unusual personalities and very compassionate, empathic, people. True greatness, true humanity, requires that one delve into one's own heart and there know the joys and sorrows, the dreams and disappointments, the victories and failures, that all humankind experiences. Knowing that, one identifies with all other human beings. There is no paradox here. The matter is readily understandable. From one point of view, as organism and psyche, one is individual; from another point of view, as self-transcending spirit, one is universal. Specify the different points of view and all apparent contradiction or inconsistency dissolves.

Or take "Dionysian and Apollonian," "rational and irrational." If the self-actualized person is understood as having achieved significant spiritual integration, delight in order and balance as well as openness to spontaneity and playfulness should both be expected. For human spirit is precisely an *open-ended* dynamism toward absolute *consistency*. Moreover, if, as it seems, "irrational" really means to say "intuitive, spontaneous, motivated by feelings," rationality and "irrationality" will be characteristic of any integrated person. For the wholesome functioning of the human, as organism, psyche, and spirit, requires that emphasis now be given to this, now to that dimension, of one's polymorphic being. Attention to the "this and that," to the "now and then," of the harmoniously interacting human system eliminates any true contradiction.

A similar explanation pertains to the false dichotomy, selfish and unselfish, discussed in the previous chapter. Therefore, what Wilber and Maslow may describe as paradox appears hardly to be that when a deeper understanding is brought to bear on the matter.

The Confounding of Psychology and Ontology

A second example of supposed paradox is more difficult. It is difficult because it moves from the personal and psychological into the epistemological and the ontological. Or at least I take it to move in this way, and I need to explain myself.

This matter is so highly ambiguous that I am not sure what to make of it. I find a pervasive ambiguity in writings about Eastern philosophy. I am never sure in the end if the statements are referring to psychology or to ontology. For me the two are very different, and I find that they are generally confounded.

Take, for example, the Buddhist teaching of *anatman/anatta*, non-self. On the one hand, this teaching is supposed to carry simple psychological wisdom that is common in spiritual and psychological circles in both East and West: "Instead of denying or negating self, achieving *anatman* is actually accepting the different side of a coin, namely the true self, without the false perceptions associated with one's ordinary mind and ordinary language" (Hong, 1995, p. 98). The point here is that one needs to avoid attachments, ego involvement, biases. No problem. But on the other hand, this teaching seems to bespeak an ontological truth; it seems to speak about what is or is not in objective reality: "Not only does it [the concept of non-self] reflect the nature of existential reality, but it also serves as an instrument which breaks down the illusion of an immortal self" (Hong, 1995, p. 98). Now, whether or not the self is immortal is not in question here. The point is simply that the doctrine of *anatman* supposedly announces the facts of the matter. This announcement is an ontological claim.

My sense is that the validity of Buddhist teaching lies more in its psychological wisdom than anywhere else. Buddhism offers a practical path for wholesome living. The fact that Mahayana Buddhism proposed the eightfold path and the six virtues or *paramita* as a practical formulation of the theoretically formulated middle path of nondualism supports this understanding (Hong, 1995). However, my judgment is that, when Buddhist teachings—or perhaps only Western renditions of them—begin making ontological statements, they run into inevitable self-contradiction; they become nonsensical.

I am aware, of course, that central to this tradition ultimately is the eschewing of all statement. Yet statements are made, and they do have ontological intent. My purpose is to show that, as such and taken literally, far from being paradoxical, they are nonsensical.

Another example is the famous argument of the eight-century Hindu philosopher, Samkara, with its theory of illusion and its notion of degrees of reality (Puhaka, 1995). Supposedly, though the phenomenal world is illusory, it is not unreal. It is not unreal because within the phenomenal world there is nothing really real against which to measure its unreality. Yet the phenomenal world is not as real as transcendent reality. The famous illustration is the snake encountered in the dark of night but by the light of day discovered to be a piece of rope. The experience of the night was unquestionably that of a snake, yet the light reveals that the experience of "snake" was illusory. Supposedly, the discrepancy between snake and rope can be resolved. Allow that the reality of the rope is more real than that of the snake and that the reality of the rope sublates the reality of the snake. But once again, psychology and ontology are confounded. Personal "reality," what something is for me, is taken to be an instance of objective reality, what something is in itself. Subjective experience and objective reality are taken to be the same thing, and representing a philosophical idealism, the statements do appear to be making ontological claims.

The Supposed Dualism between Being and Nothingness

Wilber presents what is patently a statement about ontology. He argues, "Even the term 'Being' is dualistic, taking as its opposite 'Nothingness,' and so on. But you get the point: mandalic science will always be based, in whole or in part, on paradoxes, and we had better face that fact right up front or our mandalic science will simply be called self-contradictory and dismissed by 'real scientists'" (75).

But Wilber's statement about being and nothingness is wrong. There is no paradox involved there, only confused thinking.

On the one hand, Wilber is right in suggesting that being has no opposite. On the other hand, he is mistaken to think that talk of being implies that it does. His portrayal of the matter suggests that there is some paradox involved. But no, it is simply mistaken to think that positing being implies an opposite. Nothingness is not the opposite of being, for nothingness is not. *Nothingness* is but a word, a concept; it has no correlate in reality, for if it had, it would be something, being, and not nothing. There is no paradox in this discussion of being and nothingness. There is merely the confusion of words and reality—like a classic error in Eastern spiritual wisdom: mistaking the menu for the meal (77) or the finger for the moon it points at.

Wilber says that the term *being* is dualistic. Now, the term, as a term, may be dualistic if one allows that another term *nothingness* is its opposite. But being as reality is not dualistic, for being has no opposite: nothingness does not exist. So properly understood, even to affirm being as reality is not dualistic. Propositional thinking does not always involve the supposed error of dualism.

The affirmation of being is both propositional and non-dualistic. This statement is not to suggest that no distinctions pertain *within* being, but this latter consideration is another matter, not to be mixed up in the present discussion. But adherents to a "non-dual metaphysics" believe that in ultimate reality there is no this and that; all distinction and all non-distinction is superseded. In one unique case this belief has validity, as I will show below, but this consideration is still another matter and ought not to be mixed up in the present discussion.

The implication of the "non-dual" position is that to conclude that one thing is not another would ultimately be a mistake. This mistake is called "dualism." I find the cry of "dualism" a bugaboo. It too easily functions as a cover for fuzzy thinking, even as it is used in spiritual circles to discredit other opinions. The accusation of dualism occurs within discourse, while people are speaking or writing, yet its implies that the rules of discourse—the use of affirmative or negative statements—need not be observed. The further implication is that the discourse itself has no ultimate validity. In this case, the cry of dualism disqualifies itself, for it is itself part of the discourse. There is obvious self-contradiction here, but the rejection of dualism also disqualifies even the concern for self-contradiction, for at some point Yes and No supposedly lose all significance. So instead of admitting contradiction or otherwise sorting the matter out, people say that the matter is merely paradoxical.

In rejecting the notion of being as dualistic, Wilber's rendition of the matter rejects the distinction between being and non-being. At stake in this rejection is the principle of contradiction: A thing cannot both be and not be at the same time and in the same regard. This long standing principle expresses the inviolable requirement of logical and coherent discourse. Without this principle and without coherent discourse, there is no articulate knowledge, no science of any kind. Why this is so can be explained—granted that one respects logical coherence!

According to Lonergan's analysis, the principle of contradiction expresses the focus of human consciousness as it functions on the third level. This is to say, concern about "is versus is not" is built into the functioning of the human mind. This concern is an essential structure of human consciousness. This concern surfaces in the spontaneous question that determines this third level: Is it? or Is it so? Correct answer to this question, a Yes or a No, results in human knowledge, in attainment of fact, objectivity, reality. Correct answer is the essence of science.

You cannot disagree with that analysis without in the process proving it, for your very counter-assertion, "No, it is not so," is a

No-versus-Yes statement. Only receding into silence could make your point: "Those who know, do not say; those who say, do not know" (yet even here one must question what "to know" means). But then receding into silence is not "making a point"; it is, rather, withdrawing from the discussion. And again, more on this in the following subsection.

Insistence on the third level of consciousness breaks the back of all idealism. Idealism takes ideas for reality. Idealism is content to rest in what may be merely "bright" (but mistaken) ideas emerging on the second level of consciousness and does not, like realism, by engaging the third level, go on to verify whether or not the bright ideas square with the data (Lonergan, 1972, p. 213). As is clear in the discussion of being and nothingness above, the option for idealism or for realism—for commitment to terms/ideas or commitment to reality—is at the heart of this matter. Of course, a position that is on target would not choose for either ideas or for reality but would choose for both and would carefully keep both in their appropriate place.

To reject the validity of the distinction between Yes and No, between is and is not, is to reject the principle of contradiction and perforce to reject the validity of human knowledge. It is to suggest that human knowing does not attain to the real, that the process of human knowing has no ultimate validity, that human knowing pertains only to some ultimately deluded subjectivity, that human knowledge moves in some intermediate and ultimately illusory realm. Wilber makes these very suggestions when he posits a noumenological or gnostic science of the spiritual in addition to mandalic science of the spiritual and maintains that the mandalic science—the one that deals in propositions, statements, expressions of supposed knowledge—is invalid in the face of the noumenological. This is to say, the suggestion is that ultimately— unless we give the word *know* a whole other meaning—humans really cannot know reality; what we generally call knowledge is delusionary.

Even in what Wilber calls "a perfect summary of the paradox of the ultimate," similar confusions in thinking occur. He quotes Sri Ramana Maharshi's formulation of the matter: "The world is illusory; Brahman alone is real; Brahman is the world" (154). This formulation is, indeed, astute. There is no logical inconsistency in these three premises; per se the logical form of this argument is acceptable—but only if the terms *illusory* and *real* are taken as unrelated predicates of already existing realities. However, whether the world is something real and existing, about which one could then legitimately predicate ontological qualities, is precisely the question.

Supposedly, the world is illusory. Remember, at stake is existence, being or not being. So then, does the world's being illusory mean that the world really exists but seems to be different from what it is? Or does it mean that the world really does not exist, though it seems to exist in some way? The response can only be the latter (Wilber, 1980b, p. 78). For, if Brahman alone is real, there is nothing else that is real—which is to say, nothing else exists.

So, rephrased with attention to existence and non-existence, the argument runs as follows: "The world does not exist; Brahman alone exists; Brahman is the world." Thus, the suggestion is that Brahman, which exists, is the world, which does not exist. In other words, what is, is what is not; the existent is the non-existent; being is non-being. This is not paradox. This is simple contradiction.

Paradox seems to arise only because of the supposition that saying the word *world* posits the world as existing and, further, because of obscurity in the words *illusory* and *real*. But positing something in mind or by word—*ens rationis* in the Scholastic terminology—is not the same thing as determining the actual existence of something—*ens reale*. Insight on the second level of consciousness regarding what something might be is not the same as insight on the third level of consciousness regarding the actual existence of that something as understood. Sort out the difference between concept and reality, between idealism and realism, between the second and third levels of consciousness, and the inadequacy of the argument becomes obvious.

Said still otherwise, Wilber's position exemplifies the arational mentality of the latent kind (see Chapter One). Aware that rationality matters, Wilber attempts to articulate a rational position, but in fact this position implicitly denies the validity of rationality. Indeed, Wilber's position and that of Eastern thought generally outright reject rationality as capable of real—that is, ultimately valid—knowing. The principle of contradiction is deemed ultimately inapplicable. This argued rejection of rationality, rather than being named the self-contradiction that it is, is couched in the less conspicuous term *paradox*.

The Experience of All-Without-Distinctions

From another point of view, Wilber's talk of being-without-distinction does show valid insight, and in acknowledging this fact, I want to insist that I am not writing off such talk as sheer folly. Rather, I am suggesting that such talk does not do justice to the experience. Clearly, some people do attain a unitive experience, and this experience needs to be respected. The experience itself is valid in its own realm, as an experience. But the articulation of the experience is another matter. An experience can be represented accurately or it can be misrepresented. Psychotherapists deal with this state of affairs daily: while respecting the experience of the client, they nonetheless lead the client to a new, more accurate, interpretation of it. Thus, they help the client face the full reality of the matter and free the client to live a more wholesome life. I understand and value the spiritual experience in question. What I question is the interpretation that Wilber gives it.

There is a real human experience that might be described as an experience of everything and in which, nonetheless, no distinctions pertain. Not even the distinction between Yes and No, between Is and Is-not, comes up. This experience is beyond distinctions and beyond non-distinctions, beyond "form" and beyond "non-form." Yet the experience *seems* to be an experience of all and, indeed, in some way is an experience of what does pertain to all.

The all-embracing experience in question is the experience of consciousness or spirit itself.

That experience pertains to all precisely insofar as the all in question is all that there is to be known. All that there is to be known, is known precisely and only through the human knowing instrument, consciousness. When *human* knowing is in question, there is no other option. The all in question is all potential human reality, a world of meaning and value, the reality that could be affirmed in correct judgment of fact, the reality that is not given apart from human consciousness—for as humans our consciousness, our awareness, is partially constitutive of the reality in which we live. Of course, granted that humans can know correctly, this all is in fact the objective universe; it is what really is. But "objective" here does not mean sensible or palpable; rather, it means openly experienced, insightfully understood, and correctly affirmed. So this all is not some physical reality lying "out there" on its own or some mental reality *imagined* "in here" in one's head. This all is a composite of data (whether physical, psychic, or spiritual), understanding, and judgment. This all is never given apart from human consciousness. Therefore, to experience consciousness itself is to experience that which pertains to everything that there is to be known. This unique experience is the experience in nonreflecting awareness "of" the contentless openendedness of human spirit, whose dynamism points toward, and whose four-level structure anticipates, all that there is to be known (Helminiak, 1996a, pp. 65–69. Lonergan, 1957, pp. 348–374).

Accordingly, an experience of consciousness itself—consciousness "of" consciousness, awareness "of" awareness—is in some way an experience of all reality. Insofar as all that is humanly knowable must accord with the structures of human knowing, of human consciousness, the experience of consciousness as such is a partial, heuristically anticipated, experience of all that there is to be known. As Lonergan (1957, p. xxviii)[2] suggests, Understand understanding and in some way you already understand something about everything there is to be understood.

Moreover, distinctions do not pertain in this unique experience, nor in any mere experience, precisely because this is merely an experience—and here the term *experience* is used in Lonergan's technical sense to indicate the mere availability of data, the correlate of acts of awareness on the first level of consciousness. In contrast, distinctions do pertain once questions about the data arise and insight occurs on the second level of consciousness and judgments of fact are made and knowledge results on the third level of consciousness.

I have argued that, apart from all appeal to God, an analysis of spirit can account for the many themes usually associated with spiritual matters (Helminiak, 1986b; 1987c; 1996a, pp. 121–128; 1996c). Among these themes is experience of what in some way is ubiquitous, eternal, and infinite. This experience is the experience of the self-transcending dynamism, spirit, inherent in and constitutive of humanity as such.

---

2. "Thoroughly understand what it is to understand, and not only will you understand the broad lines of all there is to be understood but also you will possess a fixed base, an invariant pattern, opening upon all further developments of understanding."

Yet this experience (first level of consciousness) is the very source of the data which, when correctly (third level of consciousness) understood and articulated (second level of consciousness), may rightly be said, now in rational statement, to be an experience of nothing other than spirit or consciousness. Such statement about spirit or consciousness, insofar as it actually is correct, retains ultimate validity as a formulation of that which was indeed experienced. This statement is a statement about reality, fact, objectivity (even though the "object" of concern in this unique case is human subjectivity itself). Indeed, I submit, this statement is about that very thing that Wilber calls "ultimate reality," that is, consciousness (though he confounds it with God)—or in any case, this statement can account for all the characteristics attributed to "ultimate reality." Moreover, this statement is logical and coherent; it needs make no appeal to paradox. Allowing for the difference between the moment of experience and the moment of pondering the experience, and sorting out the raw data of experience from insight into and statement about the data, this statement articulates the experience even while respecting the principle of contradiction.

Granted the distinction between experience and knowledge, i.e., between the conscious and the known, and granted an adequate theory of knowledge, the bugaboo "dualism" retreats. And the supposed paradox about the realm of distinctions (samsara) and the realm of no distinctions (nirvana), about the reality humans know and the reality that ultimately is—this other supposed paradox also falls away. Paradox gives way to explanation. If humans really can know reality, what is known is what actually is. As known, reality or being has no dualistic counterpart: nothingness is not real. Within mere experience, all concern about distinctions, separations, and dualisms is moot, for no questions have yet arisen: there is neither "form" nor "non-form." But within the realm of rational discourse, once questions do arise, distinctions do pertain; indeed, when intelligently posited and reasonably affirmed, the distinctions give rise to the terms that in interrelationship (that is, via implicit definition) are the ultimate means of articulating reality, including the reality of mere experience wherein distinctions do not pertain.

With these formulations I believe I have articulated the conscious experience "of" consciousness. I believe I am speaking about the same experience that Wilber intends by his "ultimate reality" or "experience of the All." If so, I respect the spiritual experience that Wilber and I intend. And I respect the principle of contradiction, I avoid paradox, as well.

Wilber insists that mandalic science, articulate treatment of transcendelia, is inevitably paradoxical. Bit by bit, I am mounting a demonstration that the matter is simply not so. I am suggesting, to use Wilber's own words, that "paradox usually means there is actually just a contradiction somewhere—it indicates sloppy thinking" (189). And I am adding that this "usually" also includes the unique case that Wilber would like to exclude, talk about the spiritual.

Wilber's Two Spiritual "Sciences"

Despite an overwhelming emphasis on mandalic science, in one place Wilber actually presents two classes of science dealing with transcendelia, side by side. But the two are incommensurate, and neither is science.

The first is mandalic science, that articulate treatment that is, supposedly, inevitably paradoxical. In its place I speak of spirituality, the systematic discipline envisaged throughout this book and elsewhere (Helminiak, 1979, 1986a, 1986b, 1987b, 1987c, 1988a, 1996a, 1996b, 1996c). While honoring Wilber's concern for a science of spirit or consciousness, spirituality as envisaged here—indeed, like all science—is not paradoxical.

The second class of transcendental sciences in Wilber's scheme is "noumenological or gnostic sciences." In the first place, they include "the methodologies and injunctions for the *direct* apprehension of transcendelia as transcendelia" (73). As such, they represent only the first strand of knowledge and lack the other two, so on Wilber's own definition these "sciences" are not even knowledge. Perforce they cannot be sciences. They are what I would call academic spirituality of the practical or pastoral or professional type, extended treatments of the "how-to's" of spiritual practice (Helminiak, 1996a, pp. 36–37). In the second place, Wilber's noumenological sciences entail "direct and intuitive apprehension of spirit, noumenon, *dharmakaya*" (73). These are not science because, as explained above, they pertain to experience, not to knowledge. They refer to the source of data, human experience "of"

consciousness—which can, of course, ground a scientific spirituality, properly conceived, as I am attempting to show.

Picture-thinking and Description

Another pervasive source of paradox in Wilber's presentation is a
consistent reliance on picture-thinking. As must be already obvious, Wilber's terminology is fuzzy. Its meaning is ever shifting. Not
theoretically defined terms, let alone fully systematic formulation
in implicit definition, but pictures, images, symbols, and metaphors
express his meaning. Wilber deals in description, not in explanation as understood here. Thus, supposedly, in the physical sciences
one uses concepts to "map" or "mirror" (52) or "match" (68) or
"picture" (193) reality.

So much is Wilber locked into description, into physical, sensible, imaginable accounts, that he holds that space and time are
aspects even of spirit: "in the physical realm, space and time are
the densest, the grossest, the most head-knockingly concrete. As
we move up the spectrum of consciousness, space and time become
subtler and subtler . . ." (79). Understood in that way, abstraction is
just a blurring of lines; having an insight, getting an idea, is just
forming a mental picture; the spiritual is just a very diffuse version
of the physical. Note how a function that is proper to psyche, namely,
imaging, is confounded with functions that are proper to spirit or
consciousness, namely, insight and judgment. (Lonergan [1976] has
provided a genetic analysis of these differing understandings of
thinking.)

Again, so much is Wilber locked into description that he ends
up obscuring one of his most important contributions. He ends up
denying the possibility of immediate experience "of" spirit. On the
one hand, Wilber speaks brilliantly of the "direct apprehension
of spirit, *by* spirit, *as* spirit" (60)—what I refer to as spirit's
nonreflecting presence "to" itself (Helminiak, 1996a, pp. 43–72). But
on the other hand, Wilber says, "Since you *are* Brahman, you obviously can't *see* Brahman, just as, for instance, an eye cannot see
itself and an ear cannot hear itself" (303). Supposedly, that human
understanding "grasps" reality is "like a hand trying to grasp itself
or a tongue trying to taste itself" (175). Somehow cognizant of spirit's

nonreflecting presence "to" itself and so, potentially, "to" all reality, Wilber nonetheless denies the possibility of such immediate self-apprehension. He seems to be able to conceive and express consciousness only in terms of the perceptible and the imaginable: consciousness is like the physical eye that sees or the ear that hears or the hand that grasps. Thus, picture-thinking betrays his most profound insights.

Ironically, despite his keen commitment to a spiritual science, Wilber's presentation lacks an appreciation of the spiritual acts beyond experience—namely, following Lonergan's model: understanding, judgment, and decision. This peculiar state of affairs probably results from Wilber's reliance on Eastern sources. Eastern concern and expertise emphasize the experience of consciousness as conscious, as nonreflecting awareness. In Lonergan's terminology, such experience is a first-level-of-consciousness affair. Emphasis on it attends to nonreflecting awareness "of" *conscious acts* themselves but by the same token easily overlooks the other levels of consciousness where the *contents of acts* are what usually grasp our attention. So Eastern emphasis is keenly aware of the experience of consciousness but not so attentive to understandings, judgments, and decisions. Thus, Jack Kornfield (1989, p. 149) explains, "The kind of attention that one develops in inner meditation is more of a passive attention where the active component is simply the brightness of your observation or investigation, but does not include the active component of choosing or deciding."

In contrast, Western concern, stereotypically more "practical," focuses more on argument, propositions, concepts, and, perhaps, their formation, and decision making. So Western concern is more likely to highlight the contents and products of acts on the second, third, and fourth levels of consciousness: concepts, judgments, and decisions.

The rare occurrence is to have a theory—like Lonergan's—that highlights and integrates both sets of concerns. Such a theory determines a "universal viewpoint" (Lonergan, 1957, pp. 564–568) from which criticism of every other theory is possible. Thus, the present analysis shows Wilber's presentation to be strong in its *appreciation* of conscious experience but weak in its *account* of conscious experience, weak regarding knowledge, science, and explanation. Picture-thinking restricts Wilber's account of things to description, precludes real explanation, perforce distorts his meaning, inevitably entails paradox, and even sometimes results in self-contradiction.

Graphic and concrete thinking does not even work for the physical sciences. So much the less will picture-thinking be adequate to the spiritual realm, which is by nature unimaginable. Then no wonder that, when Wilber attempts to express the spiritual in imageful ways, paradox results. Generally, paradox is a correlate of description; paradox pertains only when systematic explanation has not yet been achieved. Current debate about waves versus particles in quantum mechanics is a disturbing case in point. On this whole matter, recall the discussion of common sense and theory in Chapter Three.

Separation and Distinction

Crucial to systematic formulation is the realization that a separation is not a distinction. Separation implies that one thing is not close to another. Separation pertains to the realms of the sensible and the imaginable, where a spatial or temporal array is of the essence of the matter. In contrast, distinction implies an intellectual realization—insight—that one thing is not another. One thing is not another if their respective intelligibilities differ. Distinctions depend on insights, spiritual acts, yet distinctions pertain in the realms of the physical, the organic, the psychic, and the spiritual. So weight is not height; metabolism is not life; an image is not a feeling; an insight is not nonreflecting self-awareness. Yet in none of these instances is separation at stake. Things may well be distinct without being separate—though, by the nature of things, they cannot be separate without also being (really, though not necessarily conceptually) distinct.

Now, consider these statements: "Well, the absolute itself, being all-pervading and all-inclusive, is not other to any phenomenon" (163). "The absolute is different from, or set apart from absolutely nothing" (163). "The absolute . . . cannot be characterized or qualified because it is not set apart or different from anything and therefore could not be described as one thing or event among others" (169–170). "God is not One Thing set apart from the many" (170).

There is no paradox in those statements, the supposed paradox that God is both something different from, yet not set apart from, other things. There is merely the confusion of distinction and separation. Following traditional Western theology, the matter can be stated quite plainly: God is not the world (posit a distinction, namely, the inviolable one between Creator and creation), yet, since by definition the world does not exist without God not only in its beginning but also in its continued existence, God is everywhere and in no way distant or apart from the world (deny any separation).

About God and Consciousness

Discussing the hierarchy of being, Wilber suggests that the absolute is differently related to the different levels of the hierarchy: "It is, as I said, paradoxical. All of the absolute is equally at every point, *and* some points are closer to the absolute than others" (163). Note that this statement is phrased in terms of imaginable closeness, non-separations. No wonder supposed paradoxes result.

But another major confusion also influences that statement. The "absolute" in question can refer to human consciousness or to God. Granted, for Wilber they are one and the same. My insistence is that they are not and that their identification is a further source of the supposed paradox, the confusion. Or, phrasing the matter more conservatively, I propose another interpretation that seems to account for all the relevant data and that also avoids paradox or self-contradiction.

Confusing Consciousness with God

If the "absolute" in the first clause refers to God ("All of the absolute is equally at every point"), it is easy enough to understand how the absolute is equally present everywhere. That matter was just noted in the discussion three paragraphs above. On the other hand, if the "absolute" in the first clause refers to human consciousness, it is also easy enough to understand how it is equally present—not present everywhere in the real world but present to every thought a person has and so present to whatever the person knows. Or said otherwise, consciousness is present to that person's whole world, to whatever is—as far as that individual person can be concerned. In this restricted sense, speaking loosely and personally or psychologically, consciousness could be said to be present "everywhere."

Now consider the "absolute" in the second clause ("some points are closer to the absolute than others"). If the absolute here also refers to God, the clause makes no sense, for God, on the traditional understanding, is not "closer" here than there. As the necessary being that accounts for the existence of every contingent being, God is equally present to whatever exists. However, if the absolute in that second clause is taken to mean consciousness, all paradox in this statement can dissolve. For the hierarchy in question is based on levels of meditative experience. Different meditators have different experiences. The more adept experience their own human consciousness or spirit more intensely. Then, "closer to the absolute" may refer to intensity of meditative experience. On this interpretation, the matter is really quite simple.

Confusing Consciousness with Reality

Still, the hierarchy in question actually referred to levels of reality, not to levels of meditative experience, as I just interpreted it. But I submit that another confusion of issues is at stake here: levels of spiritual experience are confounded with levels of being; consciousness is confounded with reality; psychology is confounded with ontology; philosophical idealism supplants critical realism. Grant my interpretation and paradox dissolves.

Why grant my interpretation? Because, in fact, in Wilber's theory the levels of the hierarchy of being derive from levels of meditative experience (126; cf. Goleman, 1977; Kornfield, 1989). Human experience of consciousness is what those levels are originally about. That those levels are also levels of being is sheer supposition. Its basis is again, I submit, a misinterpretation of meditative experience.

In meditation one can become aware of the arising of ideas in one's consciousness—ripples on the ocean of consciousness as such (128–129)—so one might suppose that things in the world of reality also arise similarly in some consciousness. One might be inclined to make this supposition if one were comfortable believing that things are ideas (like a dream in God's mind), that everything is consciousness. Such a belief, a version of philosophical idealism, overlooks the distinction between concept and reality, as exemplified in the discussion of being and nothingness above. That is, such a belief overlooks the distinction between Lonergan's second and third levels of consciousness. Likewise, one might be inclined to make this supposition especially if one also supposed that one's own consciousness is identical with God, Absolute Consciousness. For then one's consciousness, God, could reasonably account for the existence of things. Of course, if ideas in my mind are identified with things in reality, a problematic discrepancy arises, for the ideas in my mind may not be the same as the ideas in yours, whereas things in reality are simply themselves, one and the same. Still, supposition that all minds are the one, divine consciousness would eliminate this possible problematic discrepancy, for ideas in the divine mind—that is, in your mind and my mind—are taken to be identical with things in reality. Furthermore, that everyone's consciousness was the one and the same consciousness would most seem to be the case for those who had attained full enlightenment, those who had experienced the pure experience of nonreflecting consciousness, "consciousness as such." For in this case there are no informing contents to make my consciousness different from yours. Indeed, if the structure of consciousness is the same in all people, as Lonergan's analysis suggests, everyone would have the same experience when they nonreflectingly experience pure consciousness. Then, confounding experience with knowledge, they might very easily, but erroneously, conclude that there is ontologically only one consciousness. This conclusion might seem all the more correct since in that moment of experience all logic, all distinction, is irrelevant. Reflection and distinction as to what I am and what I am experiencing or as to what I am and what you are, play no part in that experience.

Note this well. The above interpretation of meditative experience on the basis of Lonergan's analysis of consciousness can account for all the essentials of Wilber's perennial philosophy—and without gratuitous suppositions about consciousness, reality, and God. That interpretation accounts for the relevant data also without invoking paradox. Moreover, the only evidence one really has for said suppositions is one's own experience of the functioning of one's own consciousness. That this experience of one's own subjectivity should be projected into an account of the existence of the world, certainly seems far-fetched—granted, of course, that human consciousness and not God is the object of the experience.

That projection seems even more far-fetched when formulated mythically in terms of a ripple on the ocean of Consciousness as Such (128–129)—a "ripple" that can otherwise be given a fully reasonable interpretation, as just suggested above. This ripple really longs for the infinite but is afraid to loose itself again in the ocean, so it compromises and makes substitutes and moves stepwise ever further from the infinite it once was. Eventually it reduces itself to physical matter and loses itself in insentient slumber. This emergence of anthropomorphized physical matter, by the way, is supposedly identical with the moment of the Big Bang of modern physics.

One could hardly go wrong in risking another interpretation, especially when that interpretation provides a logical and coherent explanation of the very same data. So I submit that the valid meaning in talk of a hierarchy of levels is an array of possible increasing refinement of meditative experiences. On this interpretation the notion that some points are "closer" to the absolute than are others can make perfect sense. For the meaning is simply that more adept meditators have a deeper experience of human consciousness than do others. There is no paradox here but only a multiple interacting confusion of issues: imagining and understanding, separation and distinction, experience and knowledge, consciousness and reality, and then again, consciousness and God.

NonReflecting Consciousness as the "Ultimate State"

Granted that more coherent interpretation, other difficult passages in Wilber fall easily into logical order, as follows:

> The Ultimate State of Consciousness [read: the experience of nonreflecting consciousness] is not a state among other states but a state inclusive of all states. This means most emphatically that the Ultimate State of Consciousness is not an altered state of consciousness. [Obviously not, since nonreflecting consciousness is a simultaneous and inextricable concomitant of every act of human reflecting awareness.] . . . The Ultimate State of Consciousness is perfectly compatible with every state

of consciousness and altered state of consciousness [again, obviously, since consciousness as such is the condition for the possibility of any specific and content-specified experience of consciousness], and there is no state of consciousness apart or outside it [overlook the spatial metaphors here]. (297)

All of this points inescapably to the fact that you not only are already one with the Absolute [that is, consciousness, not God], you already know [that is, have available to you the experiential data pertinent to the fact that] you are. As Huang Po said, "The Buddha-Nature [that is, human consciousness, especially as experienced nonreflectingly] and your perception [that is, experience] of it are one." [Of course. For apart from any subject-object distinction, nonreflecting awareness is precisely awareness "of" awareness.] And since, as we have seen, the Buddha Nature is always present, then so is your perception of It. (297)

That the Ultimate State of Consciousness is not a state apart or in anyway different from the Present State of Consciousness is the point so many people seem to miss. [That is, the experience of consciousness or spirit is in no way an extraordinary thing. Rather, it is a concomitant of all distinctively human experience.] Hence, they misguidedly seek to engineer for themselves a "higher" state of consciousness, radically different from their present state of awareness. (298)

In short, since the Ultimate State of Consciousness is your Present State of Consciousness [that is, since nonreflecting consciousness is a simultaneous and inextricable concomitant of reflecting consciousness], there is obviously no way to cause, produce, affect, or manufacture that which is already the case. . . . But when we imagine [exactly: imagination rather than understanding is at stake] that the Ultimate State of Consciousness is different from the state of consciousness we now have [yet do not forget that the experience of nonreflecting consciousness is different from the experience of reflecting consciousness, though both are inextricable aspects of one and the same consciousness], we then foolheartedly seek ways to usher in this supposedly different and miraculous state of "higher" consciousness. (299–300)

In fact, it's only because we keep insisting that the Ultimate State of Consciousness be different from the Present

State of Consciousness [though, in fact, those who have cultivated consciousness "of" consciousness and have achieved a
meditative "moment" of contentless nonreflecting consciousness do experience something that in that contentless form is
not a part of everyday conscious experience] that makes it so
hard to admit to ourselves that we already know [read: experience; and add: to some degree] our Buddha Nature [that is,
consciousness]. (300)

I have been showing how Wilber's insistence on paradox is a
red herring. Given an adequate array of intellectual tools, the
paradoxical readily submits to consistent and logical analysis. Other
complications in Wilber's presentation may also be easily resolved.
Brief attention to these will further support the thrust of my argument. Then, in conclusion, discussion will turn to Wilber's use of
the various religious traditions.

Confusing Timelessness with Eternity

Another consideration that lends support to Wilber's perennial
philosophy is his identification of eternity—and so divinity—with
the human experience of timelessness. But that identification is
mistaken. Wilber writes,

[S]uppose . . . that the Ultimate State of Consciousness could
be attained or reached or entered. What would that imply?
Only that that state of consciousness which you *entered* would
necessarily have a beginning in time; that that state of consciousness is therefore not timeless and eternal; and that, in
short, that state of consciousness is precisely not the Ultimate
State of Consciousness. (296)
    Any state of consciousness that can be entered, or that
emerges after various practices, must have a beginning in
time, and thus is not and could never be the timeless and
eternal Ultimate State of Consciousness. (297)

Wilber's valid point is that adept meditators do have experiences of timelessness. The obvious explanation is that they experience nonreflecting consciousness. As a mere experience and as

nonreflecting, it precludes all distinctions—distinctions of is and is-not, distinctions of this and that, distinctions of here and there, as well as distinctions of now and then.

The mistake is the identification of timelessness with eternity. In popular terms, eternity implies having no beginning. More precisely, however, it implies being self-explanatory or uncreated. So only God is eternal. In contrast to eternity, there is also timelessness. The medievals called it *aevum* in explicit distinction to *eternitas* (Thomas Aquinas, *Summa Theologica*, I, q. 10, a. 5). Timelessness merely implies the absence of any change and so the absence of any possible measure of change and so the absence of time. Angels, who are pure spirits, bodiless and unchanging, experience timelessness; this does not mean they are eternal, for they are creatures. Misidentifying eternity and timelessness, Wilber's argument erroneously supposes that to experience timelessness is to experience God. So talk is of the "Ultimate State of Consciousness" and of the "Absolute," written with upper case letters, when no such implication of Divinity is warranted.

The Experience of Consciousness

Further clarification can also be made about the matter of having a beginning or not. Assume that the timelessness refers to the experience of nonreflecting consciousness. Now, from one point of view it is true that this experience is an ever-available possibility for people, as long as they are not comatose or in dreamless sleep. For nonreflecting consciousness is a simultaneous and inextricable concomitant of all reflecting human consciousness. From this point of view, granted that spirit has emerged in the maturing human form (Helminiak, 1996a, pp. 196–197), nonreflecting consciousness is there for a person to experience "from the beginning"—which is to say, from his or her beginning. The data of nonreflecting consciousness are nothing that need to be produced; they need only to be attended to.

However, one could attend or not attend to those data. Through meditative practice or in some other way, one could learn to attend. One could learn to experience in a way that one had not experienced before. So, from another point of view, one could have an experience that one did not have from the beginning. The experience of nonreflecting consciousness as such would then be something new. Purified of all explicit content, it would be the conscious experience "of" consciousness itself. As such, it would be a profound and recognized, and perhaps even named, experience of consciousness, and it would entail timelessness. This focused and recognized experience of the data was not there from the beginning, though the data to be recognized had themselves been there all along.

Note that at stake, strictly speaking, is "*recognized* experience" of those data, for the discussion is about the possibility of acknowledging and talking about that experience. Wilber (1995, p. 299) uses the words "*conscious realization*" to refer to this same matter. Discussion always presupposes reflecting consciousness. But the data in question in the present peculiar case are the very possibility of experience itself and so, in one sense, are identical with experience. This was the point of the Huang Po quote in the subsection before last. The very nature of consciousness or spirit is awareness "of" awareness, so as conscious or spiritual the human subject is always at some level aware "of" him- or herself. In this sense, the data and the experience are "always" available. That was the point of the second last paragraph. But those data as such are seldom attended to. When they are attended to, there enters the picture for the first time the possibility of recognizing the experience. Consciousness as nonreflecting passes over into consciousness as reflecting, even as the data in question this time are of consciousness itself. This is the point of the last paragraph. And this is the presupposition of the whole exposition of consciousness in Lonergan (1957), as summarized in Chapter One and detailed elsewhere (Helminiak, 1996a, pp. 43–103).

Obviously, at some particular point in time, one can begin to attend to those peculiar data and so experience timelessness and note the experience. This is just what trained meditators do.

The fact that meditators learn to attend to nonreflecting consciousness means they will experience timelessness. But the experience of timelessness does not mean that their experience is without beginning. Nor does it mean that the data they experience were without beginning. That is, it does not mean that they or their minds are eternal. It only means that what they eventually experience is something of a very peculiar kind. Its very nature is to be beyond space and time. For what they begin to experience deliberately, quite simply, is created human spirit or consciousness.

This explanation does account for all the relevant data. In contrast, a coherent argument that meditators really experience God requires the addition of significant other presuppositions, and these are absent in Wilber's presentation. These additional presuppositions were spelled out in Chapter Two. Beyond grounding any mere treatment of consciousness or spirit, these presuppositions determine the theist and theotic viewpoints.

Wilber's Position as Pantheist

Another ghost that haunts Wilber's presentation is the specter of pantheism. Wilber's bottom-line defense against the charge of pantheism is that the Absolute is more than all the things It constitutes. Wilber claims a form of panentheism, so he argues, "God contains all things but all things do not exclusively contain God—that would be pantheism" (162). Or again, "God is not the sum of those objects because you could destroy those objects and God would still exist" (170). Or said otherwise, "The whole world in and by itself is not exclusively Brahman, because you could theoretically destroy the whole world but that wouldn't destroy Brahman or Buddha Nature or Tao" (155).

In itself panentheism may be an acceptable enough notion if it intends simply to insist that God is not distant from the world but rather everything is somehow in God (Cobb, 1983; Reese, 1980, pp. 407–408). This notion is certainly more acceptable than the misunderstanding of divine transcendence (Lebmann, 1970) that imagines God to be distant from, or unconcerned about, or uninvolved in, the world; and this notion is more acceptable than strict pantheism, which imagines that God is the sum and substance of everything or that the sum and substance of everything is God. Nonetheless, an inherent difficulty with the notion of panentheism is that it is imaginative. It attempts to account for God in terms of location and distance. As such, it is but a sophisticated metaphor—though, like all metaphors, in the right situation it may be a useful metaphor.

However, Wilber goes on to say, "God is not another object in addition to [those] objects. God is not One Thing set apart from the many" (170), and "all things, including subatomic particles, are ultimately made of God" (165). "The absolute is both the highest level of reality *and* the condition or real nature of every level of reality. It is the highest rung of the ladder, *and* it is the wood out of which the ladder is made" (158). " 'All the Buddhas and all sentient beings are nothing but the One Mind, besides which nothing exists.' " " 'All the world is Brahman.' " " 'The world is nothing but Mind,' and 'All is Mind' " (290).

First, note that picture-thinking significantly obscures Wilber's attempt to deal with this matter. To contain things or not, to be apart from things or not, and to be that out of which something is made (e.g., wood), pertain to physical, spatial, and imaginable realities. Such notions are not adequate to the discussion of God. To say that God is not apart from something (no separation) or that God contains something (no imagined separation) does not necessarily imply that God is that something (no distinction). Nonetheless, that God is that something might very well be what Wilber means. For his other statement, that something is made of God (imagination), cannot but mean that the thing in question *is* God. This very conclusion was argued at the Christian Council of Nicea (325 C.E.): that the Son is *homoousios to patri*, "of the same stuff as the Father," means that the Son is God even as the Father is God (Helminiak, 1986d; Lonergan, 1964/1976). So Wilber's statement is wholly ambiguous.

Similarly, that God is "not another object in addition to those other objects" is also ambiguous. If this statement means that God is not separate, spatially distant, from those objects, then there is no problem. Likewise, if this statement means that God is not a material, physical, object as are those other objects, then, again, there is no problem. But if this statement means that God is not different from those other objects, that those objects plus God are still only one and the same thing, then there is a problem. Then the distinction between God and the objects is denied, and strict identity is affirmed. The affirmation is that God is those other things and that they are God. In reality, the one is the others; only the names are changed—like saying that Monica the *mother* (of her daughter) and Monica the *sister* (of her brother) are one and the same person. Only the names, the concepts *in the mind*—mother and sister or God and all other things—are different; but *in reality* there is no difference: Monica is Monica, the mother is the sister, God is all things and all things are God. (Note again how idealism, the identity of concept and reality, befuddles Wilber's position.) But such a position is pantheism, plain and simple. So Wilber's formulations are pantheist, and such formulations are his common fare. For example, Wilber (1995, p. 293) continues to make such inherently ambiguous statements when he speaks of "that Spirit which is within and beyond the Earth, which is prior to the Earth but *not other to* the Earth" (*emphasis added*).

Still, the matter really is difficult. An important question remains: How can God be said to be an object and an object different from other objects? The answer depends on what you understand by "object." If you can conceive "object" only imaginatively, in picture-thinking, then God cannot be an object distinct from other objects, for God is not physical, not spatio-temporal. But if you understand "object" to mean anything whose actual existence can be correctly affirmed, then there can be non-spatio-temporal things, spiritual things, as well as physical, spatial, and imaginable things; then God can be an object just as any other thing, reality, being, is an object; and then God can be affirmed as a particular something distinct from all other things (Lonergan, 1972, pp. 341–342).

On that understanding, the criterion of knowledge, reality, truth, is not sensation, perception, or imagination but rather the correct judgment of fact. The criterion is not an organic or psychic act; it is a spiritual act. At stake is distinctively human knowing, the result of an act of consciousness operating on the third level, the result of an insight that determines that an idea does indeed accurately represent the data.

That understanding of *knowing* as a correlate of existence—existence in reality and not merely in mind—is an essential which Wilber's presentation lacks. For example, he argues, "Buddha Nature or God is one with all things in the act of perceiving-creating them" (192). But creation is a matter of being and not being, of existing and not existing. Wilber's statement correlates *perception* and existence: all things are by God's "perceiving-creating" them. In effect, Wilber identifies perception with knowledge and existence: to see is to know, and to be seen is to exist. (Recall the discussion above regarding Wilber's second strand of knowledge: you see and you know.) Reality is reduced to perception. This is Berkeley revisited: *esse est percipi*, to be is to be perceived.

Now, one might defend Wilber and suggest that he speaks of "perception" and "seeing" only metaphorically and really intends to speak of knowing. But this concession would be too generous: nowhere in Wilber's writing nor in the summaries by his critics have I seen evidence of an adequate epistemology. The bugaboos of modern Western philosophy, epistemology and ontology, have surfaced repeatedly throughout this discussion, and they tangle around and strangle the heart of Wilber's argument. Though Wilber wants desperately to treat the spiritual, his epistemology is limited to the psychic: the perceptible and the imaginable. His intellectual tools are inadequate to deal with his subject matter. So his statements come out ambiguous at best, and his only defense is appeal to "paradox."

Wilber resists being classified as pantheist, but his position, at least as stated, is pantheist by any standard definition. Why is Wilber so concerned about that epithet? His goal is to present a comprehensive-integral paradigm. His treatment of God must satisfy the Western traditions as well as the Eastern. So like the Western traditions, it seems, he must reject pantheism. Sad to say, however, his argument does not hold. On this pivotal issue, there can be no reconciliation of positions. That Atman *is* Brahman, that the world *is* the Ultimate expressing itself, these notions are incompatible with the Western understanding of God as Creator. Then one last aspect of Wilber's presentation still needs to be addressed: the mixing of religious traditions.

Mixing Religious Traditions

For Wilber, the "absolute" is Mind, God, or Brahman, and all three are identified. On my understanding these three are far from equivalent. This is the pivotal difference.

Buddhism: Consciousness, not God

The above analyses make it clear that consciousness or spirit, undifferentiatedly called "mind," is no synonym for God. Adding a capital letter to Consciousness, Spirit, or Mind does not change the situation. The fundamental inconsistency at stake in this confounding is the simultaneous positing of two different absolutes. Consciousness or mind provides experiences and statements in this world of time, space, and process. These statements are what is generally taken to constitute science or knowledge. But emphasis on God in Wilber's position—really emphasis on Brahman—posits another absolute, transcendent of the first and fully ineffable. This second absolute is deemed the really real, the ultimate, and so in fact impugns the validity of the first. All manner of appeal to paradox may attempt to obscure the logical inconsistency of this position. But the above criticism has shown, I believe, not only that, but also how and why, real inconsistency does occur. Moreover, the criticism provides an alternative interpretation that seems coherently to account for the data.

The conclusion must be that it is simply a mistake to identify human consciousness with God. Indeed, Buddhism is well aware of this fact. Buddhism is non-theist (Suzuki, 1970/1976; Trungpa, 1973, 1976)—but not atheist. That is, it does not deny the existence God. It merely declines to discuss the supposed divine Absolute. It sees such discussion as distraction from the essential, the practice of meditation. It is clear that it deals with only human consciousness and means only that by "Buddha nature."

Wilber plays fast and loose with Buddhism. He extrapolates from its treatment of consciousness or Buddha nature and identifies Buddha nature with God. He appeals to real similarities, discussed here and in detail elsewhere (Helminiak, 1986d, 1996a). But in identifying the spiritual with the divine, he overlooks and obscures the essential determinant of the theist, in contrast to the philosophic, viewpoint: creation, the fact of contingent existence. The Buddhist tradition avoids this mistake. It humbly and wisely pleads deliberate ignorance about the question of God. In this it remains, in my opinion, a thoroughly authentic tradition. It squares with the philosophic viewpoint. Wilber's presentation too easily conflates this non-theist religion with the others.

The God of Western Religion without Paradox

I take "God" to be the Western notion pertinent to Judaism, Christianity, and Islam. Talk of God introduces the question about existence and non-existence. Creation is the key to the theist viewpoint, as explained in Chapter Two. Wilber overlooks this key issue and so confounds the notion "God" with consciousness or spirit. Why he does so is easy to explain. Without an adequate theory of knowledge—one that correlates knowledge with fact, reality, objectivity, truth, what *is*—one could not have a clear understanding of creation, of being and not-being. Likewise, without clear commitment to the principle of contradiction, one could not adequately treat questions of being and non-being. Thus, for a confluence of reasons, already detailed above, Wilber confounds the Western notion of God with notions in Eastern religions.

However, one aspect of Western theology seems to support Wilber's insistence that all treatment of the Absolute ultimately results in paradox. Of course, here I take "Absolute" to mean God and not consciousness, Brahman, or something else. That aspect is the doctrine of analogy.

As Thomas Aquinas so often repeated in his *Summa Theologica*, we can know *that* God is, but we cannot know *what* God is. As explained in Chapter Two, we can know *that* God is, because "God" is the required answer to the question about the existence of things. There must be some such answer if human questioning is a valid enterprise and if the universe is perforce intelligible. But we cannot know *what* God is, for to know that would be to understand the explanation of everything about everything. Though our dynamic human spirits do tend toward such understanding, no one has understood everything about everything, so no one knows what such understanding would be like. Said otherwise, we lack the data to allow us to elaborate the matter; we simply do not have experience of God, Explanation of Everything about Everything, such that we could say what God is.

Obviously, this talk of God as Explanation of Everything about Everything is a theory; it is a hypothesis for treating the matter of "God." But far from just any old hypothesis, this one appears to be the best available opinion of the day. This theory is grounded in an analogy. The prime analogue is dynamic human consciousness. "God" is hypothesized to be the terminus of dynamic human consciousness, the explanation of everything about everything.

Now, since we do experience dynamic human consciousness and since we do have some idea about what kind of terminus consciousness must have, yet since we have not in fact experienced that terminus, we are left to speak about that terminus, about "God," only in a rather peculiar way. We extrapolate from the experience of human consciousness and, to this extent, know clearly what we intend. Yet, as regards ultimate implications, we must admit we do not comprehend what we are projecting. Such talk about "God" is analogical. It speaks of "God" on the basis of analogy with consciousness. And such talk does seem to be paradoxical.

Yet even here, the paradox is only apparent. Traditional treatment of analogy notes three aspects of predication about God. First, one makes affirmations about God—such as, "God exists," "God is good," "God is wise." These statements are true and have absolute validity. Otherwise, "God" could not be the Explanation of Everything about Everything. But second, one must deny that these statements pertain to God in the same way that they pertain to other beings. For That which Explains Everything about Everything is unlike anything else we know. So whatever is said of It must apply in a peculiar way. Nonetheless, that peculiar way can be elaborated. Insofar as "God" is the terminus of dynamic human consciousness, whatever is said of God must apply in all perfection, supereminently. So, third, one must affirm that these statements about God apply in a perfection that surpasses our understanding.

Thus, there are three aspects to predication about God: affirmation, denial, and supereminence. Note that the denial is not the cancellation of the affirmations about God. The denial is merely the clarification that the affirmations pertain to God in a way different from other things, namely, supereminently. So there is valid content in the statements made about God. But there is also the realization that the full import of those statements is beyond our understanding.

Note also, then, that there is no real paradox here, the possible paradox of both affirmation and denial. For the affirmation is about one aspect of the matter and the denial, about another. And the emphasis on supereminence in the third place serves precisely to explain the denial. So one can correctly and coherently affirm that God exists while also affirming that one does not comprehend what that existence means. Lonergan's distinction between the third and the second levels of consciousness neatly focuses the difference between *that* and *what* something is. So distinction, not paradox, is in question here.

Note, thirdly, why we do not and cannot comprehend our own valid statements about God—because we do not have experience of God per se. We can know anything on which we have data. But our data on God is always mediate: we know of God only by means of other things whose existence requires an explanation; and to provide that explanation, we can extrapolate Explanation of Everything about Everything because we have experience of limited explanation and we have experience of the open-ended dynamism of our own consciousness. But we have no direct experience of God. Or at least, there is no cogent reason for supposing direct experience; all the relevant data can be accounted for otherwise, namely, in terms of human consciousness. I believe I have intimated such an accounting above, and I have provided a fuller treatment elsewhere (Helminiak, 1996a).

However, from another point of view, one could still argue that we do have direct experience of God, but this argument would hold only granted additional presuppositions—such as those that constitute, for example, a Christian theotics. Thus, elsewhere (Helminiak, 1982) I reminded Christians that they can correctly speak about the direct experience of God but only because they also affirm that the divine Holy Spirit has been poured into the human heart.

Misrepresentation of Christianity

Now and again, but rather rarely, Wilber makes explicit reference to Christianity to support his overall presentation. Understandably, Wilber does not conceive the essence of Christianity, the possibility of human deification, as presented in Chapter Two and elsewhere (Helminiak, 1979, 1982, 1986a, 1986b, 1986d, 1987b, 1987c, 1988a, 1989b, 1996a, 1996c). Yet even otherwise, his is a reductionist picture.

Wilber dismisses core Christian doctrines as merely symbolic (35) without ever questioning their possible ontological implication. He disparages Aquinas's "proofs" for the existence of God (18) without appreciating the subtlety of Aquinas's argument. Aquinas never thought he was proving anything. Rather, he was providing a reasonable account of the faith for those who already believe, and he was providing arguments that might incline toward faith those who do not believe. This is to say, Aquinas was only proposing plausibility arguments, which Wilber (63) does allow.

Even Wilber's use of Bonaventure's "three eyes" is suspect. Bonaventure's understanding about experiencing God through the eye of contemplation depends on major Christian presuppositions:

divine illumination, the grace of Christ, and the effect of the sac-
raments, especially Baptism and Eucharist, as well as a person's
passage through the "three ways" of the spiritual life, the purga-
tive, illuminative, and unitive (Brady, 1967). These presuppositions
are completely foreign to Wilber's presentation, yet they alone
explain Bonaventure's understanding of contemplation. Bonaventure's full argument squares with the one I made in the third
last paragraph.

Similarly, Wilber quotes the Christians, Saint Bernard and
Pascal, in specious support of his own argument, identifying the
Christian God with Buddha. In the process he misrepresents Bud-
dhism, too (299).

Wilber supports his argument, that "all the world is really
Brahman," by citing words attributed to Christ in the *Gospel of St.
Thomas*: " 'I am the Light that is above them all, I am the All, the
All came forth from Me and the All attained to Me. Cleave a piece
of wood, I am there; Lift up the stone and you will find me there' "
(309). But this gospel is not in the Christian canon. Why not?
Because early Christian thinkers found this gospel's thought incompatible with core Christian beliefs. Indeed, the *Gospel of St.
Thomas* is gnostic. As such, its thought follows the same basic
position as Wilber's perennial philosophy, as Hinduism, neo-
Platonism, and all Great-Chain-of-Being philosophies. But the basic incompatibility between such philosophies and Christianity needs
to be noted, and Wilber's gross misrepresentation of Christianity
needs to be flagged.

Wilber continues to turn out such distortions. His recent in-
corporation of the mystic writings of Teresa of Avila and John of
the Cross into his integral paradigm (Wilber, 1995, pp. 292–301)
depends on obscuring the same distinctively Christian issues as in
the case of Bonaventure. For example, Wilber (1995, p. 299) completely misunderstands the meaning of "supernatural" in those
Christian writings. As explained in Chapter Two, this technical
Christian term bespeaks God's presence through grace, the gift of
the Holy Spirit, poured out in human hearts (Romans 5:5) and
implies a deliberate and precise contrast to God's presence in all
things as their Creator. Attempting to support his point, Wilber
quotes Teresa as saying, "God is *in all things by presence and
power and essence*." But Teresa's listing repeats an absolutely standard and centuries-old Scholastic formula, which Aquinas explained

in his *Summa Theologica* (I, q. 8, a. 3): God is in all things by presence insofar as they lay open to God's view, by power insofar as all things are under God's sway, and by essence insofar as God, the necessary existent, causes and sustains all things in their contingent existence. Elaborating how God is present in all creation, this formula has nothing to do with the possibility of human union with God, which is Wilber's concern. These matters mark the difference between the theist and theotic viewpoints.

Wilber shows profound ignorance regarding these matters. He, a defender of spirituality, does not recognize the spiritual issues that are at stake in the Christian doctrines of Incarnation, Resurrection, Trinity, and Grace. Worse than ignorant, he is also unmannered, rude, and offensive (McDermott, 1996). Not understanding Christianity, he caricatures its central tenets, and then he dismisses his caricature with ridicule (Wilber, 1995, pp. 350–355).

Brahman/Consciousness in the Perennial Philosophy

Discussion thus far has made clear that consciousness and God—as understood respectively in Buddhism and in the Western religions—are not identical. The final consideration is of Brahman, associated with Hinduism. Neither is Brahman to be identified with either consciousness or God, as understood in those other religions. According to the celebrated Hindu maxims, at the core of Wilber's perennial philosophy, "Thou art that" and "Atman is Brahman." That is, human mind or spirit or consciousness is the Absolute. This identification of consciousness and the Absolute is in clear contrast to the differentiated treatment of these two in the other religious traditions. Buddhism speaks of consciousness or Buddha nature but chooses not even to consider God. Judaism, Christianity, and Islam acknowledge consciousness and God but as two different realities. Hinduism identifies consciousness with God. Obviously, the latter is a very different understanding.

My point is simply that these are very different notions: consciousness, spirit, or Buddha nature; God; and Brahman. Yet Wilber has treated them as different formulations of one and the same thing.

In *Beyond Theology*, Alan Watts (1964) uses the image of a Chinese box to suggest how different religions can relate to one another. Wilber (1982, pp. 63–64) has employed the same metaphor. For example, Judaism fits within the bigger "box" that is Christianity, but not vice versa. The Chinese-box metaphor is similar to the system of successively higher analytic viewpoints, presented in Chapter Two. Watts suggests how Hinduism is able to incorporate Christianity, but Christianity, he argues, cannot accommodate Hinduism. The implication, the claim, is that Hinduism is therefore the more comprehensive, the more adequate, position.

Watts's presentation is impressive. It makes a beautiful, delightful, and profoundly insightful homily. Every thinking theist and Christian ought to read it! It is a useful corrective for much of the nonsense passed off as theism and Christianity, and I find little in its invectives and exhortations truly incompatible with these religious positions.

But by the very same token, Watts's implied conclusion, his theoretical claim, is unwarranted and dubious. Granted that the above criticism of Wilber's perennial philosophy is sound and assuming that Hinduism and the perennial philosophy do more or less coincide, the reason the "box" of Hinduism can incorporate any other religion may not be something to be celebrated—at least not when science is at stake. As the above criticism would suggest, the reason is fuzzy thinking.

For religious preaching, Watts scores A+, but for scientific account he fails. But the concern here is precisely the possibility of coherent interdisciplinary science. Of course, to this criticism Watts, along with Wilber, might well reply, "So what? After all, metaphor, image, and provocative suggestion are the only adequate way to express the religious." In Watts's (1964, p. 26) words, a basic principle of any overarching treatment of religion "is to deal with the subject naively, at its mythic, imagistic, or anthropomorphic level." For "to be or not to be is *not* the question, since the one endlessly implies the other" (Watts, 1964, p. 33). "The answer is always 'Yes/ No,' because existence itself is a vibratory or wavelike affair, a 'now-you-see-it-now-you-don't,' a back/front, up/down, here/there situation. . . . To be *quite* sure, to be set, fixed, and firm is to miss the point of life" (Watts, 1964, p. 22).

So, as Watts is well aware, the bottom-line issue is a question of epistemology. The question is whether or not people are capable of knowing correctly: Is there "is" and "is-not," or not? Is there truth, and can we know it? Said otherwise, Is a science of the spiritual—or of anything else, for that matter—possible? For Watts, the answer must be "Yes/No." But is he *quite* sure of his answer? While he insists that pursuit of the one, true understanding of things is ultimately folly, he nonetheless argues mightily for his own understanding of things. The self-contradiction in such an argument has already been noted above, and the reasons for it and the way out of it have also been discussed.

The position developed in this book is compatible with the Buddhist tradition as well as with the Western theist religions, Judaism, Christianity, and Islam. However, because of its distinctions between the spiritual and the divine, between creature and Creator, and between being and non-being, this position is simply incompatible with Wilber's perennial philosophy and the traditions it expresses, like Hinduism. Wilber's perennial philosophy does not fit into the "boxes" of Buddhism, theism, or Christianity, and they do not fit into it. In light of the analyses presented here, this incompatibility should require no further explanation.

However, that incompatibility does not imply that there is no further room for dialogue. Nor does it mean that substantial consensus could not be achieved. Just as I find most of Watts's presentation compatible with my theist and Christian belief, I could also embrace most of the profound spiritual wisdom of Hinduism within my understanding of Christianity. Unfortunately, this much must be granted to Watts: the Christian religion is too commonly typified by guilt, fear, sinfulness, punishment, legalism, and alienation from self, the universe, and God. In contrast stand the freedom, the delight, the playfulness, the trust, and the divine adventure that Hinduism sees in the human role in the universe, understood as an expression of God and as moving people toward ultimate union with God. But these practical teachings of Hinduism, these inspirational messages, are not foreign to the Christian tradition. On this score there is no fundamental difference.

Ah, but how one would explain those practical teachings, what theoretical account of them one would give—that is where the difference lies. If one could grant that there is a difference between the functional role of commonsense religion and the ontological intent of systematic theological account—the very distinction that Wilber and Watts and others speaking for the East consistently pooh-pooh—we might all be able to have our cake and eat it, too.

We might find a union of East and West. We might be able to preserve the practical spiritual wisdom of the East within a coherent scientific account, the desideratum of the West. Detailed discussion of this possibility goes far beyond the limits of this book. Such discussion would be more theology and theotics than interdisciplinary method, the topic here. But because of my belief in the capacity of the human spirit, a major presupposition of my work (Lonergan, 1957), I must at least insist on this possibility here. Let no one take my highlighting fundamental theoretical differences between Hinduism and Judeo-Christianity as a hard-headed and self-righteous positing of irreconcilable division.

Conclusion Regarding Wilber

Lest sectarian bickering shamefully enter the discussion at this late stage, let it be clear once again what the real issue is. Discussion here has recently turned to world religions, but religion is not the issue. The broader and more important issue is the possibility of an insightful, coherent, comprehensive, consistent, and accurate account of things spiritual. The issue is the interrelationship of religion and the human sciences.

Throughout, the broad possibility of a science of spirituality has been the concern of this book. On this score, Wilber's presentation has been found wanting. The data Wilber presents certainly do need explanation. His concern for a scientific treatment of the spiritual also deserves a standing ovation. His profound insight into certain aspects of consciousness needs to be credited. Still, the metaphor of three eyes plus a notion of three strands of knowledge or science and an additional appeal to unified "knowledge" beyond all distinctions, all facets of the perennial philosophy, do not cover the intricacies of the matter. Moreover, the claim that paradox must reign in this realm does not legitimate the inability to order these intricacies, and the conflation of significantly different religious traditions, far from shedding light on the matter, is only another symptom of the methodological problem.

These flaws lie at the heart of Wilber's position. They continue to hold sway and they debilitate the presentation in his later massive study, *Sex, Ecology, Spirituality* (Wilber, 1995; for useful summaries see Rothberg, 1996b; Walsh, 1996). Some brief criticism here will make my point, consolidate the argument presented thus far, and connect this chapter with the growing, recent discussion about Wilber's thought.

In *Sex, Ecology, Spirituality*, Wilber speaks of three realms of reality: physiosphere, biosphere, and noosphere. The noosphere incorporates undifferentiatedly what I would distinguish as psyche and spirit. As a result, all of the confounds discussed in this book come into play in Wilber's ongoing theorizing. In particular, Wilber conceives the spiritual or transpersonal realm as, in some way, extending into a still-further dimension of the noosphere, and that further dimension gains its specificity by being identified with Ultimate Consciousness. Yet, consistent with Wilber's version of the perennial philosophy, the Ultimate is still thought to be an aspect of the human—but then, of course, it is an aspect of everything else, as well: all is Consciousness, or, more ambiguously phrased, all is an expression of Consciousness. Said in Western terms: God and the universe, Creator and creation, are confounded.

It follows that in *Sex, Ecology, Spirituality* the ontological continues to be confounded with the conscious; philosophical idealism reigns (Walsh, 1996). So when Wilber spells out his thirteen levels of interior-individual development and matches them, step for step, in the three other quadrants of his master diagram—the physical-biological, the social, and the cultural realms—he also proposes thirteen corresponding ontological realities in each realm. The very achievement of this overall symmetrical schema, which Wilber calls the Four Quadrants of the Kosmos, is an amazing feat of creativity. Still, it seems that much of the achievement depends more on imagination than on appeal to empirically verifiable data. What the schema demands, Wilber finds, but the validity of these findings is debatable. Thus, questioning whether or not real-life issues match the sequencing that the schema proposes, others have criticized one or another facet of this overall schema and have begun to chip away at the credibility of the supposed synthesis (Grof, 1996; Kelly, 1996; Kremer, 1996; Rothberg, 1996a; Washburn, 1996; Wright, 1996; Zimmerman, 1996). Much more radically, I would suggest that the effort to discern four realms that match, step for step, is misguided. This effort rests on the mistaken assumption that levels of reality are parallels and expressions of levels of consciousness. I already criticized this assumption and proposed an alternative explanation of the relevant data. The implication here is that the individual glitches in Wilber's comprehensive schema are not mere glitches but natural symptoms of a major misconception.

The root of that misconception lies in Wilber's elaboration of the levels of interior-individual development. These levels are essentially the same as those guiding Wilber's methodological position in *Eye to Eye*. They are the levels of conscious experience and their supposed corresponding levels of reality. As noted early in this chapter, the three eyes of flesh, reason, and spirit, plus the further level of the Ultimate, are but a shorthand version of a more detailed continuum, which Wilber refers to in *Sex, Ecology, Spirituality* as physiosphere, biosphere, and noosphere and details in thirteen levels. Corresponding to these levels, these spheres, and these eyes, are the different types of "science" that Wilber proposes.

The terms *mandalic* science and *noumenological* or *gnostic* science do not occur in the Index, but the substantive matters recur in *Sex, Ecology, Spirituality*. Noumenological or gnostic science would correspond with the Nondual level, which is off Wilber's chart, beyond the thirteenth level of conscious development. Kelly (1996, p. 22) confirms this understanding when he explains that "Nondual" is Wilber's recently preferred term for the "Ultimate," the "Absolute," or "Spirit." At that point of awareness, in the Nondual, one realizes that all things are one, beyond all conception, distinction, and proposition.

On the other hand, mandalic science would correspond with what Wilber calls "vision-logic." It is hard to say exactly what vision-logic is. Wilber (1995, p. 185) suggests that to use vision-logic is to "not just reasonably decide the individual issues, but hold them all together at once in mind." But this holding together is peculiar, for "vision-logic can hold in mind contradictions, it can unify opposites, it is dialectical and nonlinear, and it weaves together what otherwise appear to be incompatible notions." Vision-logic is supposedly a level beyond post-formal operational thinking, on which already there is no consensus (Commons, Richards, & Armon, 1984). Moreover, in Wilber's own portrayal of the matter, without being " 'irrational' or 'non-rational' or 'arational' " (Rothberg, 1996, p. 3), vision-logic is clearly supposed to transcend rationality. Puhakka's (in press) profound analysis suggests that Wilber's notion of vision-logic does indeed entail movement beyond the constraints of the principle of contradiction. But how a cognitive process could countenance contradictions and still not be irrational, non-rational, or arational is itself a mystery beyond rationality—which is, indeed, the point; but to me this assertion seems to be mere words without substance, whistling in the dark, a product of the arational mentality.

My sense is that vision-logic is but another way to talk about the supposed inevitability of paradox when one attempts to reason about spirit. This is to say, vision-logic is a construct parallel to Wilber's mandalic science, and Kelly (1996, p. 22) confirms this assessment. As such, vision-logic is an alchemical amalgam of conceptual cognitive concern and aconceptual meditative experience and as such entails a fanciful notion of transrational knowledge. In other words, the argument in *Sex, Ecology, Spirituality* rests on the same slippery epistemological presuppositions presented in *Eye to Eye*.

More specifically, the flaw in Wilber's presentation is that, in his proposed levels of interior development, he mixes together stages of cognitive development and levels of meditative experience. In the process, he calls "knowledge" what is merely experience, that is, data that *could* be questioned in a process that *could* lead to understanding and knowledge but that in themselves are not knowledge. This confounding allows him to place on a single continuum matters that are really very different. In a line he lays out apples after oranges and claims that they belong together since they are all fruits. And, indeed, his levels all do have something or other to do with consciousness. But apples are not a further expression of oranges, and levels of meditative experience are not further stages of cognitive development. As Kelly (1996, p. 20) expresses the matter, "Clearly, the transpersonal 'levels' as a whole are of a completely different order than the ones that 'precede' them [in Wilber's hierarchy]."

Precisely because he adds meditative levels to the list of cognitive stages, Wilber—along with centuries of fuzzy thinking about mysticism—is able to maintain that meditative experiences constitute knowledge. Moreover, since the wildly variably conceived post-formal operational thought marks the passage between the two sets, the claim to knowledge in the later levels easily slips in. Then, in the supposed highest attainment, the Nondual, all the known characteristics of knowledge disappear; all concepts, distinctions, and propositions become irrelevant; but this phenomenon is nonetheless presented as a kind of knowledge. The implication—and explicit claim—is that all distinctions are ultimately irrelevant. I criticized this matter above. My point here is that it continues to control Wilber's theorizing, and it discredits his theorizing for any-one who believes that knowledge and science entail articulate ex-planation. I also suggested how one could achieve such articulate explanation even regarding these spiritual matters.

Lonergan (1972, pp. 85–99) also proposes an evolutionary ac-count of the ongoing differentiation of consciousness (something akin to Wilber's specification of a spectrum of consciousness). Lonergan's "stages of meaning" are three: common sense, theory, and interiority. I already characterized common sense as a way of understanding that relates things to oneself, and I highlighted its association with metaphor, myth, ritual, image, symbol, story, description, and sug-gestive, inspirational, and paradoxical statement. And I character-ized theory as a way of understanding that relates things to one another; I exemplified its epitome, implicit definition, in the equa-tion for a circle (Helminiak, 1996a, Chapter 5); and I associated theory with rigorous science, ongoing methodical explanation.

Thirdly, following Lonergan, all along I have been operating out of the stage of interiority. It is characterized initially by the modern "turn toward to the subject" and ultimately by a theoreti-cally precise understanding of understanding. Once achieved, the latter allows one to appreciate and account for both common sense and theory as differing ways of understanding, each valid in its own right, each limited in its own way. Herein is a similarity to Wilber's vision-logic, for the stage of interiority can interrelate and hold together different perspectives. However, nowhere in Lonergan's position does the principle of contradiction get superseded. Inte-grating different perspectives is not the same thing as accepting contradictions. Moreover, insisting that contradictions are mere paradoxes is to confine thinking to the realm of common sense.

To some extent, Lonergan's three stages of meaning parallel stages of cognitive development: concrete-operational, formal op-erational, and post-formal operational thinking, which also feature in Wilber's levels of interior development. If Lonergan's analysis of intentional consciousness is taken as an account and an instance of post-formal operational thinking (Helminiak, 1988b), there arise important contrasts with Wilber's presentation. First, as already noted, the principle of contradiction remains ever valid. But sec-ondly, in post-formal operational thinking cognitive development reaches its summit. When cognition—understanding and knowing—is the project, there can be no further stage of development once one has understood understanding itself, for then one knows the very source and generic form of all possible knowledge (see note 2 above). In contrast, Wilber allows further levels beyond post-formal operational thinking. But his further levels move beyond rationality, that is, they no longer deal with cognition. Rather, they are in fact levels of possible refinements of meditative experience. As such, however, they do not necessarily follow nor do they presuppose the stages of cognitive development. They are apples being compared with oranges. On this very point and from different points of view, Grof (1996), Kelly (1996), Kremer (1996), Rothberg (1996a), and Washburn (1996) all find problems with Wilber's spectrum of consciousness. I believe I am pinpointing the underlying theoretical problem in Wilber's account.

On a Lonerganian analysis, post-formal operational thought would represent the final stage of cognitive development. But on this basis Lonergan would not write off the levels of meditative experience that Wilber indicates. These Lonergan (1972, pp. 258–262, 302–305) would treat under the category of "differentiations of consciousness." For cognition is but one possible avenue for the cultivation of human consciousness. In addition to common sense and then theory and interiority, people can also cultivate, for example, aesthetic awareness or else mystical awareness (which I have been referring to as meditative experience). These different kinds of cultivated awareness, different specializations of conscious capacity, represent differentiations of consciousness, and each is not to be compared to the others in some hierarchical listing as are the documented stages of cognitive development. To be sure, mystical awareness also has documented stages or levels or degrees, and these Wilber invokes to propose the highest levels in his spectrum of consciousness. But he is mistaken to propose these as further kinds of cognition. They are, indeed, sources of very specialized data on consciousness/spirit itself, but they are not new means of knowing.

On this same Lonerganian analysis, another important consideration emerges. Image, symbol, metaphor, myth, ritual, and the like are hardly prerational expressions of consciousness. They are, rather, the common coinage and expression of commonsense thinking, especially when consciousness is undifferentiated—that is, in cultures where theory has not yet emerged and among people whom critical thinking has hardly influenced. But insofar as image

and metaphor and the like are but alternative *expressions* of meaning, they do represent a form of knowledge and they also participate in and abide by their own rules of rational—that is, reasoned
and argued—discourse. For example, details in the mythic accounts
of creation in the Book of Genesis stand in provocative contrast to
parallel accounts in Mesopotamian myth. The contrasts are deliberate, represent a polemic, and propose a particular understanding
of God (McKenzie, 1990, 77:25–29). They evince rational argument
via symbol and myth.

   Although Wilber (1995, p. 173) notes the ambiguity in the term
rationality, his account of this matter is questionable in that he sees
magical and mythic thinking as prerational. But by understanding
understanding, by working within the stage of interiority, Lonergan's
analysis recognizes the validity and preserves the dignity of primordial styles of thought and reasoning. Thus, this Lonerganian analysis gives theoretical grounding to Kremer's (1996) criticism of Wilber
in defense of indigenous peoples. And on still another front this
analysis indicates how Wilber's spectrum of consciousness confounds
important and distinct sets of matters, lining them up in a mistaken
hierarchical array. This time, myth and ritual and other expressions
of meaning (including concepts [cf. Helminiak, 1996a, pp. 134–135])
are peaches, expressions of meaning, set out on the hierarchy before
oranges, stages of cognitive development, which in turn precede
apples, levels of meditative experience. Wilber has at least three
different kinds of things strung together in one continuum.

   In some way sensitive to the same matter, Grof (1996), Kelly
(1996), Rothberg (1996a), and Washburn (1996) criticize Wilber's
hierarchical model for restricting the possibility of spiritual experiences to the higher levels of his continuum. For children also
often have profound spiritual experiences, and adult spiritual experiences often entail elements that pertain only on the lower levels of Wilber's continuum, which Wilber must then see as regressive
and depreciate as an entry into the spiritual realm through the
"back door" (Grof, 1996). Understanding the matter in terms of
various and possibly parallel differentiations of consciousness rather
than in terms of a continuous sequence of levels or stages already
brings clarity to the matter.

   But another consideration is also relevant—Wilber's model of
the human being. Overlooking the difference between spirit and
psyche within the human mind, Wilber identifies the spiritual with

Ultimate Consciousness or God. Then all spiritual development must look like a very advanced affair, and in Wilber's scheme "advanced" means high up the ranks in the supposed Great Chain of Being. For if all things in our mundane experience are but an "involuted" expression of Ultimate Consciousness, advance toward Consciousness must entail ascent away from the physiosphere and biosphere and into the noosphere and beyond. The implication is that spirit is not available or is not so richly available in those lower spheres, for according to Wilber's perennial philosophy, the physical is the crassest expression of Consciousness in the Great Chain of Being. In contrast, if human spirit is not identified with God and if the human is conceived as inherently spiritual, then spirit is available to be experienced at every stage of human development, and profound spiritual experiences, far from implying some flight from the physical and psychological, would entail precisely the ever-further integration of the organic, psychic, and spiritual in the human being. A this-worldly, "incarnational," rather than an other-worldly, spirituality results (Helminiak, 1987a). So spiritual experiences would *routinely* involve "descent" into the "lower" dimensions of human makeup, "regression" into the psychic undergirdings of the human mind.

In *The Human Core of Spirituality,* I detailed that process of spiritual integration and development. My point here is that this account not only stands in contrast to Wilber's but also provides a theoretical grounding for Grof's (1996), Kelly's (1996), Kremer's (1996), Rothberg's (1996b), and Washburn's (1996) criticism of Wilber's model. This is not to say that I would completely agree with the analyses of these other theorists. For example, as in the case of Freud's psychoanalytic constructs (Helminiak, 1996a, Chapter 17), the distinction between psyche and spirit cuts through both Washburn's (1995) *Dynamic Ground* and his *ego,* revealing both that and why Dynamic Ground, despite elaborate verbal specification, remains an amorphous and ultimately unworkable construct. This is only to say that, granted my alternative model, their criticisms of Wilber can stand on coherent theoretical grounds as well as on empirical and intuitive ones.

Clearly, Wilber's model needs radical revision. Its hierarchical backbone, the so-called spectrum of consciousness, involves numerous and serious ambiguities, and sorting out the ambiguities actually dismantles the proposed hierarchy. Then the other quadrants of Wilber's grand scheme of the Kosmos in *Sex, Ecology, Spirituality* also come undone. The core problem is Wilber's perennial philosophy; it is epistemologically incoherent; it provides no solid basis for the superstructure that Wilber would build upon it. Said otherwise, there are "fundamental problems with the root metaphor of the Great Chain of Being" (Kelly, 1996, p. 23). Or echoing Kremer (1996, p. 44), the considerations elaborated here "not only require, if they are to be integrated, a fine-tuning of Wilber's theory, but, if taken seriously, a rethinking of the entire model."

Coming from a Western approach and opting for a critical realism, this book has proposed an alternative model—a system of four viewpoints that presumes a tripartite understanding of the human, including an analysis of dynamic consciousness or spirit as both reflecting and nonreflecting and as operating on four levels, all within a context that distinguishes description and explanation, or common sense and theory, and that also allows for non-cognitive differentiations of consciousness. This alternative model seems better able than Wilber's to integrate the broad concerns that he addresses.

But whether there can even be a science of the spiritual—this is the question at stake in this book and in Wilber's extensive writings. Both this book and Wilber's agree that the answer is Yes, but this answer will not hold until a coherent account of spirituality can actually be demonstrated and the coherent interrelationship of religion and the human sciences can be delineated. Finding Wilber's proposal wanting, I have provided another. It outlines a scientific spirituality and ipso facto delineates the relationship between religion and the human sciences. If this alternative proposal holds even though Wilber's fails, Wilber's dogged Yes to a science of spirituality is nonetheless vindicated. Transpersonal psychology can have a coherent theoretical core. A credible science of spirituality is actually emerging. Religion and science can be reconciled.

Epilogue

eligion used to be everything, but not anymore. As history progressed, various strands of living branched off and became independent. The seventeenth century saw the emancipation of the natural sciences. The eighteenth century saw the emergence of the social or human sciences. They continue to struggle for their independence. Part of their difficulty is an uncertainty about the nature of social science itself.

But technological advances in the twentieth century have wrought an epochal change. The world is shrinking to one global village. In the process, religions have encountered one another. The common man and woman are aware of a range of beliefs and practices that differ from their own. So certainty in religious commitments has been challenged, and people have begun to distinguish between spirituality and religion. People discern commonalities among the various religions and tend to prize religious wisdom more highly than their religious affiliation.

This state of affairs has important implications for the self-understanding of the human sciences, and this study of religion and the human sciences has capitalized on them. If spirituality is not identical with religion but is rather something that the religions carry, spirituality appears to be a human phenomenon more than a theological one. Then, if spirituality can be specified in some more or less precise way, spirituality not only appears as a link between religion and social science but also clarifies the nature of both of them. The strictly theological dimensions of religion get sorted out from the human dimensions, and within the human dimensions a similar differentiation occurs. Those aspects of religion that claim universal validity stand out in contrast to those that are simply the products of particular histories. This latter differentiation also suggests something about the human sciences, for it applies to them as well as to religion. Thus, there emerges an analytic schema for sorting out the various interrelated aspects of religion, and this very schema simultaneously suggests the interrelationship of religion and the human sciences.

Refined and nuanced, the schema in question is the system of higher viewpoint presented in this book. Differentiation and interrelation of the positivist, the philosophic, and the theist viewpoints, as well as the theotic, form the theoretical core of this book's position on the relationship of religion and the human sciences. Other positions on religion and the human sciences are available, and this book examined them in light of its own: the integration project of Evangelical Christianity, the debate about the difference between theology and religious studies, the distinction between the *Geistes-* and *Naturwissenschaften*, the implementation of a revised critical correlation, and the appeal to a perennial philosophy. This book criticized all of them while remaining consistently true to its own position—which suggests that this position may be more incisive and more comprehensive than the rest.

To be sure, in order to do its work, this book employed a host of other intellectual tools, borrowed from Bernard Lonergan, in addition to the notion of higher viewpoints. There are

- the elaboration of the bimodal and four-level structure of dynamic and openended human consciousness or spirit, which grounds the nontheist conceptualization of spirituality;

- the specification of authenticity as a normativity built into the structure of the human spirit;

- the specification of the authentic human subject as the key to any successful scientific enterprise, even one within the supposedly "subjective" realms of the humanities and the human sciences;

- the elimination of the supposed conflict between faith and reason by specification of different horizons of faith, presuppositional stances, variously characteristic of all of the four viewpoints;

- the difference between separation and distinction;

- the specification of explanation as successful implementation of implicit definition or systematic statement, wherein terms and their relations codefine one another and thus precisely express an intended meaning;

- the distinction between common sense and theory and the parallel distinctions between description and explanation and between "interpretation" and "explanation" (*Geistes-* and *Naturwissenschaft*) and the parallel specification of the realm of symbol, metaphor, and paradoxical statement on the one hand and the realm of systematic formulation on the other;

- the distinction and interrelation between data and knowledge and the parallel distinction between experience and knowledge and the related indication of differentiations of consciousness—for example, mystical differentiation—in contrast to stages of cognitive development;

- the understanding of knowledge as a composite of data, understanding, and judgment; and

- the specification of verification or judgment of fact as the criterion of truth in contrast to mere communal or social consensus.

But granted all that—and not only is this presupposition massive but none of its elements is optional, for they all hang together—this book and its companion volumes (Helminiak, 1987c, 1996a) propose what appears to be a coherent and comprehensive paradigm for human and religious studies. This proposal has far-reaching implications.

If spirituality can be specified as a specialization within psychology, the essential nature of the human sciences as "human" has been clarified. Then there may ensue a fully scientific enterprise dedicated to genuine human well being. This enterprise would rest on sound theory and appeal to empirical evidence. Like the blades of a scissors, theory and evidence would close together to sharpen one another and to produce ongoing advance (Lonergan, 1972, p. 293).

Attending to what have traditionally been valid religious concerns, a science of spirituality would indicate what is humanly wholesome and how the farthest reaches of human potential might be attained. That is to say, a spiritual technology would emerge (Feingold & Helminiak, 1996), and it could be shared universally. Just as technologies for production, travel, communication, and so on have transformed the face of modern living around the world, so a spiritual technology might transform postmodern life. By breaking free of the category *religion*, which has been separated so clumsily from the modern state and secular society, a spirituality worthy of all humanity would actually inform secular culture without imposing the particularities of the various religions. Then the possibility of a truly global community would emerge.

Of course, this vision is a dream. At the present time the human sciences and the world's nations are as fragmented as the religions. The hope for consensus in human science is no nearer than that in religion. Yet, if the analyses in this book are correct, we are not left to chance or to grace in the task of forming a global society. If these analyses are correct, we have broken the code, and we know the way.

Unlike in former days, we are not left to await a prophet who would arise to show the way. Indeed, no prophet could successfully arise in our age. Penetrating analyses, critical thinking, unscrupulous pandering, and shrewd cynicism make a mockery of the most sacred of things. If one bumper sticker reads, "Visualize World Peace," another counters with, "Visualize Whirled Peas." If one says, "Jesus died for our sins," another adds, "Then make it worth his while." No other generation has been so self-aware, so equipped with sound knowledge, so burdened with self-doubt, and so frighteningly capable of shaping or even obliterating history. And on no other generation has the weight of pivotal choices lain so squarely and so heavily.

The choices are ours. The world is in our own hands today. *Commitment must be to the process of openness, honesty, and love— in a word, authenticity. The process need only be named and embraced and implemented up front. The matter is as simple as that. There is nothing mysterious or miraculous about it. The mere willingness to deliberately own this commitment is the key to its successful collective fulfillment.*

The denouement of *Angels in America* (Kushner, 1993) was right on target. There was no angel, and the Magician God was not to be found; this God had long since been away from the celestial office. In the end there was only a community of concerned and decent human beings, and this was enough to make life as fulfilling as one could ever hope.

The creation of the new spiritual base must be an explicit undertaking. It must be deliberate, up front, and down to earth. The result of this deliberate creation must be some consensus about vision and virtue, about what is to be believed and what is really worthwhile. Such consensus could only rest on what is objectively true and what is objectively good. Nothing else could maintain universal and ongoing support.

But those very criteria are what is built into the position presented in this book. So this dream of a united global community does have a basis in reality.

A crucial role in making this dream come true lies with the world's religions. Religion resisted the visions of Bacon, Kepler, and Galileo when natural science was first emerging. Even though they expressed their new outlook in terms compatible with the reigning Christianity of the day, it took centuries before religion and inherited speculation finally relinquished their claim over "natural philosophy." The vision being ventured here takes the scientific revolution another giant step forward. It will probably take a long time for the religions to acknowledge this vision, too, even though, again, in the full picture the religions lose nothing of their function—except their political power and their controlling mystique over people.

A differential analysis within the four viewpoints respects religious customs and particular traditions—unless they are actually humanly destructive. It highlights the value of human authenticity that has, under other names, always characterized religion at its best. It acknowledges God and allows for belief in God for those who understand life in this way. And it leaves room for matters of human deification, as is explained, for example, in classical Christian orthodoxy and as occurs in other forms in Hinduism and other religions. Within this overall perspective the desideratum is that the religions would stop their bickering and recognize their common spiritual core. Then all kinds of humanists and theists could live together in harmony. Along with the human sciences and secular agencies, they could publicly rally around authenticity, and at the same time a myriad of different religious forms could privately express and advance this common spiritual core. The only condition would be that the forms not violate authenticity. If this is too much to ask of a religion, then this religion could hardly be of God, and it would be patently unworthy of human respect.

This vision resembles August Comte's Global Society, based on altruism, and Saint-Simon's "new Christianity," centered around ethics and fraternity, and also the French Revolution's Religion of Reason, and to this extent this dream might seem to be a recurrent nightmare. But the times have changed, our understanding is deeper, and there are significant differences in these visions. The openended dynamism of the questioning human spirit is a far cry from rationalistically conceived eighteenth-century reason. The Christianity of the theotic viewpoint, unlike that of Saint-Simon, is not stripped of all metaphysical beliefs. And the altruism of August Comte is recognized as an inadequately conceived ethical ideal.

The suggestion is that in the delineation of human spirit there has been a scientific breakthrough. As Newton's synthesis structured a new physics, as Mendeleev's periodic table launched modern chemistry, as Darwin's theory of evolution gave biology its paradigm, so Lonergan's analyses may be the beginnings of truly methodical social science, including spirituality, theology, and theotics. We may actually be entering a new human era and not just a new millennium. It will be characterized by the genuine integration of the human sciences and religion.

REFERENCES

Abbagnano, N. (1967). Positivism. In P. Edwards (Ed.), *The encyclopedia of philosophy*, vol. 6 (pp. 414–419). New York: Macmillan Publishing Co.

Andrews, L. M. (1987). *To thine own self be true: The rebirth of values in the new ethical therapy*. New York: Doubleday, Anchor Press.

Armstrong, K. (1993). *A history of God: The 4000-year quest of Judaism, Christianity and Islam*. New York: Ballantine Books.

Assagioli, R. (1976). *Psychosynthesis: A manual of principles and techniques*. New York: Penguin. (Original work published 1965).

Barbour, I. (1974). *Myths, models, and paradigms*. New York: Harper & Row.

Bain, H. A. (1987). Review of Helminiak's *Spiritual development. The Journal of Pastoral Care, 41,* 281–283.

Barth, K. (1960). *The humanity of God*. Richmond, VA: John Knox Press.

Beauchesne, R. J. (1990). Heeding the early Congar today, and two recent Roman Catholic issues: Seeking hope on the road back. *Journal of Ecumenical Studies, 27,* 535–560.

Bellah, R. N. (1970). Confessions of a former establishment fundamentalist. *Bulletin for the Council on the Study of Religion, 1,* 1–6.

Bellah, R. N., Madsen, R., Sullivan, W. M., Swindler, A., & Tipton, S. M. (1985). *Habits of the heart: Individualism and commitment in American life*. New York: Harper & Row.

Benson, P. L., & Spilka, B. (1973). God images as a function of self-esteem and locus of control. *Journal for the Scientific Study of Religion, 12,* 297–310.

Bergin, A. E. (1980). Psychotherapy and religious values. *Journal of Counseling and Clinical Psychology, 48,* 95–105.

———. (1991). Values and religious issues in psychotherapy and mental health. *American Psychologist, 46,* 394–403.

Bergin, A., & Jensen, J. (1990). Religiosity of psychotherapists: A national survey. *Psychotherapy, 27,* 3–7.

Bergin, A. E., Masters, K. S., & Richards, P. S. (1987). Religiousness and mental health reconsidered: A study of an intrinsically religious sample. *Journal of Counseling Psychology, 34,* 197–204.

Bernstein, R. J. (1976). *The restructuring of social and political theory.* Philadelphia: University of Pennsylvania Press.

Borg, M. J. (1995). *Meeting Jesus again for the first time: The historical Jesus and the heart of contemporary faith.* San Francisco: Harper San Francisco.

Boswell, J. (1980). *Christianity, social tolerance, and homosexuality: Gay people in western Europe from the beginnings of the Christian Era to the fourteenth century.* Chicago: University of Chicago Press.

Bouma-Prediger, S. (1990). The task of integration: A modest proposal. *Journal of Psychology and Theology, 18,* 21–31.

Bracken, J. A. (1997). Book review: Daniel A. Helminiak, *The human core of spirituality: Mind as psyche and spirit. Dialogues* (Interdisciplinary Dialogue Group), *2*(2), 7–8.

Brady, I. C. (1967). St. Bonaventure. *New Catholic encyclopedia,* vol. 2 (pp. 658–664). Washington, DC: The Catholic University of America.

Brown, D. (1994). Believing traditions and the task of the academic theologian. *Journal of the American Academy of Religion, 62,* 1167–1179.

———. (1997). Academic theology and religious studies. *Bulletin of the Council of Societies for the Study of Religion, 26,* 64–66.

Browning, D. A. (1987). *Religious thought and the modern psychologies: A critical conversation in the theology of culture.* Philadelphia: Fortress Press.

Bufford, R. K. (1981). *The human reflex: Behavioral psychology in biblical perspective.* San Francisco: Harper & Row.

Butler, K. (1990). Spirituality reconsidered. *The Family Therapy Networker, 14*(5), 26–27.

Canda, E. R. (1988a). Conceptualizing spirituality for social work: Insights from diverse perspectives. *Social Thought, 14,* 30–46.

———. (1988b). Spirituality, religious diversity, and social work practice. *Social Casework, 69,* 238–247.

Carter, J. D. (1977). Secular and sacred models of psychology and religion. *Journal of Psychology and Theology, 5,* 197–208.

Carter, J. D., & Mohline, R. J. (1976). The nature and scope of integration: A proposal. *Journal of Psychology and Theology, 4,* 3–14.

Chandler, C. K., Holden, J. M., & Kolander, C. A. (1992). Counseling for spiritual wellness: Theory and practice. *Journal of Counseling and Development, 71,* 168–175.

Cobb, J. (1983). Panentheism. In A. Richardson & J. Bowden (Eds.), *The Westminster dictionary of Christian theology* (p. 423). Philadelphia: The Westminster Press.

Collins, G. R. (1983). Moving through the jungle: A decade of integration. *Journal of Psychology and Theology, 11,* 2–7.

Commons, M. L., Richards, F. A., & Armon, R. (1984). *Beyond formal operations: Late adolescent and adult development.* New York: Praeger.

Conn, J. W. (1989). *Spirituality and personal maturity.* Lanham: University Press of America, Inc.

Countryman, L. W. (1988). *Dirt, greed and sex: Sexual ethics in the New Testament and their implications for today.* Philadelphia: Fortress Press.

Crabb, L. J. (1975). *Basic principles of biblical counseling.* Grand Rapids: Zondervan Publishing House.

———. (1977). *Effective biblical counseling.* Grand Rapids: Zondervan Publishing House.

Crossan, J. D. (1993). *The historical Jesus: The life of a Mediterranean Jewish peasant.* San Francisco: Harper San Francisco.

Crowe, F. E. (1980). *The Lonergan enterprise.* Cambridge, MA: Cowley Publications.

Curran, C. E., & McCormick, R. A. (1980). *The distinctiveness of Christian ethics.* New York: Paulist Press.

Dan, D. (1990). Recovery: A modern initiation rite. *The Family Therapy Networker, 14*(5), 28–29.

DeCoulanges, F. (1972). *The ancient city: A study of the religion, laws, and institutions of Greece and Rome.* Garden City, NJ: Doubleday & Co., Inc.

Deikman, A. J. (1982). *The observing self: Mysticism and psychotherapy.* Boston: Beacon.

Denzinger, H., & Schonmetzer, A. (1965). *Enchiridion symbolorum definitionum et declarationum de rebus fidei et morum,* 23rd ed. Freiburg im Breisgau: Verlag Herder.

Department of Psychology (1995). *West Georgia College: Master's Degree: Psychology.* Carrollton, GA: Department of Psychology, West Georgia College.

DeVries, M. J. (1982). The conduct of integration: A response to Farnsworth. *Journal of Psychology and Theology, 10,* 320–325.

Doherty, W. J. (1995). *Soul searching: Why psychotherapy must promote moral responsibility.* New York: Basic Books.

Doran, R. M. (1977a). Psychic conversion. *The Thomist, 41,* 200–236.

———. (1977b). *Subject and psyche: Ricoeur, Jung, and the search for foundations.* Washington: University Press of America.

———. (1977c). Subject, psyche, and theology's foundations. *The Journal of Religion, 57,* 267–287.

———. (1981). *Psychic conversion and theological foundations: Toward a reorientation of the human sciences.* Chico, CA: Scholars Press.

———. (1990). *Theology and the dialectics of history.* Toronto: University of Toronto Press.

Dueck, A. (1989). On living in Athens: Models of relating psychology, church and culture. *Journal of Psychology and Christianity, 8,* 5–18.

Eck, B. E. (1996). Integrating the integrators: An organizing framework for a multifaceted process of integration. *Journal of Psychology and Christianity, 15,* 101–115.

Ellis, A. (1980). Psychotherapy and atheistic values: A response to A. E. Bergin's "Psychotherapy and religious values." *Journal of Counseling and Clinical Psychology, 48,* 635–639.

Ellison, C. W., & Smith, J. (1991). Toward an integrative measure of health and well-being. *Journal of Psychology and Theology, 19,* 35–48.

Erikson, E. (1963). *Childhood and society* (2nd ed.). New York: W. W. Norton.

———. (1978). Reflections on Dr. Borg's life cycle. In E. Erikson (Ed.), *Adulthood.* New York: W. W. Norton & Co.

Farnsworth, K. E. (1974). Embodied Integration. *Journal of Psychology and Theology, 2,* 116–124.

———. (1982). The conduct of integration. *Journal of Psychology and Theology, 10,* 308–319.

———. (1996). The devil sends errors in pairs. *Journal of Psychology and Christianity, 15,* 123–132.

Feingold, B. D. (1994, October). *Spirituality: A credible scientific approach?* Paper presented at the First International Conference: Prevention: The Key to Health for Life, sponsored by the World Health Organization, Charleston, WV.

———. (1995). Towards a science of spirituality: Six arguments for an authenticity oriented approach to research and therapy. *NOVA-Psi Newsletter* (National Organization of Veterans Administration Psychologists), *13*(1), 13–21.

Feingold, B. D., & Helminiak, D. A. (1996). A credible scientific spirituality: Can it contribute to wellness, prevention, and recovery? (paper submitted for publication)

Feurherd, J. (1991, April 26). Hill and Knowlton's influence on bishops' pro-life choices. *National Catholic Reporter,* p. 3.

Flannery, A. (Ed.) (1975). *Vatican Council II: The conciliar and post conciliar documents.* Northport, NY: Costello Publishing Co.

Frankl, V. E. (1988). *The will to meaning: Foundations and applications of logotherapy.* New York: New American Library. (Original work published 1969.)

Freud. S. (1975). *The future of an illusion* (J. Strachey, Ed. & Trans.). New York: Norton. (Original work published 1927)

———. (1968). *The interpretation of dreams.* In *The standard edition of the complete psychological works of Sigmund Freud,* vols. 4 & 5. London: Hogart Press. (Original work published 1900)

Freud, S. (1964). *New introductory lectures on psychoanalysis,* (J. Strachey, Trans.). New York: W. W. Norton & Co., Inc. (Original work published 1933)

Fromm, E. (1947). *Man for himself: An inquiry into the psychology of ethics.* New York: Rinehart & Co.

———. (1973). *The anatomy of human destructiveness.* New York: Rinehart & Co.

Fowler, J. W. (1981). *Stages of faith: The psychology of human development and the quest for meaning.* San Francisco: Harper & Row.

Fuller, A. R. (1994). *Psychology and religion: Eight points of view* (3rd ed.). Lanham, MD: Rowman & Littlefield Publishers, Inc.

Furnish, V. P. (1994). The Bible and homosexuality: Reading the texts in context. In J. S. Siker (Ed.), *Homosexuality in the Church: Both sides of the debate* (pp. 18–35). Louisville, KY: Westminster John Knox.

Gadamer, H.-G. (1989). *Truth and method* (rev. ed.) (J. C. Weinsheimer & D. G. Marshall, Trans.). New York: Crossroad Publishing Company. (Original work published 1960)

Gahr, E. (1991, April 26). Hickey calls Georgetown to disown pro-choice group. *National Catholic Reporter,* p. 5.

Geuss, R. (1981). *The idea of a critical theory: Habermas and the Frankfurt School.* Cambridge, MA: Harvard University Press.

Gilkey, L. (1975). *Catholicism confronts modernity: A Protestant view.* New York: Seabury Press.

Gill, S. (1994). The academic study of religion. *Journal of the American Academy of Religion, 62,* 965–975.

Goleman, D. (1977). *Varieties of meditative experiences.* Garden City, NY: E. P. Dutton.

Grof, S. (1996). Ken Wilber's spectrum psychology: Observations from clinical consciousness research. *ReVision, 19*(1), 11–24.

Gula, R. (1989). *Reason informed by faith: Foundations of Catholic morality.* New York: Paulist Press.

304 REFERENCES

Gustafson, J. M. (1990). Explaining and valuing: An exchange between theology and the human sciences. Eleventh Annual University Lecture in Religion. Arizona State University.

Gutierrez, G. (1973). *A theology of liberation: History, politics and salvation* (C. Inda & J. Eagleson, Trans.). Maryknoll, NY: Orbis Press.

Habermas, J. (1991). *On the logic of the social sciences.* (S. Weber Nicholsen & J. A. Stark, Trans). Cambridge, MA: The MIT Press. (Original work published 1970)

Hedges, L. V. (1987). How hard is hard science, how soft is soft science? The empirical cumulativeness of research. *American Psychologist, 42,* 443–455.

Heller, D. (1986). *The children's God.* Chicago: University of Chicago Press.

Helminiak, D. A. (1979). *One in Christ: An exercise in systematic theology.* Unpublished doctoral dissertation, Boston College and Andover Newton Theological School.

———. (1982). How is meditation prayer? *Review for Religious, 41,* 774–782.

———. (1984a). Consciousness as a subject matter. *Journal for the Theory of Social Behavior, 14,* 211–230.

———. (1984b). Neurology, psychology, and extraordinary religious experiences. *Journal of Religion and Health, 23,* 33–46.

———. (1986a). Four viewpoints on the human: A conceptual schema for interdisciplinary studies, I. *Heythrop Journal, 27,* 420–437.

———. (1986b). Lonergan and systematic spiritual theology. *New Blackfriars, 67,* 78–92.

———. (1986c). Modern science on pain and suffering: A Christian perspective. *Spirituality Today, 38,* 136–148.

———. (1986d). *The same Jesus: A contemporary christology.* Chicago: Loyola University Press.

———. (1987a). Catholicism's spiritual limbo: A shift in "incarnational" spirituality. *Spirituality Today, 39,* 331–348.

———. (1987b). Four viewpoints on the human: A conceptual schema for interdisciplinary studies, I. *Heythrop Journal, 28,* 1–15.

———. (1987c). *Spiritual development: An interdisciplinary study.* Chicago: Loyola University Press.

———. (1988a). Human solidarity and collective union in Christ. *Anglican Theological Review, 70,* 34–59.

———. (1988b). Parallels in Bickhard and Lonergan: Parallels in Piaget and Aquinas. (unpublished paper)

———. (1989a, Feb. 11). Doing right by women and the Trinity too. *America, 160*(5), 110–112, 119–122.

———. (1989b). Jesus' humanity and human salvation. *Worship, 63,* 429–446.

——. (1989c). The quest for spiritual values. *Pastoral Psychology, 38,* 105–116.

——. (1992). To be a whole human being: Spiritual growth beyond psychotherapy. *Human Development, 12*(3), 34–39.

——. (1994a). *Men and women in midlife transition and the crisis of meaning and purpose in life, a matter of spirituality.* Unpublished doctoral dissertation, University of Texas at Austin.

——. (1994b). *What the bible really says about homosexuality.* San Francisco: Alamo Square Press.

——. (1995). Non-religious lesbians and gays facing AIDS: A fully psychological approach to spirituality. *Pastoral Psychology, 43,* 301–318.

——. (1996a). *The human core of spirituality: Mind as psyche and spirit.* Albany, NY: The State University of New York Press.

——. (1996b). Response to Doran and Richardson on "A scientific spirituality." *Journal for the Psychology of Religion, 6,* 33–38.

——. (1996c). A scientific spirituality: The interface of psychology and theology. *The International Journal for the Psychology of Religion, 6,* 1–19

——. (1997a). Christian (read: Fundamentalist): A case for mistaken identity. *Ecumenical Trends, 26,* 114–122.

——. (1997b). Killing for God's sake: The spiritual crisis in religion and society. *Pastoral Psychology, 45,* 365–374.

Hiatt, J. F. (1986). Spirituality, medicine, and healing. *Southern Medical Journal, 79,* 736–743.

Hill, P. C., & Kauffmann, D. R. (1996). Psychology and theology: Toward the challenge. *Journal of Psychology and Christianity, 15,* 175–183.

Holewa, L. (1991, May 10). Abortion-debate issue grips Catholic campuses. *National Catholic Reporter,* p. 3.

Hong, G. (1995). Buddhism and religious experience. In R. W. Hood, Jr. (Ed.), *Handbook of religious experience* (pp. 87–121). Birmingham, AL: Religious Education Press.

Huxley, A. (1945) *The perennial philosophy.* New York: Harper and Brothers, Publishers.

James, W. (1961). *The varieties of religious experiences.* New York: Macmillan. (Original work published 1902)

Janssens, L. (1977). Norms and priorities in a love ethics. *Louvain Studies, 6,* 207–238.

Jeeves, M. A. (1969). *The scientific enterprise and Christian faith.* Downers Grove, IL: Inter-Varsity Press.

John Paul II (1993). *The splendor of truth: Veritatis splendor* (Vatican trans.). Boston: Pauline Books & Media.

Johnson, T. (1992). *The myth of the great secret: An appreciation of Joseph Campbell* (revised ed.). Berkeley, CA: Celestial Arts.

Jones, S. (1994). A constructive relationship for religion with the science and profession of psychology: Perhaps the boldest model yet. *American Psychologist, 49*, 184–199.

———. (1996). Reflections on the nature and future of the Christian psychologies. *Journal of Pscyhology and Christianity, 15*, 133–142.

Kass, J. D., Friedman, R., Leserman, J., Zuttermeister, P., & Benson, H. (1991). Health outcomes and a new index of spiritual experience. *Journal for the Scientific Study of Religion, 30*, 203–211.

Kelly, S. M. (1996). Revisioning the mandala of consciousness. *ReVision, 18*(4), 19–24.

Kemp, H. V. (1985). Psychotherapy as a religious process: A historical heritage. In E. M. Stern (Ed.), *Psychotherapy and the religiously committed patient* (pp. 135–146). New York: Haworth Press.

Kremer, J. W. (1996). The shadow of evolutionary thinking. *ReVision, 19*(1), 41–48.

Kornfield, J. (1989). Obstacles and vicissitudes in spiritual practice. In S. Grof & C. Grof (Eds.), *Spiritual emergency: When personal transformation becomes a crisis* (pp. 137–169). New York: G. P. Putman's Sons.

Kukla, A. (1989). Nonempirical issues in psychology. *American Psychologist, 44*, 785–794.

Kushner, T. (1993). *Angels in America: A gay fantasia on national themes.* New York: Theatre Communications Group.

Lebmann, K. (1970). Transcendence. In K. Rahner (Ed.), *Sacramentum mundi: An encyclopedia of theology*, vol. 6 (pp. 275–281). New York: Herder & Herder.

Loevinger, J. (with Blasi, A). (1977). *Ego development.* San Francisco: Jossey-Bass Publishers.

Lonergan, B. J. F. (1957). *Insight: A study of human understanding.* New York: Philosophical Library.

———. (1958). *De constitutione Christi ontologica et psychologica.* Rome: Gregorian University Press.

———. (1964). *De Deo trino: II. Pars systematica.* Rome: Gregorian University Press.

———. (1967a). Cognitional structure. In F. E. Crowe (Ed.). *Collection: Papers by Bernard Lonergan* (pp. 221–239). Montreal: Palm.

———. (1967b). Dimensions of meaning. In F. E. Crowe (Ed.). *Collection: Papers by Bernard Lonergan* (pp. 252–267). Montreal: Palm.

———. (1967c). Finality, love, marriage. In F. E. Crowe (Ed.). *Collection: Papers by Bernard Lonergan* (pp. 16–53). Montreal: Palm.

———. (1967d). The natural desire to see God. In F. E. Crowe (Ed.). *Collection: Papers by Bernard Lonergan* (pp. 84–95). Montreal: Palm.

———. (1967e). *Verbum: Word and idea in Aquinas* (D. B. Burrell, Ed.). Notre Dame, IN: University of Notre Dame Press.

———. (1971). *Grace and freedom: Operative grace in the thought of St. Thomas Aquinas.* New York: Herder and Herder.

———. (1972) *Method in theology.* New York: Herder & Herder.

———. (1976). *The way to Nicea: The dialectical development of trinitarian theology* (C. O'Donavan, Trans.). Philadelphia: The Westminster Press. (Original work published 1964)

Lowenthal, M. F., Berkman, P. L., & Associates. (1967). *Aging and mental disorder in San Francisco: A social psychiatric study.* San Francisco: Jossey-Bass, Inc.

Lyotard, J.-F. (1984). *The postmodern condition: A report on knowledge* (G. Bennington & B. Massumi, Trans.). Minneapolis: University of Minnesota Press.

MacIntyre, A. (1984). *After virtue: A study of moral theory,* 2nd edition. Notre Dame, IN: Notre Dame University Press.

Mackey, J. P. (1979). *Jesus the Man and the Myth: Contemporary Christology.* New York: Paulist Press.

Malony, H. N. (Ed.). (1991). *Psychology of religion: Personalities, problems, possibilities.* Grand Rapids, MI: Baker Book House.

Manaster, G. J. (1990). On spirituality. *Individual Psychology, 46,* 277–279.

McDargh, J. (1983). *Psychoanalytic object relations theory and the study of religion: On faith and the imaging of God.* Lanham, MD: University Press of America.

McDermott, R. (1996). The need for philosophical and spiritual dialogue: Reflections on Ken Wilber's *Sex, Ecology, Spirituality. ReVision, 19*(2), 8–9.

McFadden, S. H. (1991). Spiritual assessment: Uses in research and practice with older adults. Unpublished paper presented for the American Psychological Association, San Francisco, CA.

McKenzie, J. L. (1982). *The New Testament without illusion.* New York: Crossroad.

———. (1990). Aspects of Old Testament thought. In R. E. Brown, J. A. Fitzmyer, & R. E. Murphy (Eds.), *The new Jerome biblical commentary* (article 77). Englewood Cliffs: Prentice Hall.

McManus, J. (1991, April 26). Does abortion help women? Kissling, Alvare debate. *National Catholic Reporter,* p. 4.

McQuilkin, J. R. (1975). The behavior sciences under the authority of Scripture. Unpublished paper presented for the Evangelical Theological Society, Jackson, MS (December 30).

Meadows, M. J., & Kahoe, R. D. (1984). *Psychology of religion: Religion in individual lives.* New York: Harper & Row.

Menninger, K. (1973). *Whatever became of sin?* New York: Hawthorn Books.

Miller, W. R. (1990). Spirituality: The silent dimension of addiction research. *Drug and Addiction Review, 9,* 259–266.

Miller, W. R., & Martin, J. E. (Eds.). (1988). *Behavior therapy and religion: Integrating spiritual and behavioral approaches to change.* Newbury Park, CA: Sage Publications.

Minor, R. N., & Baird, R. D. (1983). Teaching about religion at the state university: Taking the issue seriously and strictly. *Bulletin of the Council on the study of Religion, 14*(3), 69–72.

Moberg, D. O. (1978). Subjective measures of spiritual well-being. *Review of Religious Research, 25,* 351–364.

Moberg, D. O., & Brused, P. M. (1978). Spiritual well-being: A neglected subject in quality of life research. *Social Indicators Research, 5,* 303–323.

Mohr, R. D. (1995). The perils of postmodernism. *The Harvard Gay & Lesbian Review, 2*(4), 9–13.

Murray, H. A., & Morgan, C. D. (1945). A clinical study of sentiments. *Genetic Psychology Monographs, 32,* 3–311.

Myers, D. G. (1996). On professing psychological science and Christian faith. *Journal of Psychology and Christianity, 15,* 143–149.

Myers, D. G., & Jeeves, M. A. (1987). *Psychology through the eyes of faith.* San Francisco: Harper & Row.

Myrdal, G. (1958). *Value in social theory: A selection of essays on methodology* (P. Streeten, Ed.). New York: Harper and Brothers.

National Conference of Catholic Bishops. (1983). *The challenge of peace: God's purposes and our response: A pastoral letter on war and peace.* Washington, DC: United States Catholic Conference.

———. (1986). *Economic justice for all: A pastoral letter on Catholic social teaching and the U.S. economy.* Washington, DC: United States Catholic Conference.

Niebuhr, H. R. (1951). *Christ and culture.* New York: Harper and Row.

O'Donahue, W. (1989). The (even) bolder model: The clinical psychologist as metaphysician-scientist-practitioner. *American Psychologist, 44,* 1460–1468.

Ogden, S. M. (1995). Religious studies and theological studies: What is involved in the distinction between them? *Bulletin of the Council of the Societies for the Study of Religion, 24*(1), 3–4.

Overheard (1991, May 13). *Newsweek,* p. 17.

Palmer, R. (1969). *Hermeneutics: Interpretation theory in Schleiermacher, Dilthey, Heidegger, and Gadamer.* Evanston, IL: Northwestern University Press.

Paloutzian, R. F. (1996). *Invitation to the psychology of religion.* Boston: Allyn and Bacon.

Paloutzian, R. F., & Ellison, C. W. (1982). Loneliness, spiritual well-being and quality of life. In L. A. Peplau and D. Perlman (Eds.), *Loneliness: A sourcebook of current theory, research, and therapy*. New York: Wiley.

Pals, D. L. (1987). Is religion a *sui generis* phenomenon? *Journal of the American Academy of Religion, 55*, 259–282.

Patterson, R. B. (1992). *Encounters with angels: Psyche and spirit in the counseling situation*. Chicago: Loyola University Press.

Perry, W. G. (1970). *Forms of intellectual and ethical development in the college years*. New York: Holt, Rineholt and Winston.

Popper, K. R. (1985). *Popper selections*, D. Miller (Ed.). Princeton, NJ: Princeton University Press.

Puhakka, K. (1995). Hinduism and religious experience. In R. W. Hood, Jr. (Ed.), *Handbook of religious experience* (pp. 122–143). Birmingham, AL: Religious Education Press.

———. (in press). Contemplating everything: Wilber's evolutionary theory in dialectical perspective. In D. Rothberg & S. M. Kelly (Eds.), *The mandala of consciousness: Leading transpersonal thinkers in conversation with Ken Wilber*. Wheaton, IL: Quest Books.

Rahner, K. (1970). Theology, II. History. In K. Rahner (Ed.), *Sacramentum mundi: An encyclopedia of theology*, vol. 6 (pp. 240–246). New York: Herder and Herder.

Reese, W. L. (1980). Panentheism. *Dictionary of philosophy and religion: Eastern and western thought*, pp. 407–408. Atlantic Highlands, NJ: Humanities Press.

Richardson, F. C., & Guignon, C. B. (1991). Individualism and social interest. *Individual Psychology, 47*, 66–71.

Ricoeur, P. (1967). *The symbolism of evil* (E. Bushanen, Trans.). New York: Harper & Row.

Rizzuto, A. (1979). *The birth of the living God: A psychoanalytic study*. Chicago: University of Chicago Press.

Rothberg, D. (1996a). How straight is the spiritual path? Conversations with Buddhist teachers Joseph Goldstein, Jack Kornfield, and Michele McDonald-Smith. *ReVision, 19*(1), 25–40.

———. (1996b). Ken Wilber and contemporary transpersonal inquiry: An introduction to the *ReVision* conversation. *ReVision, 18*(4), 2–8.

Rosenau, P. M. (1992). *Post-modernism and the social sciences: Insights, inroads and intrusions*. Princeton: Princeton University Press.

Saxe, L. (1991). Lying: Thoughts of an applied social psychologist. *American Psychologist, 46*, 409–415.

Schneiders, S. M. (1989). Spirituality in the Academy. *Theological Studies, 50*, 676–697.

Schussler Fiorenza, F. (1991). Theological and religious studies: The contest of the faculties. In B. Wheeler & E. Farley (Eds.), *Shifting boundaries: Contextual approaches to the structure of theological education* (pp. 119–149). Louisville, KY: Westminster/John Knox Press.

———. (1993). Theology in the university. *Bulletin of the Council of Societies for the Study of Religion, 22*(2), 34–39.

Schussler Fiorenza, F. (1994). A response to Donald Wiebe. *Bulletin of the Council of Societies for the Study of Religion, 23*(1), 6–10.

Scroggs, R. (1983). *Homosexuality in the New Testament: Contextual background for contemporary debate.* Philadelphia: Fortress Press.

Segal, R. A. (1983). In defense of reductionism. *Journal of the American Academy of Religion, 51*, 98–124.

———. (1997). From theology to social science: The case of William Robertson Smith. *Bulletin of the Council of Societies for the Study of Religion, 26*, 61–64.

Segal, R. A., & Wiebe, D. (1989). Axioms and dogmas in the study of religion. *Journal of the American Academy of Religion, 58*, 591–605.

Segundo, J. L. (1973). *Grace and the human condition.* Maryknoll, NY: Orbis Books.

Shafranske, E. P., & Gorsuch, R. L. (1984). Factors associated with the perception of spirituality in psychotherapy. *The Journal of Transpersonal Psychology, 16*, 231–241.

Shafranske, E. P., & Malony, H. N. (1990). Clinical psychologists' religious and spiritual orientations and their practice of psychotherapy. *Psychotherapy, 27*, 72–78.

Sharma, A. (1997). On the distinction between religious studies and theological studies. *Bulletin of the Council of Societies for the Study of Religion, 26*, 50–51.

Sharpe, E. J. (1997). The compatibility of theological and religious studies: Historical, theoretical, and contemporary perspectives. *Bulletin of the Council of Societies for the Study of Religion, 26*, 52–60.

Sheehan, T. (1986). *The first coming: How the kingdom of God became Christianity.* New York: Random House.

Shelly, J. A., & Fish, S. (1988). *Spiritual care: The nurse's role,* 3rd edition. Downers Grove, Illinois: InterVarsity Press.

Shepard, R. N., & Metzler, J. (1971). Mental rotation of three-dimensional objects. *Science, 171*, 701–703.

Skinner, B. F. (1953). *Science and human behavior.* New York: Macmillan.

———. (1971). *Beyond freedom and dignity.* New York: Bantam Books.

Smart, N. (1997). Religious studies and theology. *Bulletin of the Council of Societies for the Study of Religion, 26*, 66–68.

Smith, J. Z. (1997). Are theological and religious studies compatible? *Bulletin of the Council of Societies for the Study of Religion, 26,* 60–61.

Spretnak, C. (1991). *States of grace: The recovery of meaning in the postmodern age.* New York: Harper Collins.

Streeter, C. M. (1990). Review of Helminiak's *Spiritual development. Spiritual Life, 42,* 171–173.

Sykes, S. W. (1983). Theology. In A. Richardson and J. Bowden (Eds.), *The Westminster dictionary of Christian theology,* pp. 566–167. Philadelphia: The Westminster Press.

Suzuki, S. (1976). *Zen mind, beginner's mind.* New York: Weatherhill. (Original work published 1970)

Taylor, C. (1989). *Sources of the self: The making of the modern identity.* Cambridge, MA: Harvard University Press.

———. (1992). *The ethics of authenticity.* Cambridge, MA: Harvard University Press.

Thistlethwaite, S. (1994). Settled issues and neglected questions: How is religion to be studied? *Journal of the American Academy of Religion, 64,* 1037–1045.

Tillich, P. (1951). *Systematic theology,* vol. 1. Chicago: University of Chicago Press.

———. (1952). *The courage to be.* Hew Haven, CT: Yale University Press.

Tracy, D. (1970). *Blessed rage for order.* New York: Seabury Press.

Trungpa, C. (1973). *Cutting through spiritual materialism.* Berkeley: Shambhala.

———. (1976). *The myth of freedom: And the way of meditation.* Berkeley: Shambhala.

Vande Kemp, H. (1996). Psychology and Christian spirituality: Explorations of the inner world. *Journal of Psycholosy and Christianity, 15,* 161–174.

Van Leeuwen, M. S. (1996). Five uneasy questions, or: Will success spoil Christian psychologists? *Journal of Psychology and Christianity, 15,* 150–160.

Virkler, H. A. (1982). Response to "The conduct of integration." *Journal of Psychology and Theology, 10,* 329–333.

Walsh, R. (1996). Developmental and evolutionary synthesis in the recent writings of Ken Wilber. *ReVision, 18*(4), 9–18.

Walsh, R., & Vaughan, F. (1994). The worldview of Ken Wilber. *Journal of Humanistic Psychology, 34*(2), 6–21.

Washburn, M. (1995). *The ego and the Dynamic Ground,* 2nd ed. Albany: State University of New York Press.

———. (1996). The pre/trans fallacy reconsidered. *ReVision, 19*(1), 2–10.

Watts, A. (1964). *Beyond theology: The art of godmanship.* New York: Vintage Books.

Weber, M. (1949). *The methodology of the social sciences* (E. A. Shils & H. A. Finch, Eds. & Trans.). Glencoe, IL: Free Press.

Wicks, R. J. (1991). *Seeking perspective: Weaving spirituality and psychology in search of clarity.* Mahwah, NJ: Paulist Press.

Wiebe, D. (1984). The failure of nerve in the academic study of religion. *Sciences Religieuses / Studies in Religion, 13,* 401–422.

———. (1986). The "academic naturalization" of religious studies: Intent or pretence? *Science Religieuses / Studies in Religion, 15,* 197–203.

———. (1994). On theology and religious studies: A response to Francis Schussler Fiorenza. *Bulletin of the Council of Societies for the Study of Religion, 23*(10), 3–6.

Wilber, K. (1977). *The spectrum of consciousness.* Wheaton, IL: Quest.

———. (1980a). *The Atman project: A transpersonal view of human development.* Wheaton, IL: Quest.

———. (1980b). The nature of consciousness. A developmental model of consciousness. In R. N. Walsh and F. Vaughan (Eds.), *Beyond ego: Transpersonal dimensions in psychology* (pp. 74–86, 99–114). Los Angeles: Tarcher.

———. (1981). *Up from Eden.* New York: Doubleday/Anchor Books.

———. (1982). Odyssey: A personal inquiry into humanistic and transpersonal psychology. *Journal of Humanistic Psychology, 22,* 57–90.

———. (1995). *Sex, ecology, spirituality: The spirit of evolution.* Boston: Shambhala.

———. (1996). *Eye to eye: The quest for the new paradigm,* 3rd ed. Boston: Shambhala.

Wogaman, J. P. (1989). *Christian moral judgment.* Louisville, KY: Westminster/John Knox Press.

Wolfe, A. (1989). *Whose keeper? Social science and moral obligation.* Berkeley: University of California Press.

———. (1993). *The human difference: Animals, computers, and the necessity of social science.* Berkeley: University of California Press.

Wright, P. A. (1966). Gender issues in Ken Wilber's transpersonal theory. *ReVision, 18*(4), 25–37.

Wulff, D. M. (1997). *Psychology of religion: Classic and contemporary,* 2nd ed. New York: John Wiley & Sons.

Yalom, I. D. (1980). *Existential psychotherapy.* New York: Basic Books.

Zimmerman, M. E. (1996). A transpersonal diagnosis of the ecological crisis. *ReVision, 18*(4), 38–48.

INDEX

Abbagnano, N., 73
abortion, 117
Absolute, The, 224, 263, 281
absolutes, 100, 183, 275–276;
  epistemological and ethical,
  16–17, 95
abstraction, 261
adulthood, xi, 192–193. *See also*
  post-formal operational
  thinking
advance, scientific, 295
aesthetics, 289
affect, *see* emotion
agape, 177
AIDS, 202
Alexander the Great, 124
All, The, experience of, 257–260
Allport, G., 193
altruism, and A. Comte, 298; and
  selfishness, 88, 169–171, 188–
  189, 192–194
American Catholic Bishops, 117
analogy, doctrine of, 277–279
ananda, 194
anatman, 251, 252
anatta, 251
Anderson, K., 59
Andrews, L. M., 88

angels, 270
anthropology, 2, 3, 32, 61, 89,
  158, 227, 233; philosophical,
  122, 165, 179, 180; philosophical, and spirituality, 190
apprehension, direct, of knowledge, 221, 226, 235–237, 241,
  260, 261
Aquinas, Thomas, *see* Thomas
  Aquinas
arationality, 75–79, 85, 147, 254,
  256, 286–287; forms of, 76–78;
  latent, and religion, 77; post-
  scientific, latent and overt,
  76–78; prescientific, 76; and
  universality of grace, 137
architecture, 69
archetypes, 164
Aristotle, 18, 82, 98, 188, 218
Arius, 35
Armon, R., 286
Armstrong, K., 123, 130
art, 119, 233
Assagioli, R., 214
atheism, and nontheism, 276
Atman, 132, 275, 281
atonement, 42
Augustine, Saint, 100, 114, 169

313